SUSSEX COAST FROM THE AIR

Published titles in this series:

Dorset Coast from the Air

North Devon Coast from the Air

South Devon Coast from the Air

North Cornwall Coast from the Air

South Cornwall Coast from the Air

Somerset Coast from the Air

Isle of Wight & Hampshire Coast from the Air

Essex Coast from the Air

Forthcoming titles in this series:

Isle of Wight from the Air

Kent Coast from the Air

Oxfordshire from the Air

Hertfordshire from the Air

Berkshire from the Air

Essex from the Air

Kent from the Air

SUSSEX COAST
from the Air

PHOTOGRAPHY BY JASON HAWKES

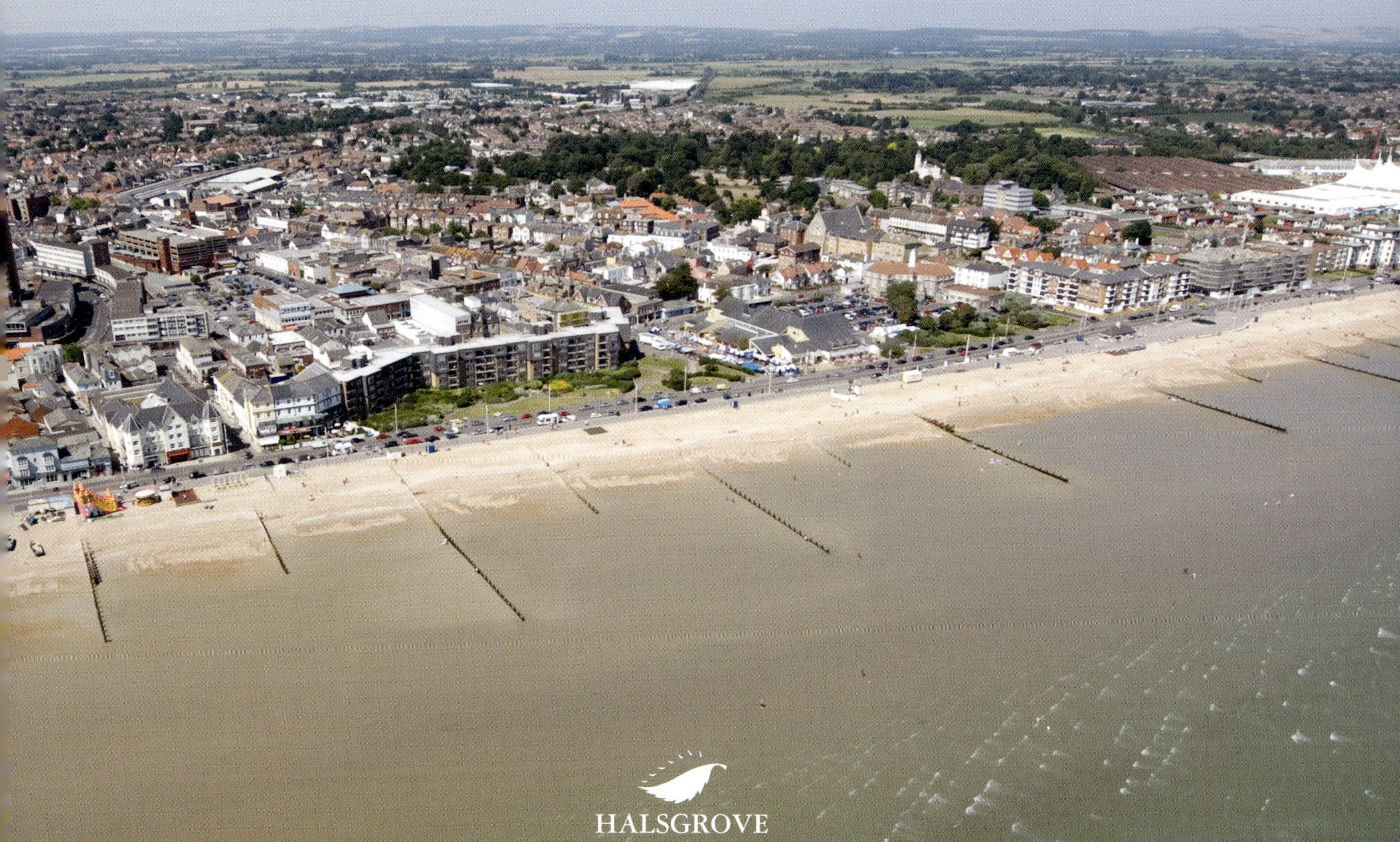

HALSGROVE

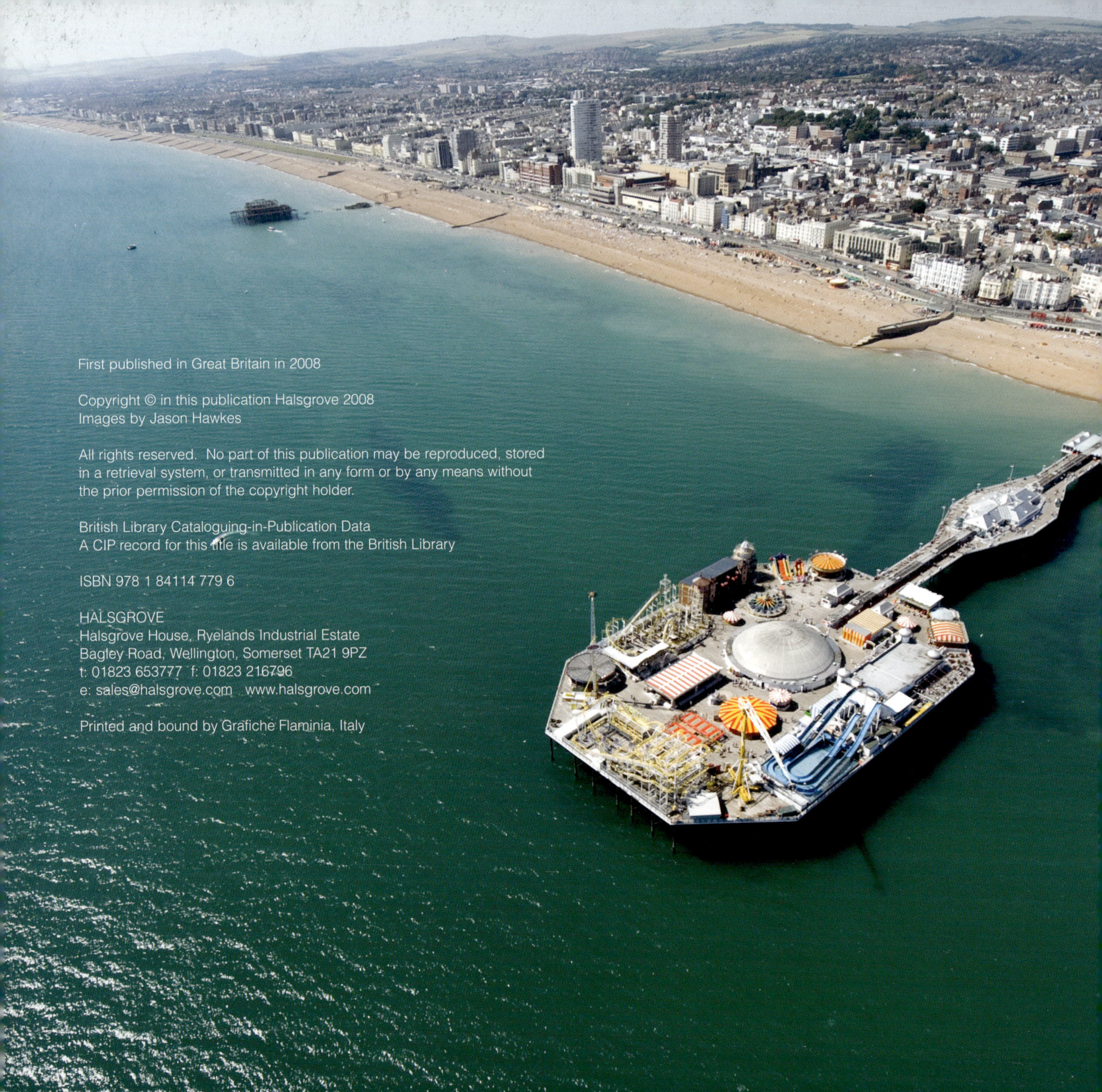

First published in Great Britain in 2008

Images by Jason Hawkes

British Library Cataloguing-in-Publication Data
A CIP record for this title is available from the British Library

ISBN 978 1 84114 779 6

HALSGROVE
Halsgrove House, Ryelands Industrial Estate
Bagley Road, Wellington, Somerset TA21 9PZ
t: 01823 653777 f: 01823 216796
e: sales@halsgrove.com www.halsgrove.com

Printed and bound by Grafiche Flaminia, Italy

INTRODUCTION

Sussex's coastline stretches eastwards from Hampshire some 90 miles (145km) from Thorney Island within Chichester Harbour to the Kent boundary near Camber Sands. The coast faces the English Channel and is largely built-up, with a variety of resort towns and ports. It has two main sections, between Selsey Bill and Beachy Head, and then from Beachy Head to Dungeness (over the border in Kent). The conurbation of Brighton, Hove, Worthing and Littlehampton has a population of over 450,000, and stretches for some 30 miles (50km) from Littlehampton in the west to Seaford in the east. Other major settlements on the coastline are Chichester, Bognor Regis, Eastbourne and Hastings.

Alongside this development, the Sussex coast contains some of the finest scenery in Southern England, including the magnificent white chalk cliffs of Beachy Head and the Seven Sisters. It was on these shores that momentous events in English history took place. The Roman legions landed here, to be followed by the Saxons, the Viking raiders and the Norman invasion of 1066; only since the eighteenth century has the coastline's reputation as a fashionable resort for tourism and leisure been developed.

The superb aerial photographs in this book provided a fascinating overview of this historic coastline which these days provides the means for thousands to enjoy leisure pursuits including watersports of all kinds, birdwatching, or simply walking the coastal footpaths.

The principal attraction of aerial photographs is that they are literally a bird's-eye view, allowing us to look down on the landscape from a perspective that we never normally see. Such pictures reveal to us things that are normally hidden from view, and often surprise us when we find that what we had imagined the layout of the land to be is in reality quite different. The best practitioners of this genre of photography also strive to capture an aesthetic in the images they take, and these pictures, sometimes quite abstract in appearance, are often strikingly beautiful in their own right.

Jason Hawkes is one of the country's best-known photographers specialising in aerial photography. From his base near London he travels worldwide to produce images for books, advertising and design. Since 1991 he has provided photographs for major international companies including Nike, HSBC, Ford, Rolex, Toyota and BP. The images in this book and the sister publications in the series were specially commissioned by Halsgrove.

For more information regarding Jason Hawkes' work visit www.jasonhawkes.com. For a complete list of titles in this series and other Halsgrove titles visit www.halsgrove.com.

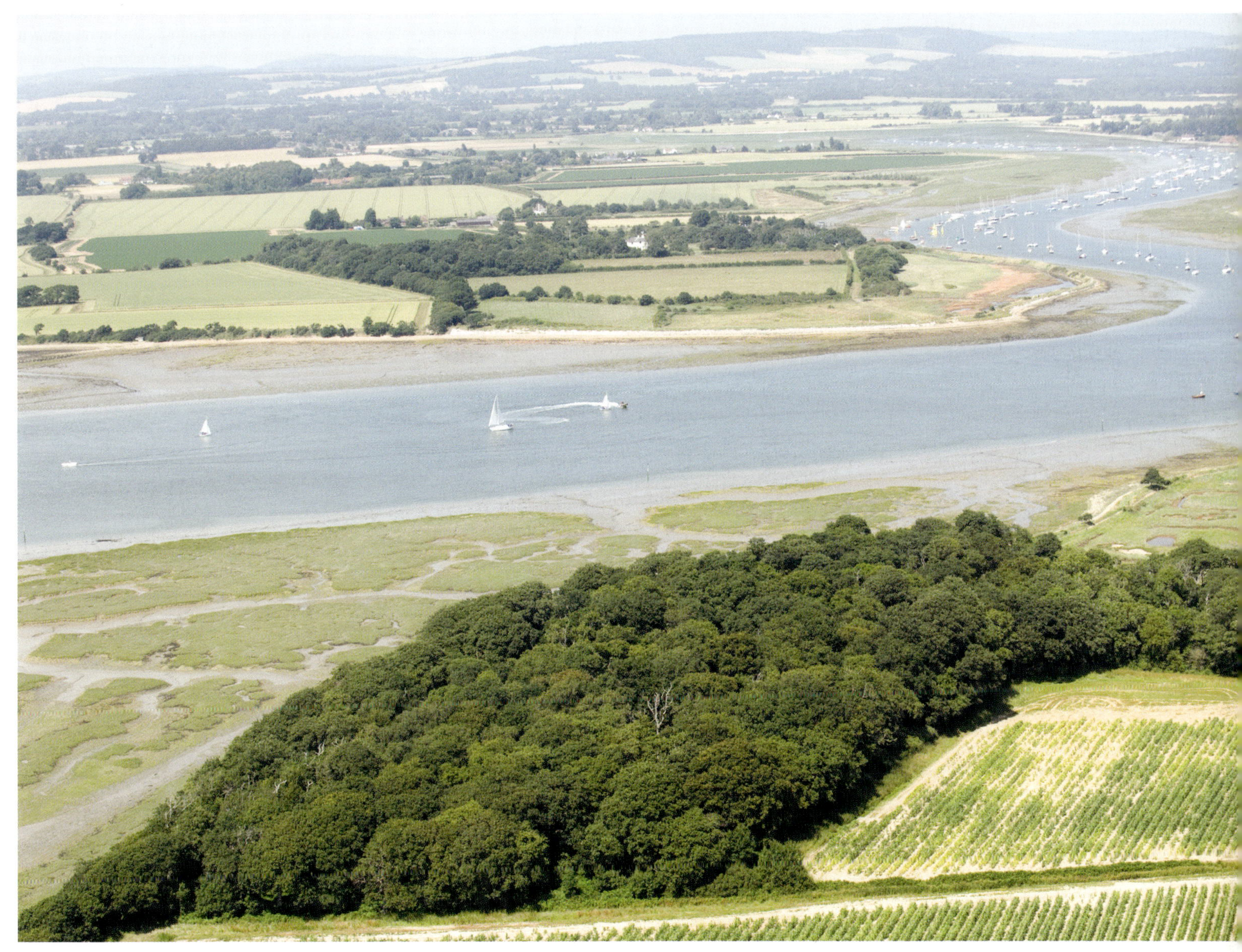

Near West Itchenor, Chichester Harbour.

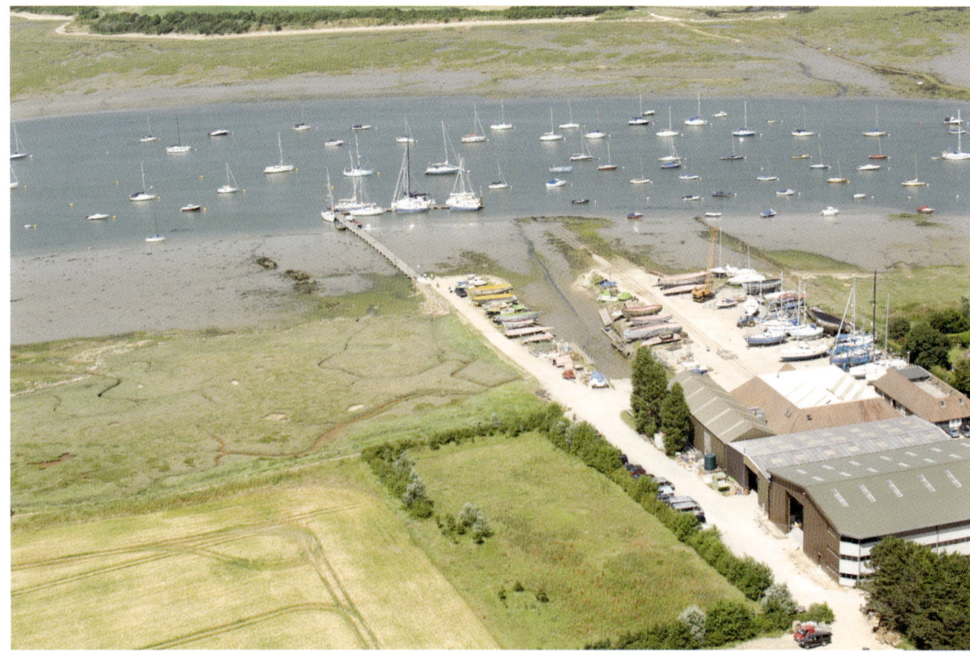

West Itchenor, in the Chichester Channel.

Following page: Dinghies and tenders lie tumbled on the foreshore at West Itchenor.

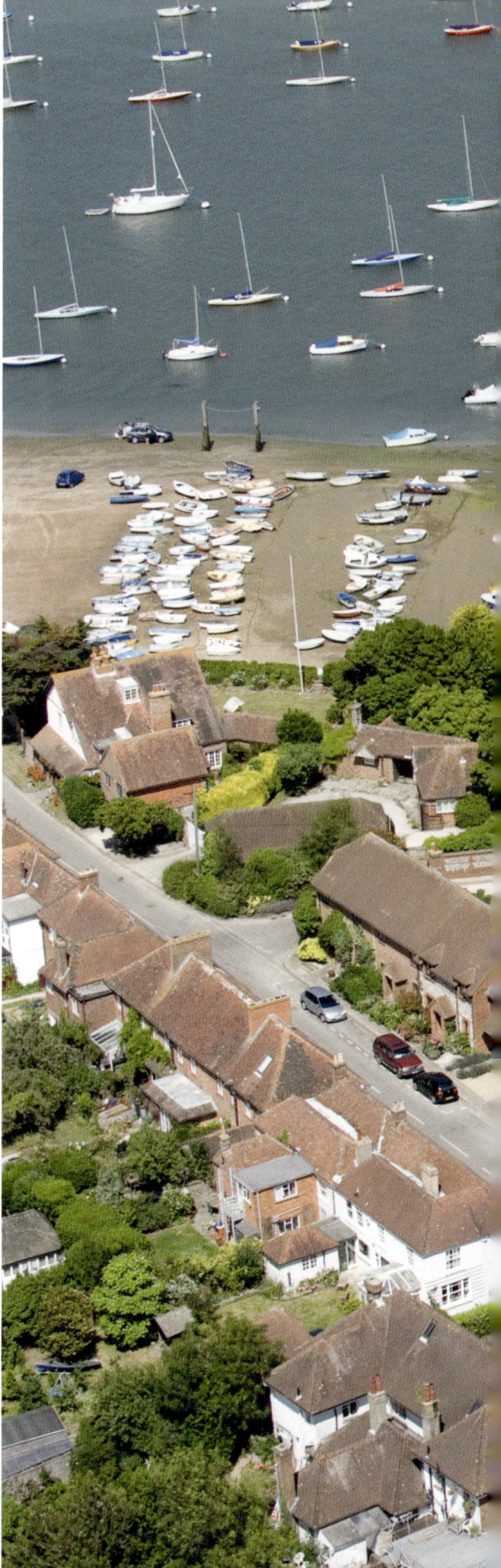

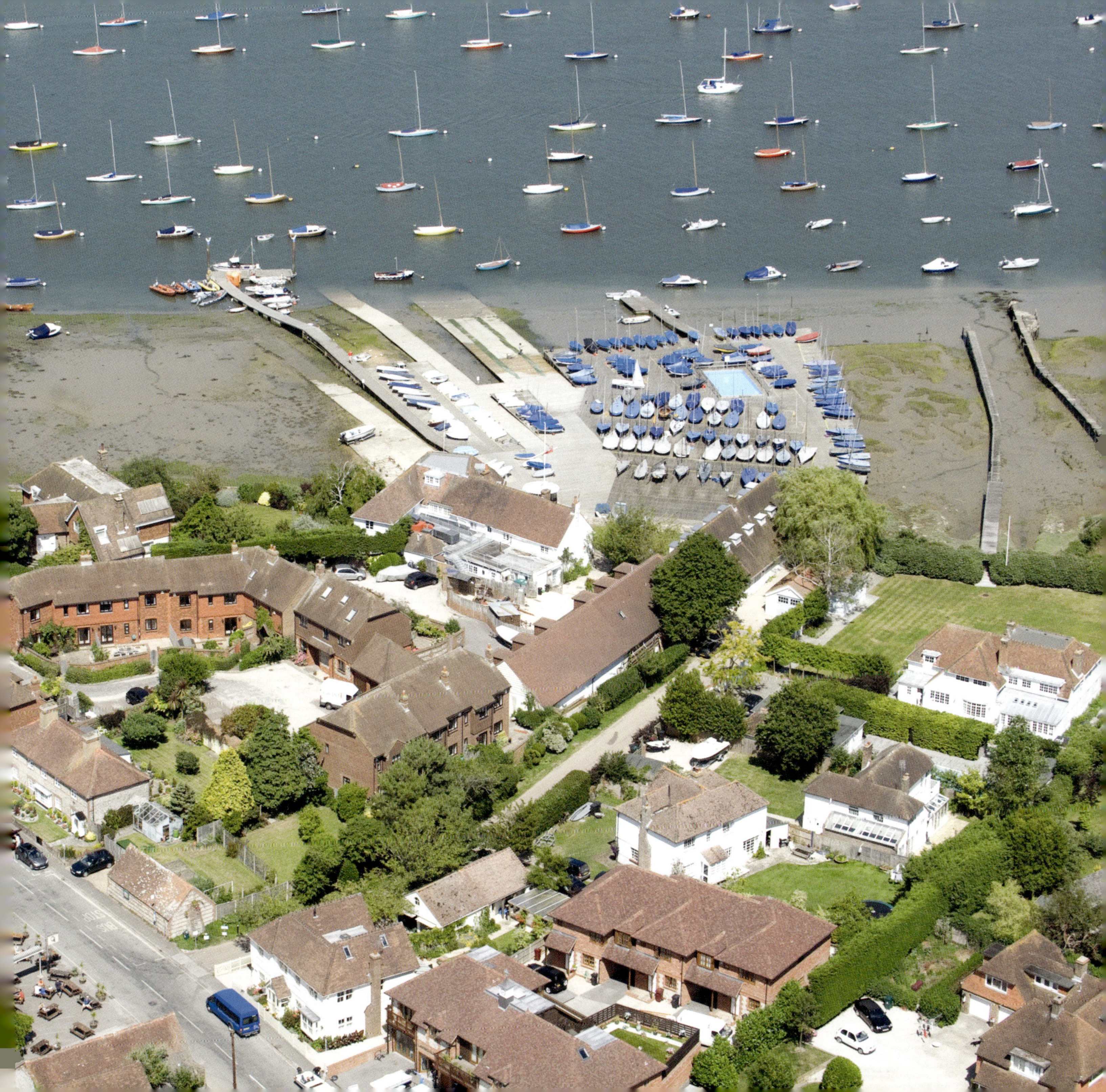

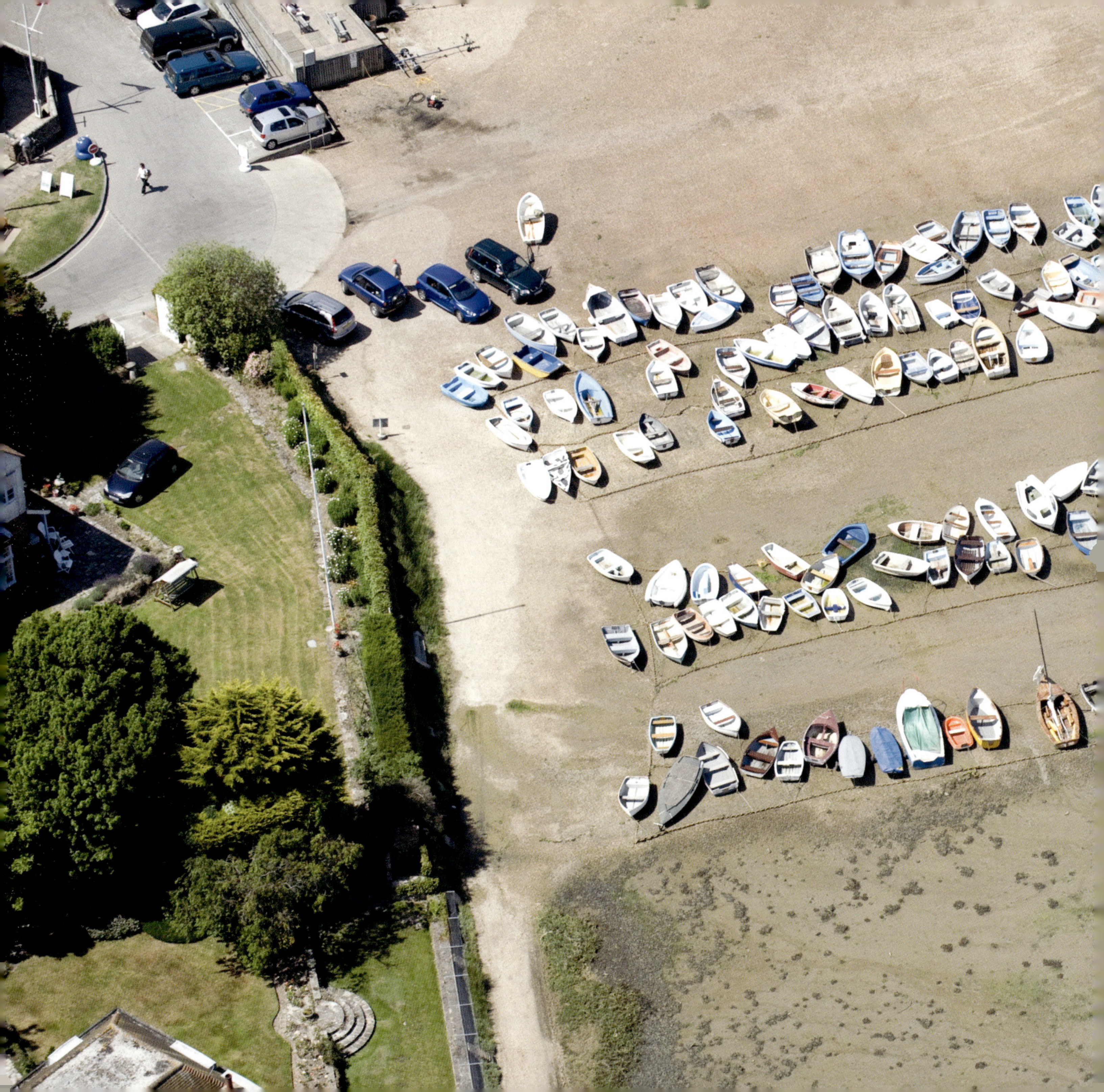

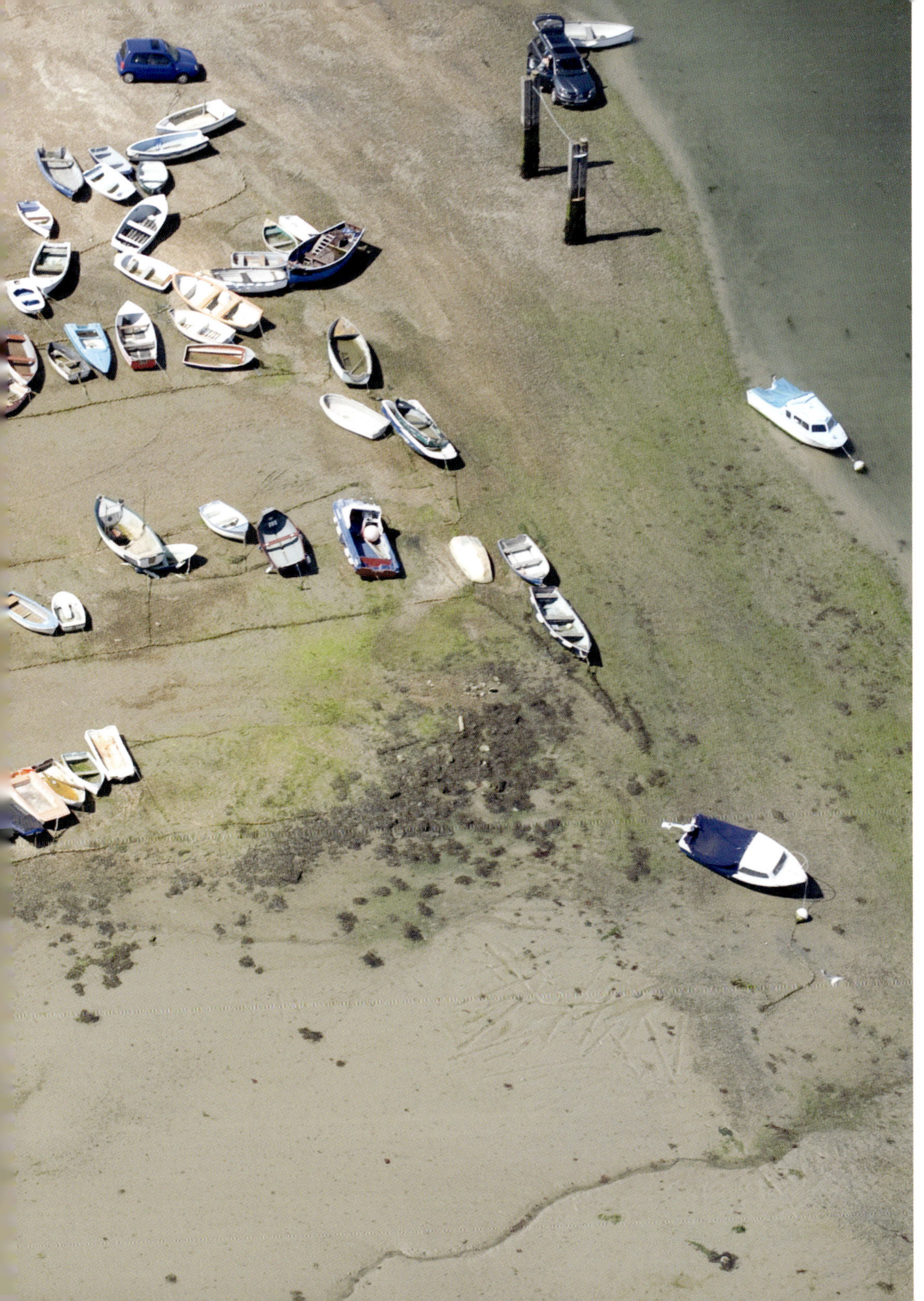

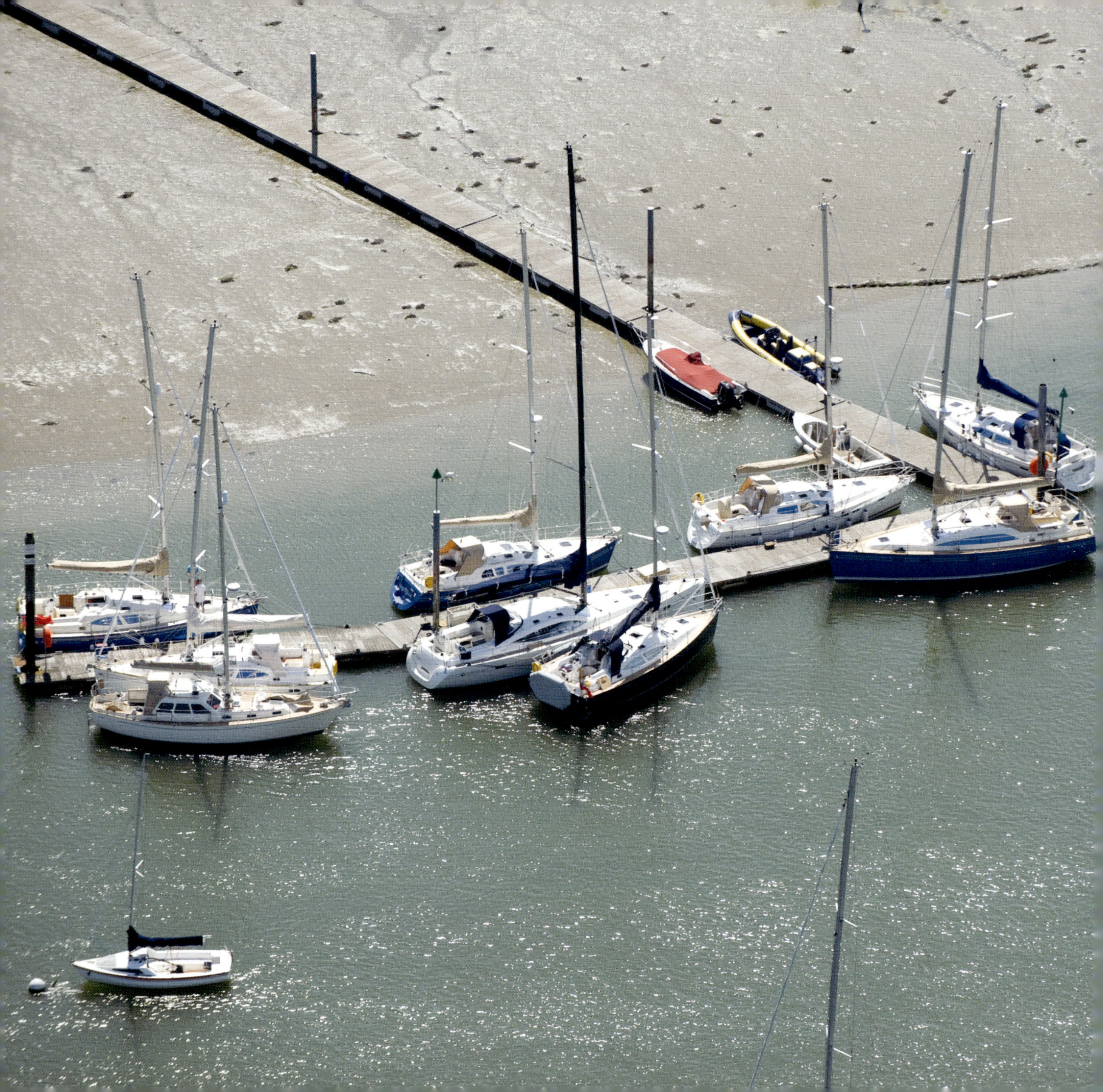

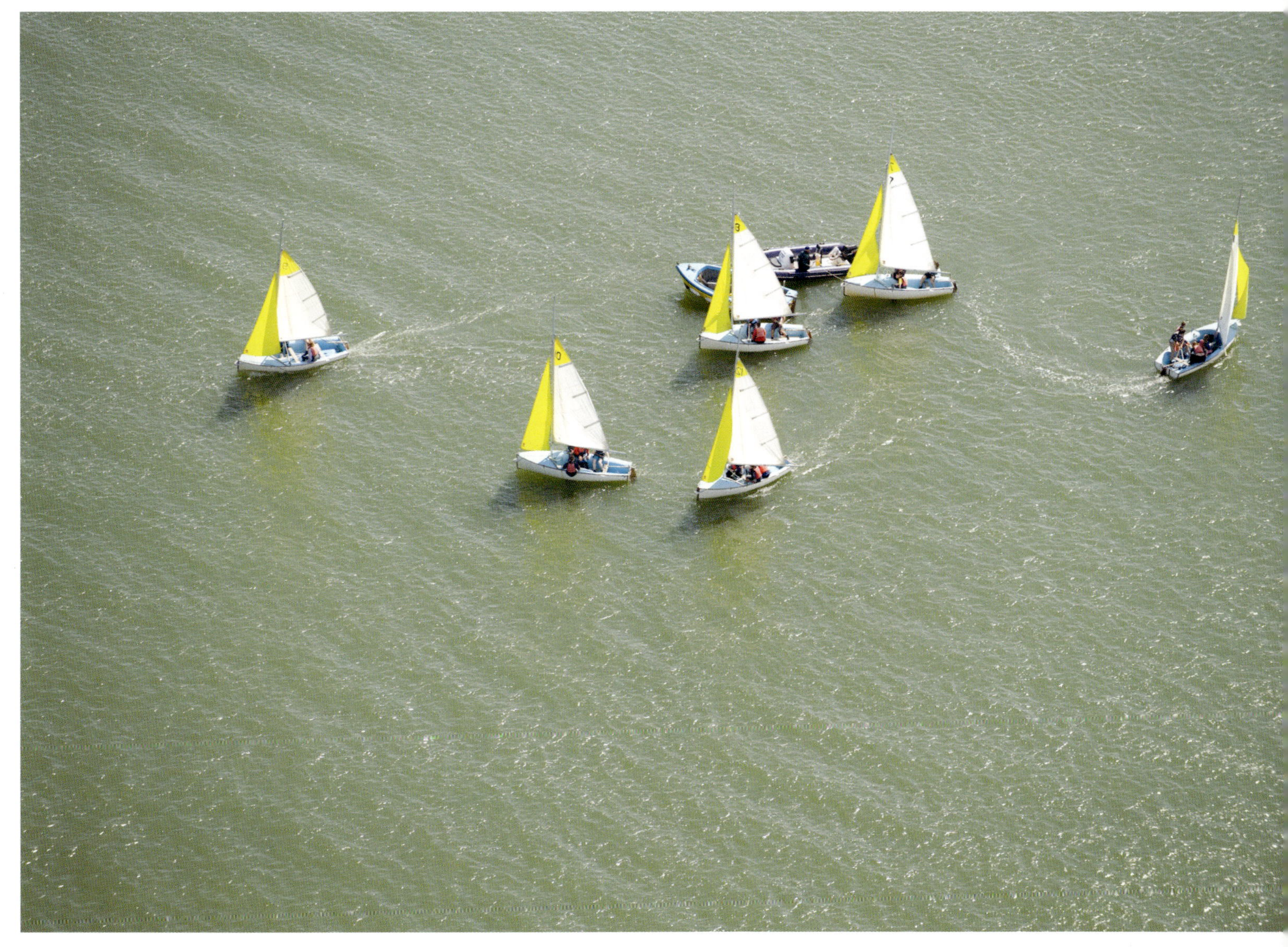

The sheltered waters of Chichester Harbour make for perfect sailing.

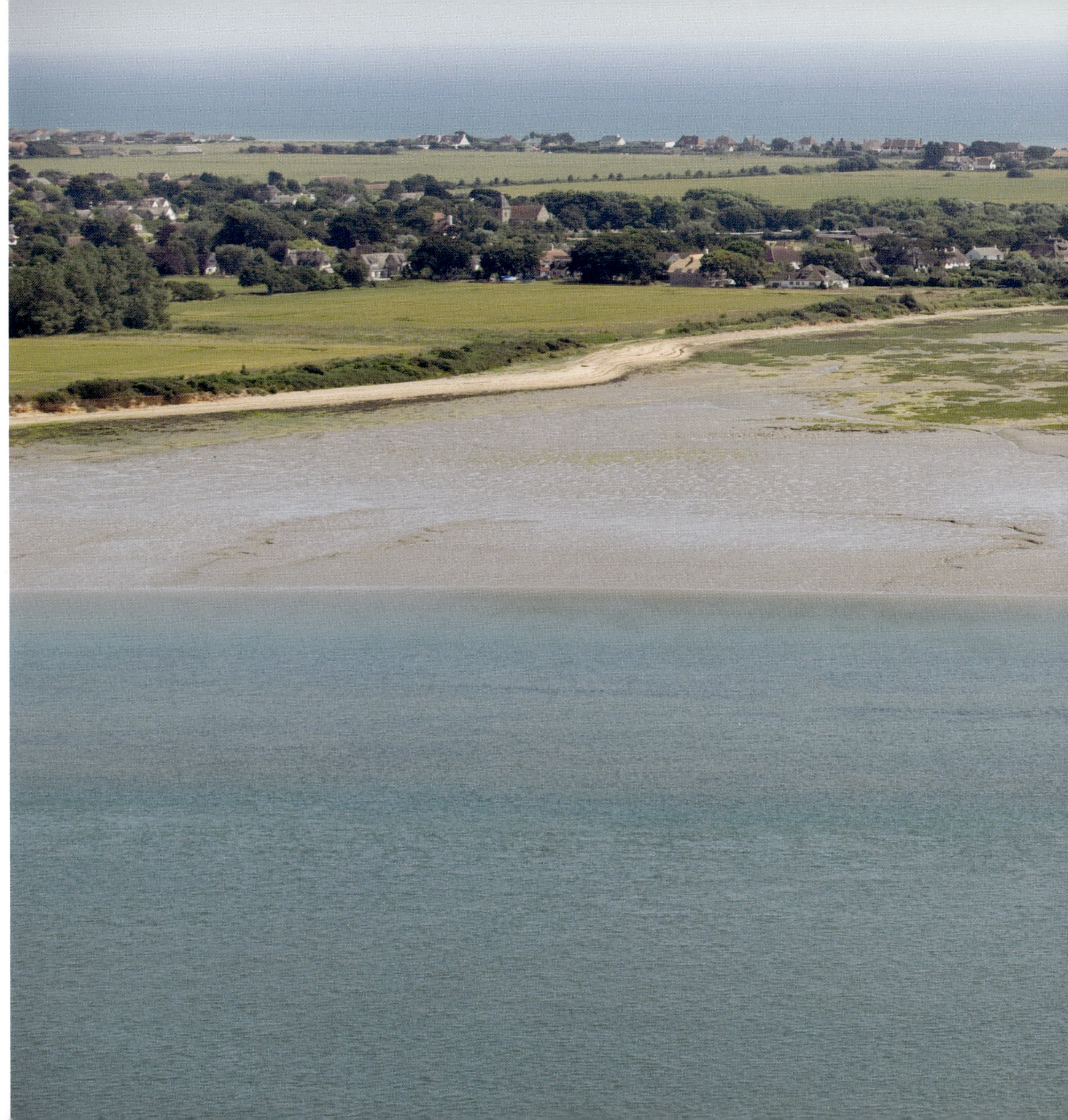

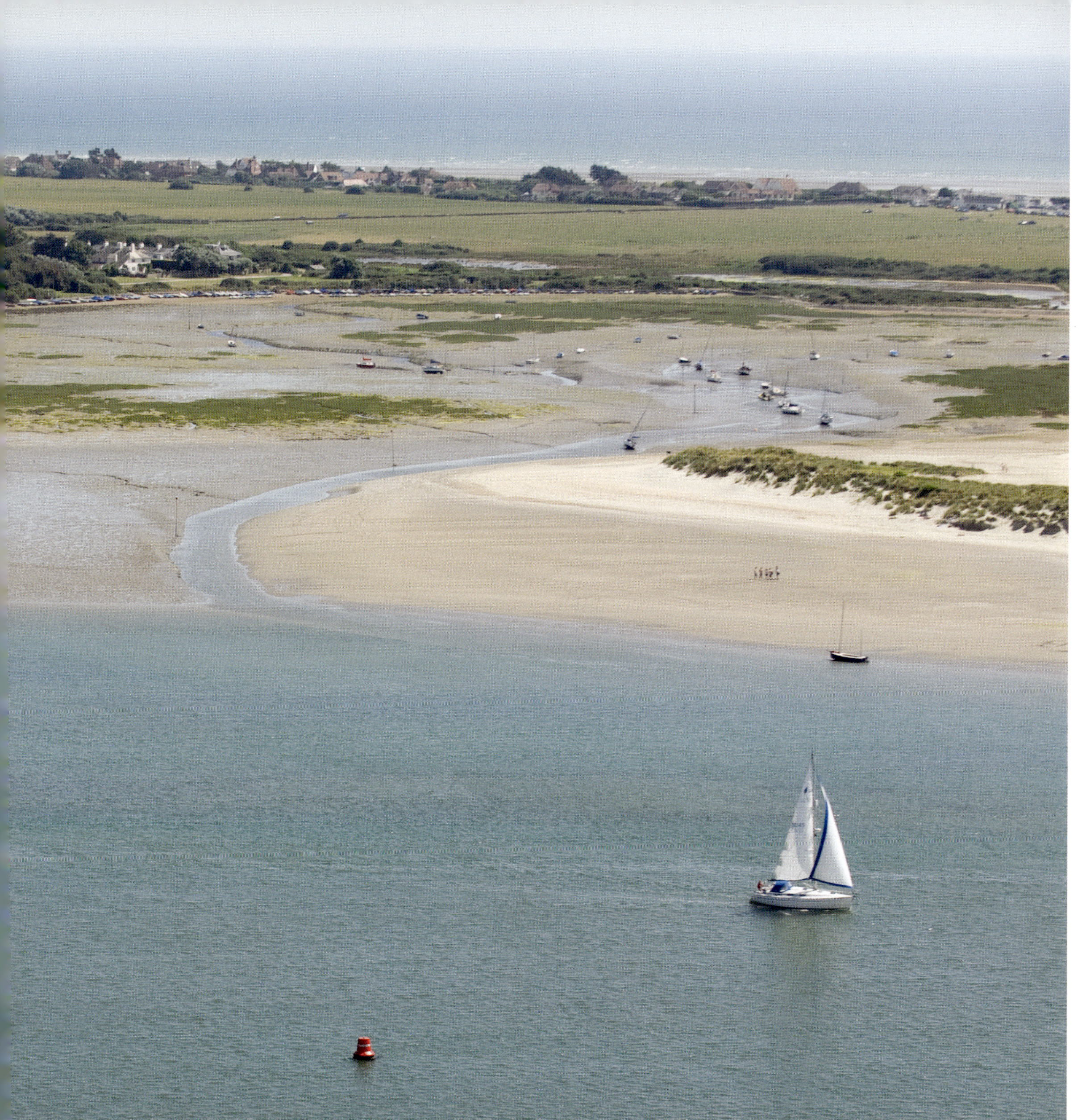

Previous page: Low water in Chichester Harbour.

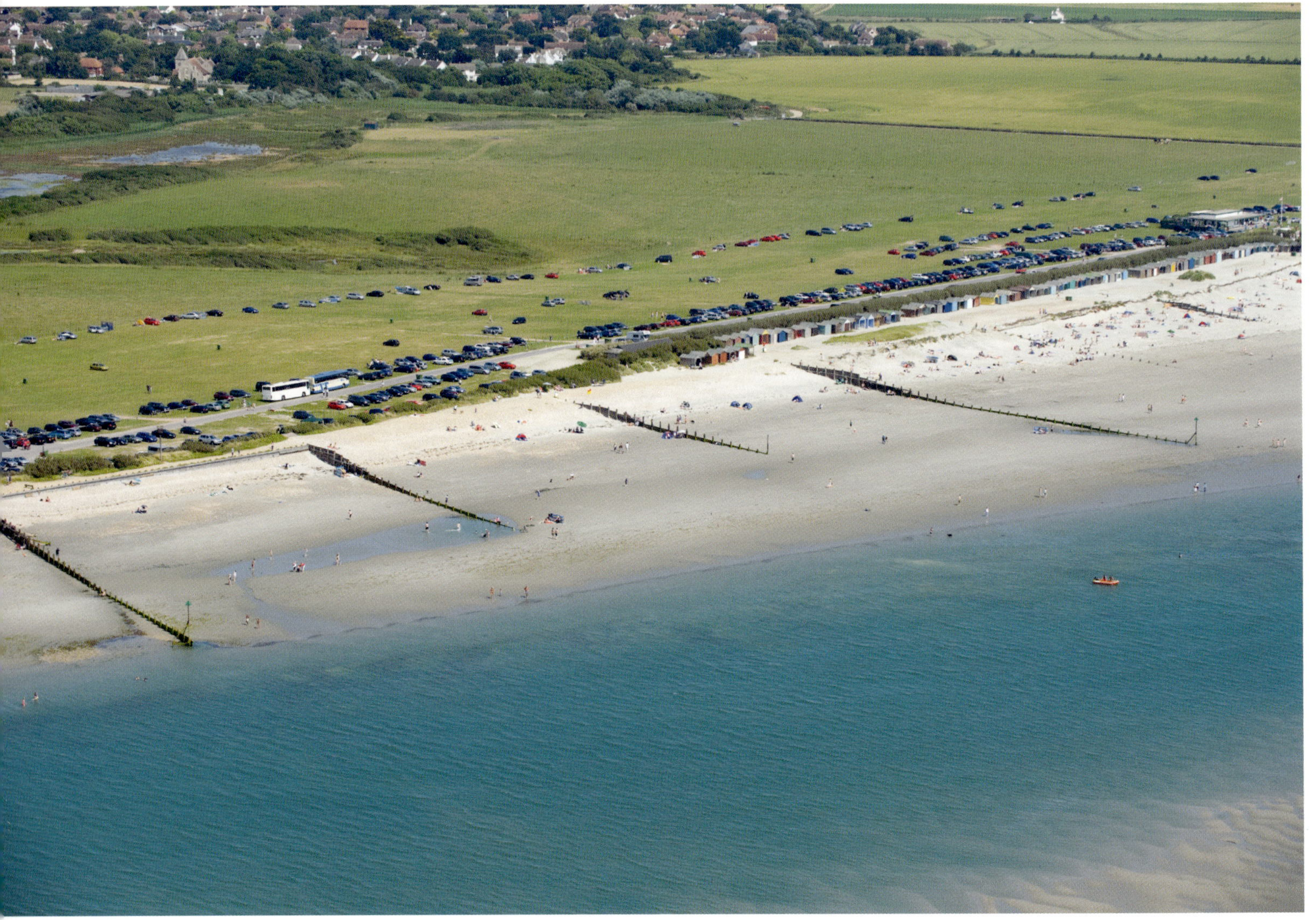

West Wittering lies at the eastern mouth of Chichester Harbour. It offers safe beaches, ideal for holidaymakers and wind surfers.

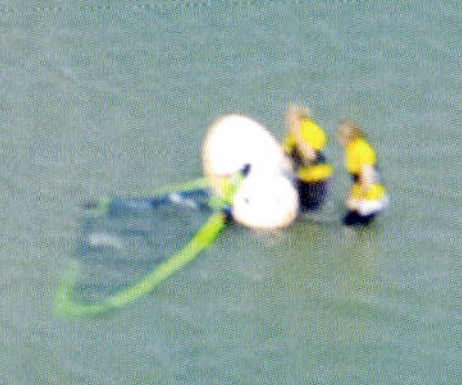
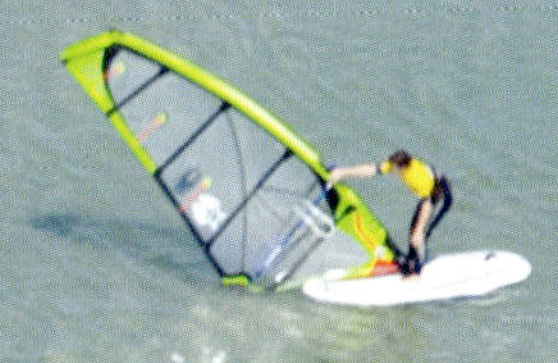
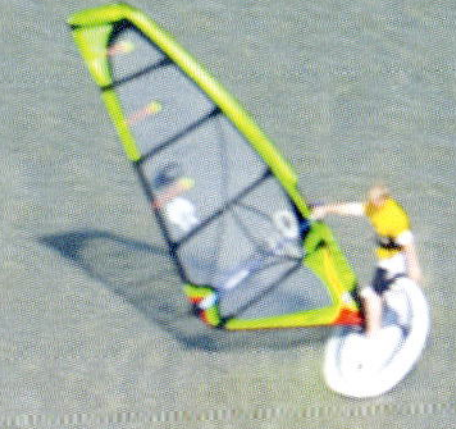
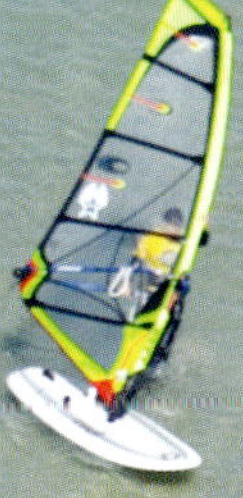

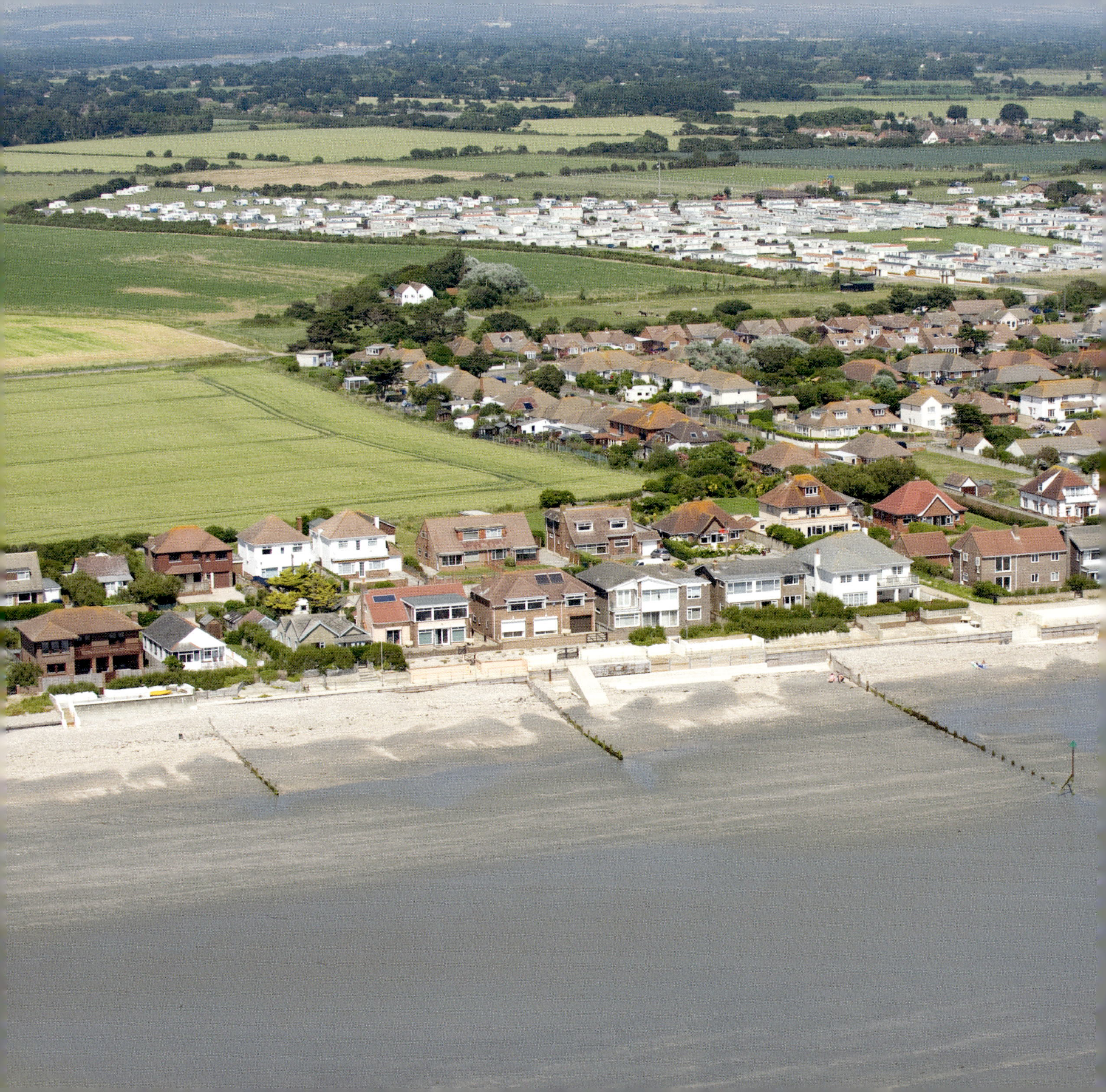

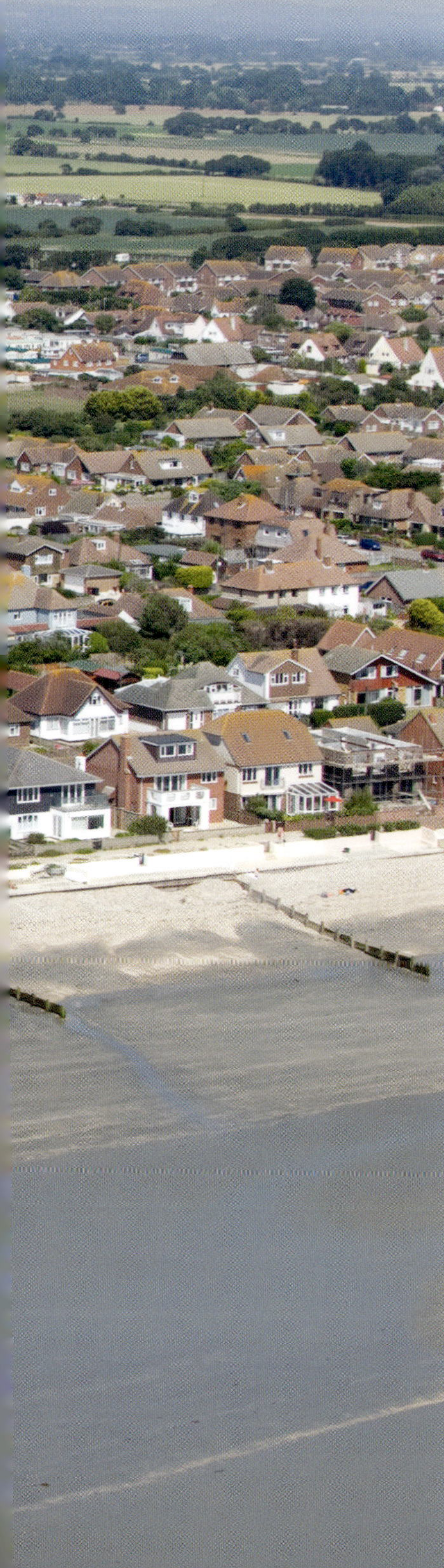

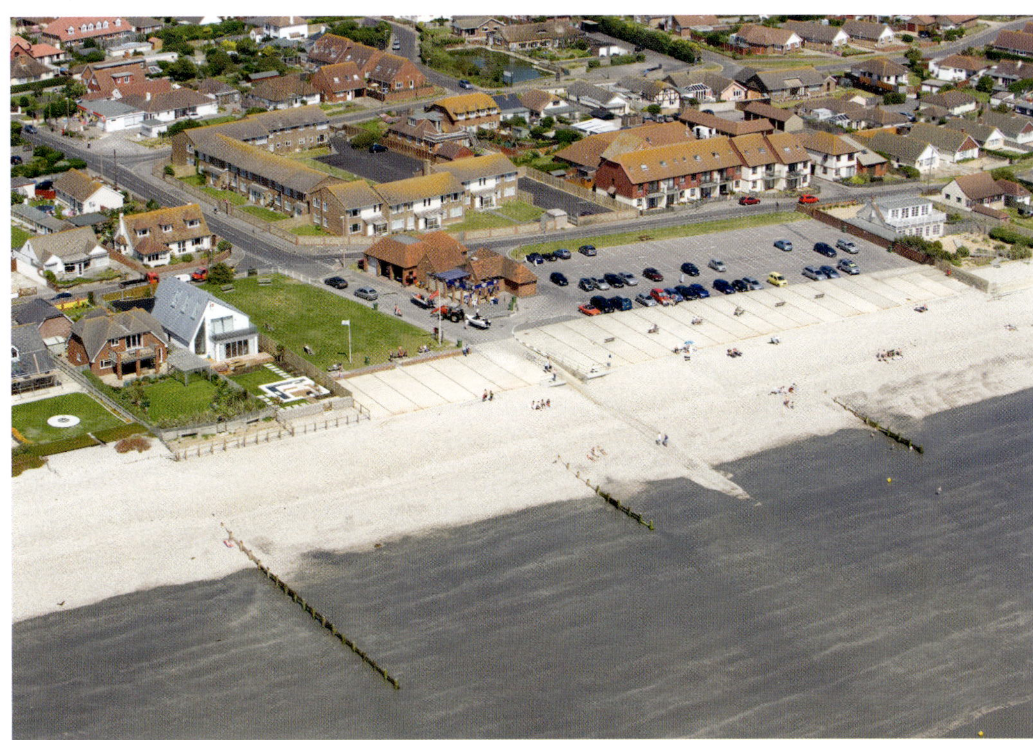

Like its neighbour, East Wittering is a popular destination for holidaymakers.

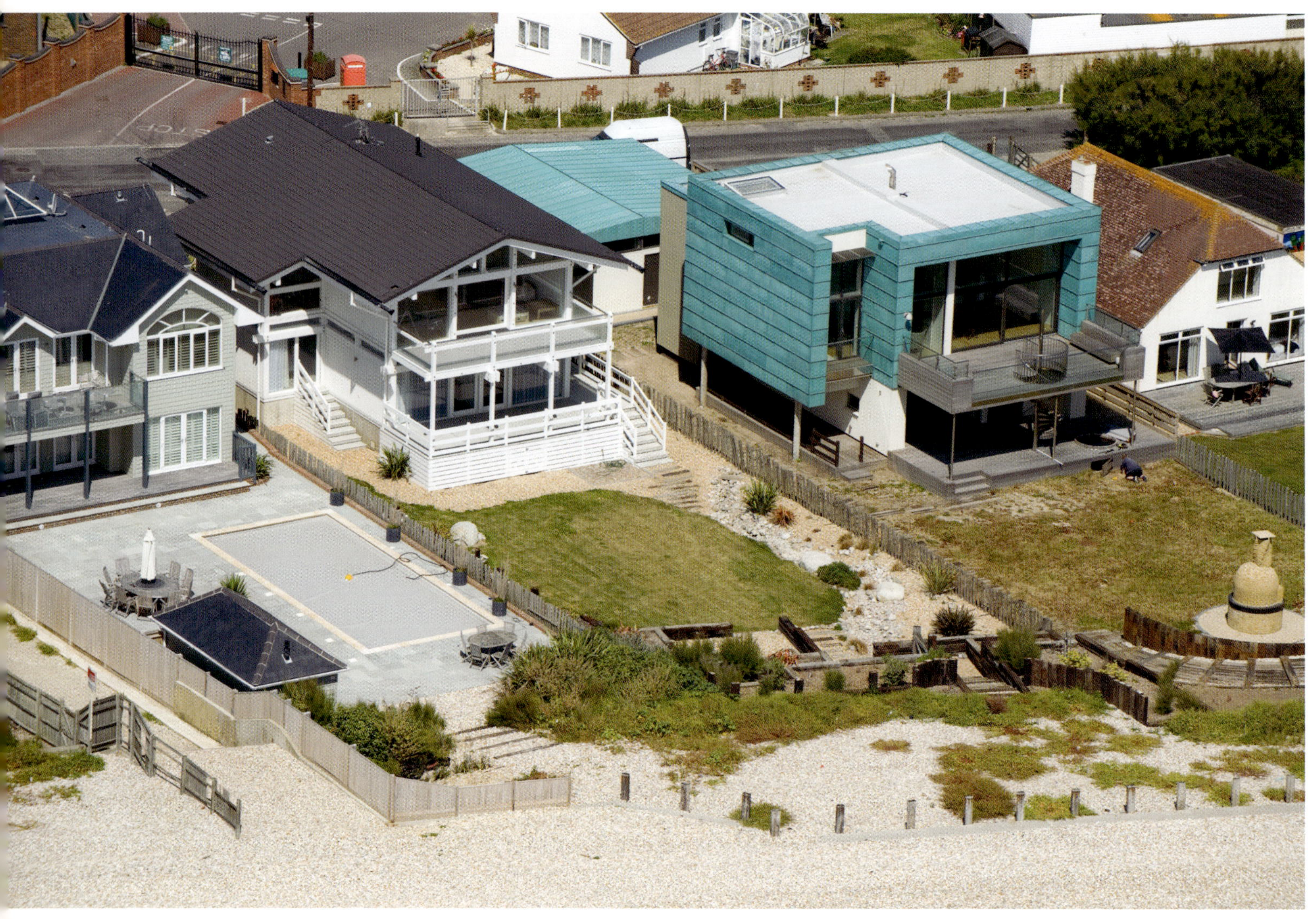

Bracklesham lies east of East Wittering. These beach-side homes offer superb views of the English Channel and westwards to the Isle of Wight.

The Waterfront Complex at West Sands which lies just to the east of Selsey. This holiday park is said to be the largest of its kind in Europe.

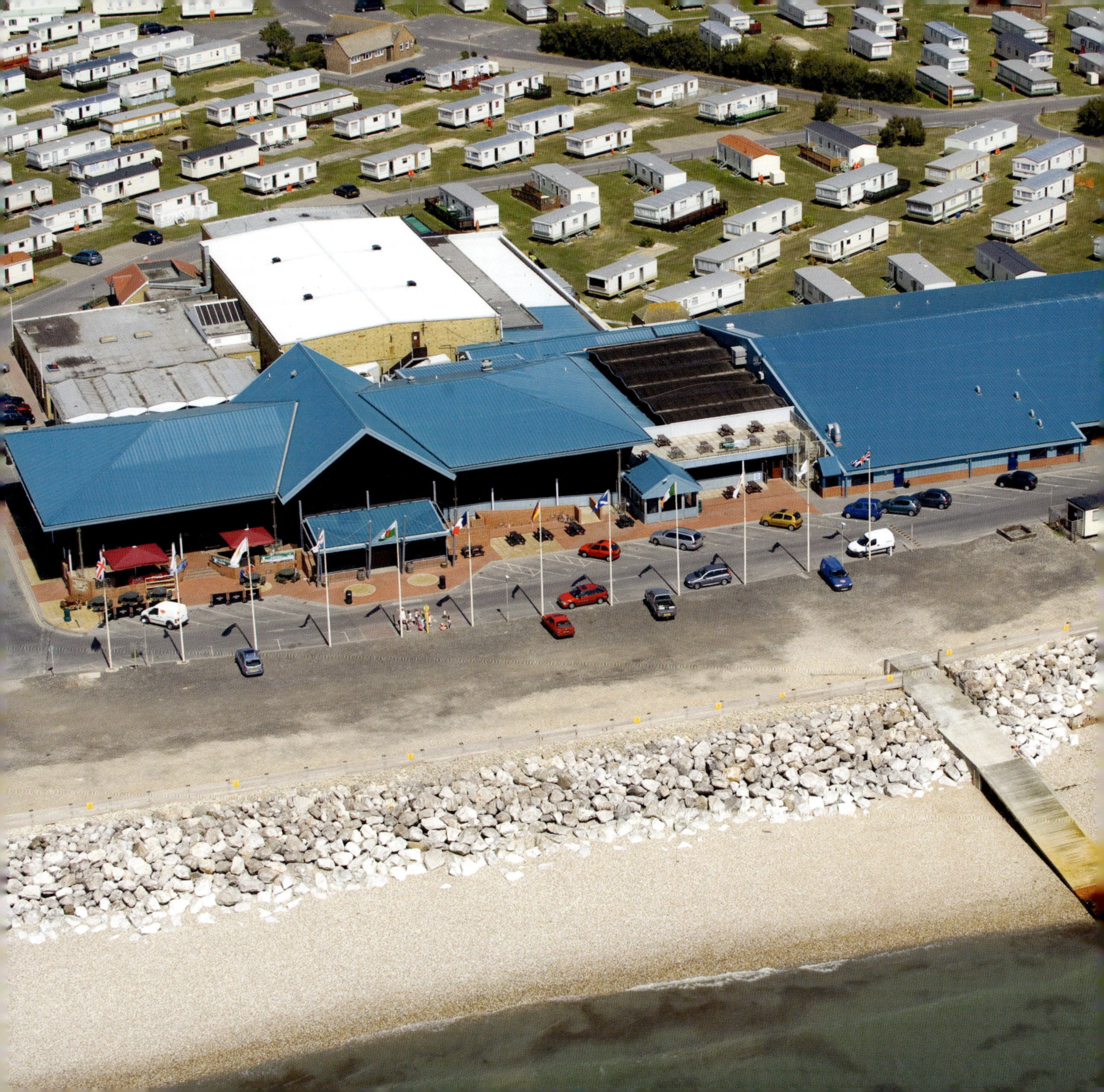

The fun fair at West Sands.

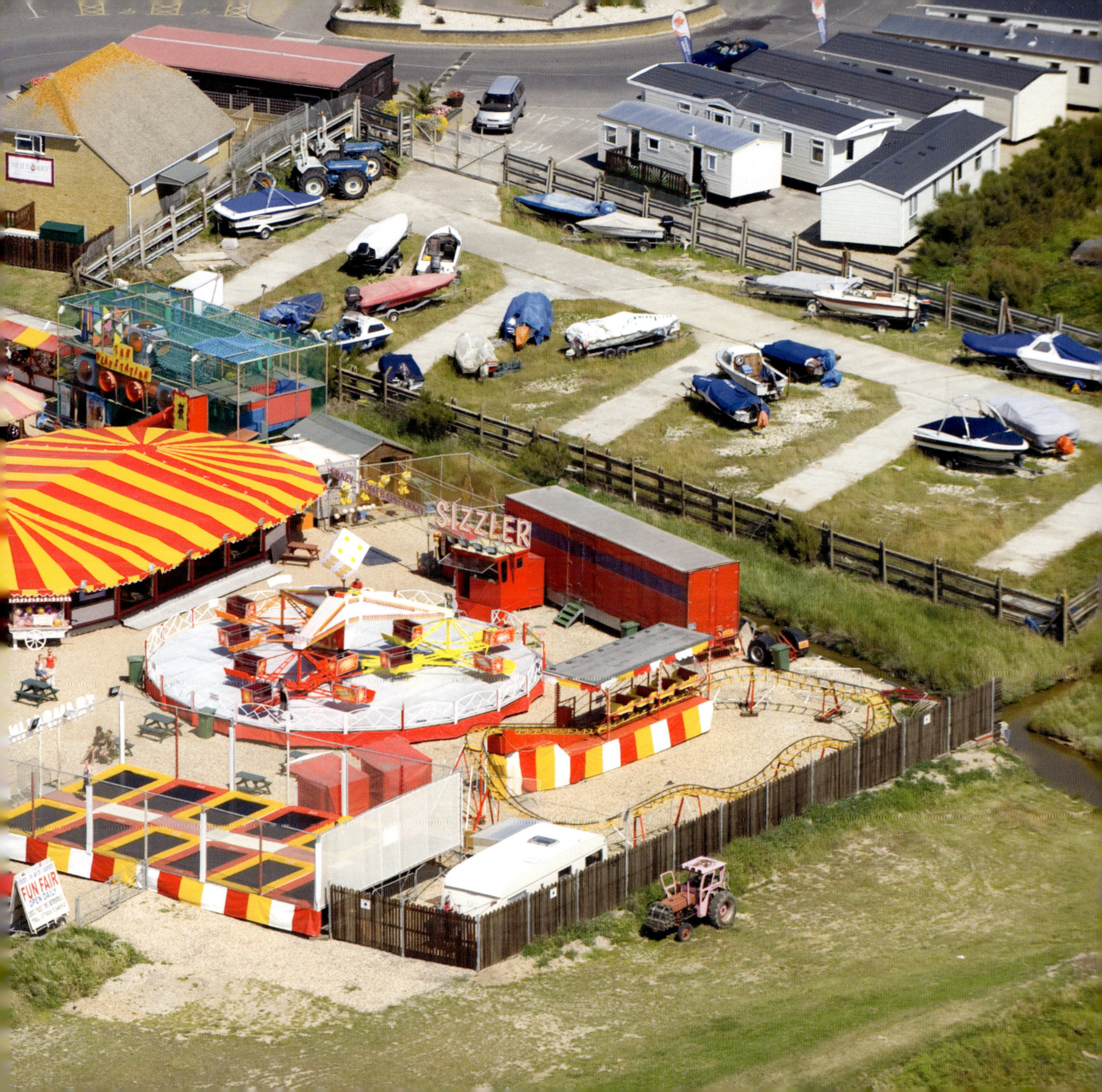
SIZZLER
FUN FAIR
OPEN DAILY

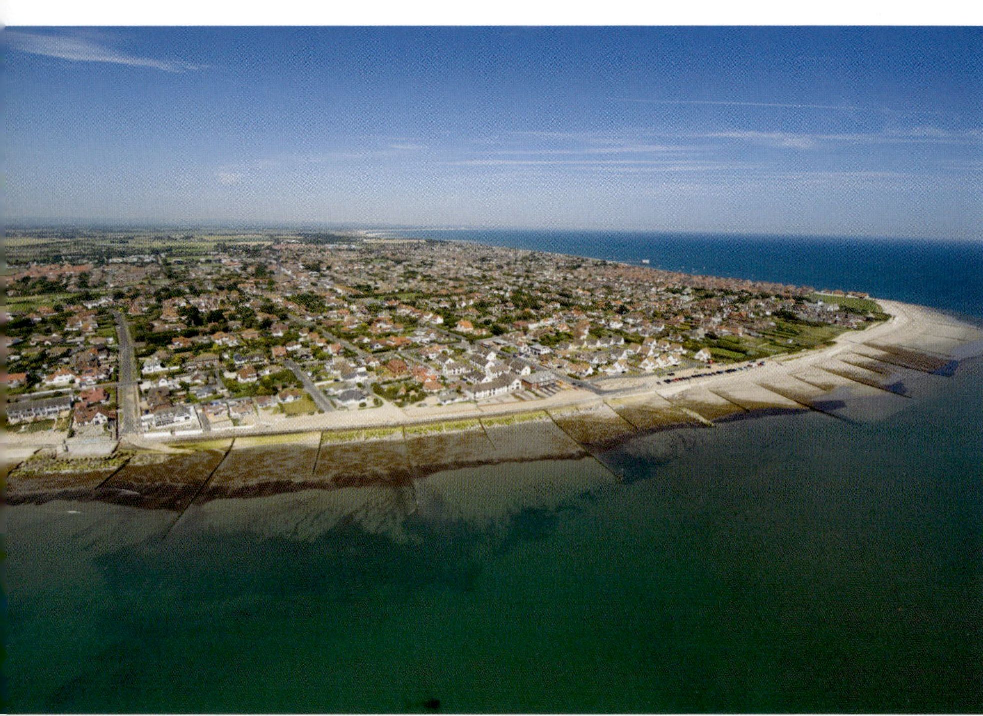

Lying a few miles south of Chichester, Selsey sits at the southern-most tip of the Manhood Peninsula. The settlement's name derives from 'Seal Island.'

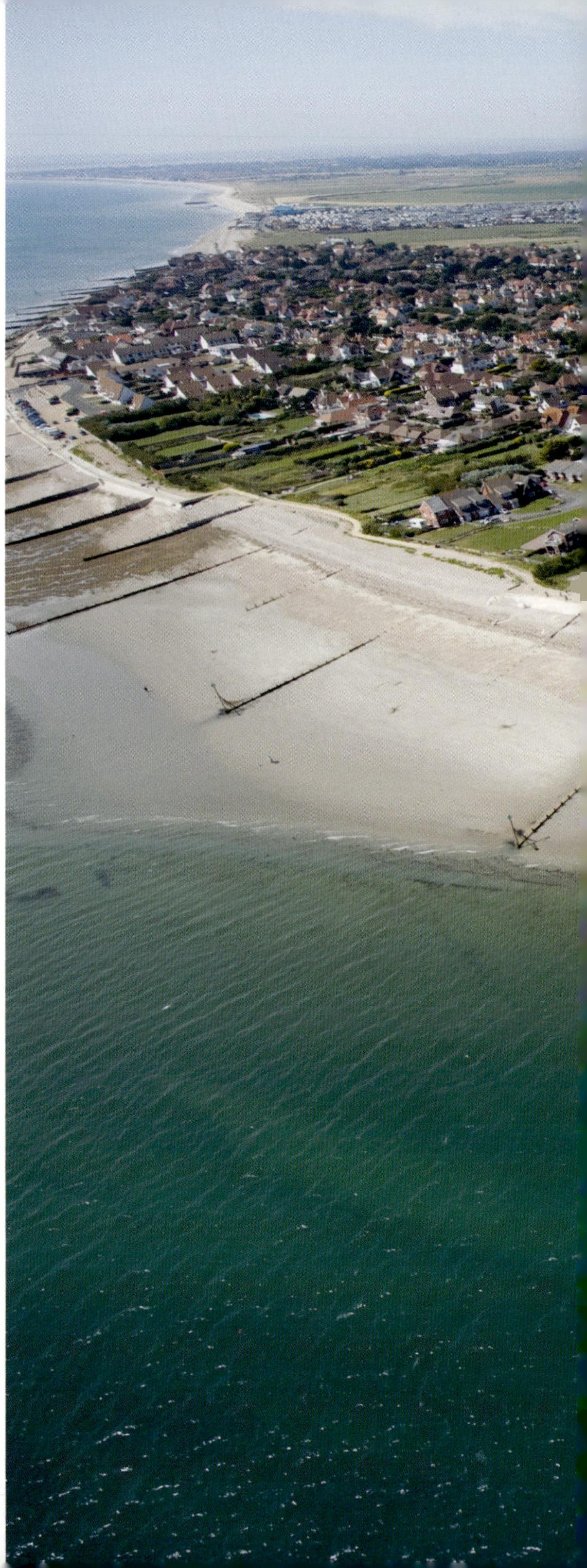

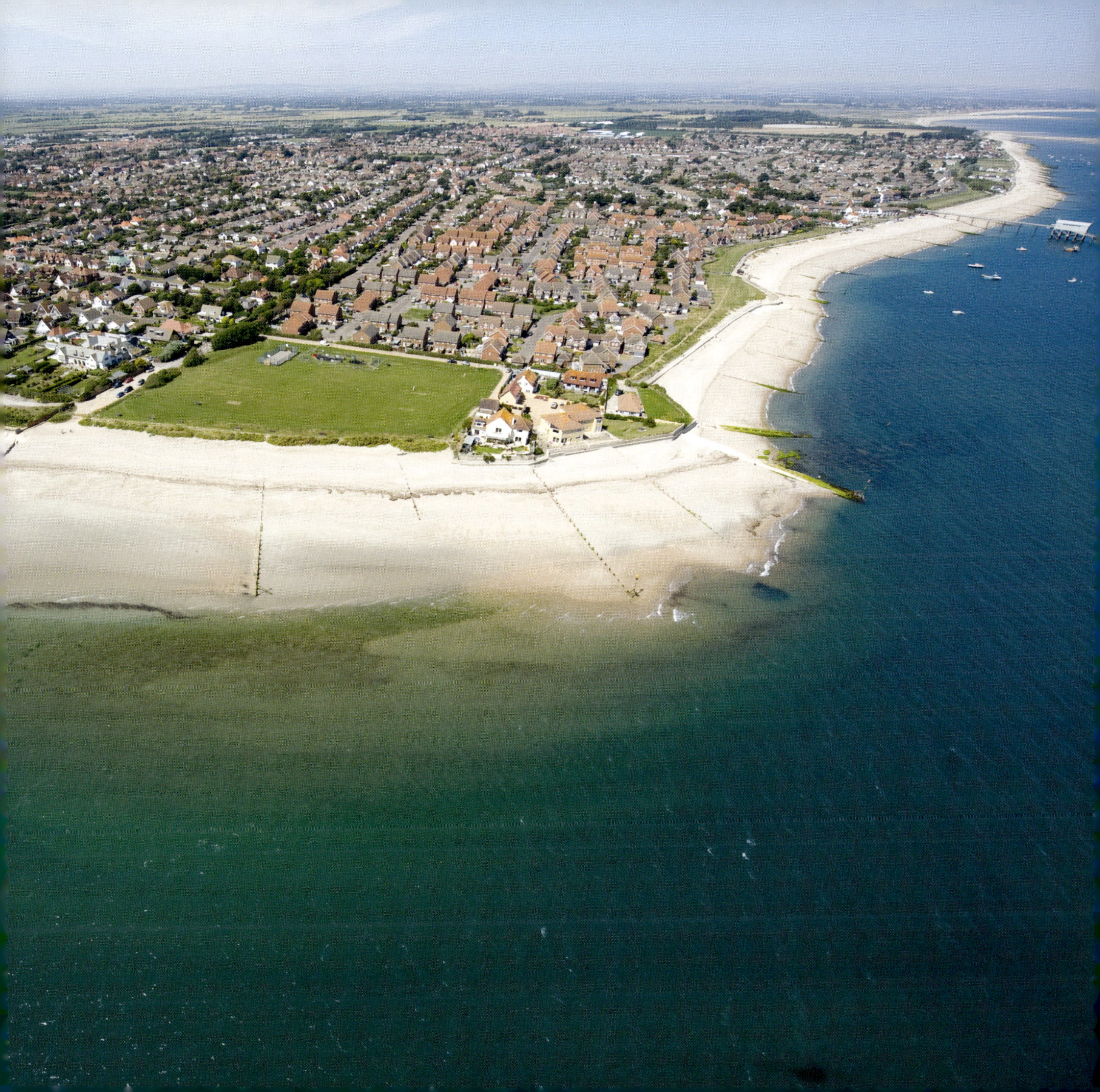

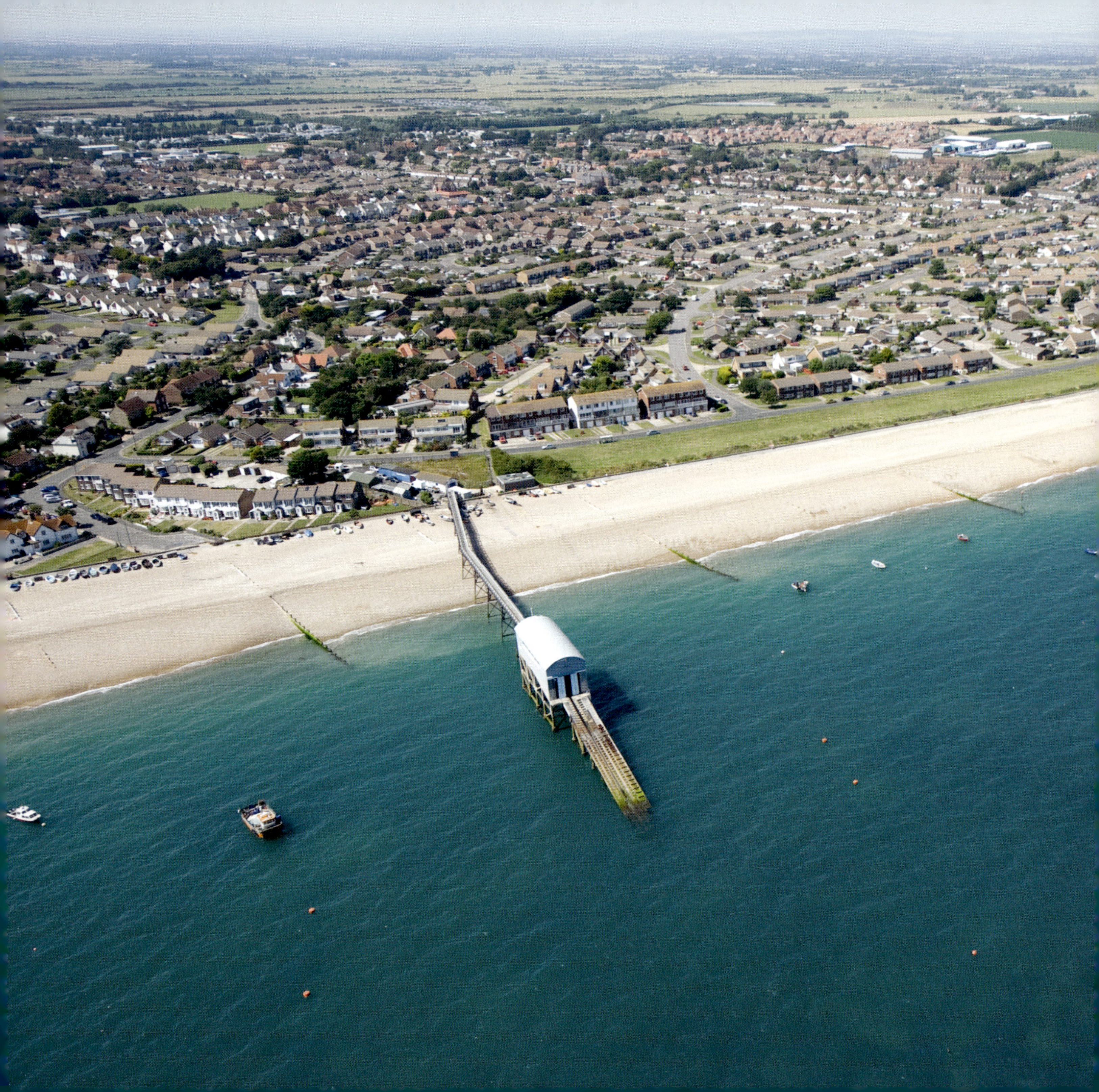

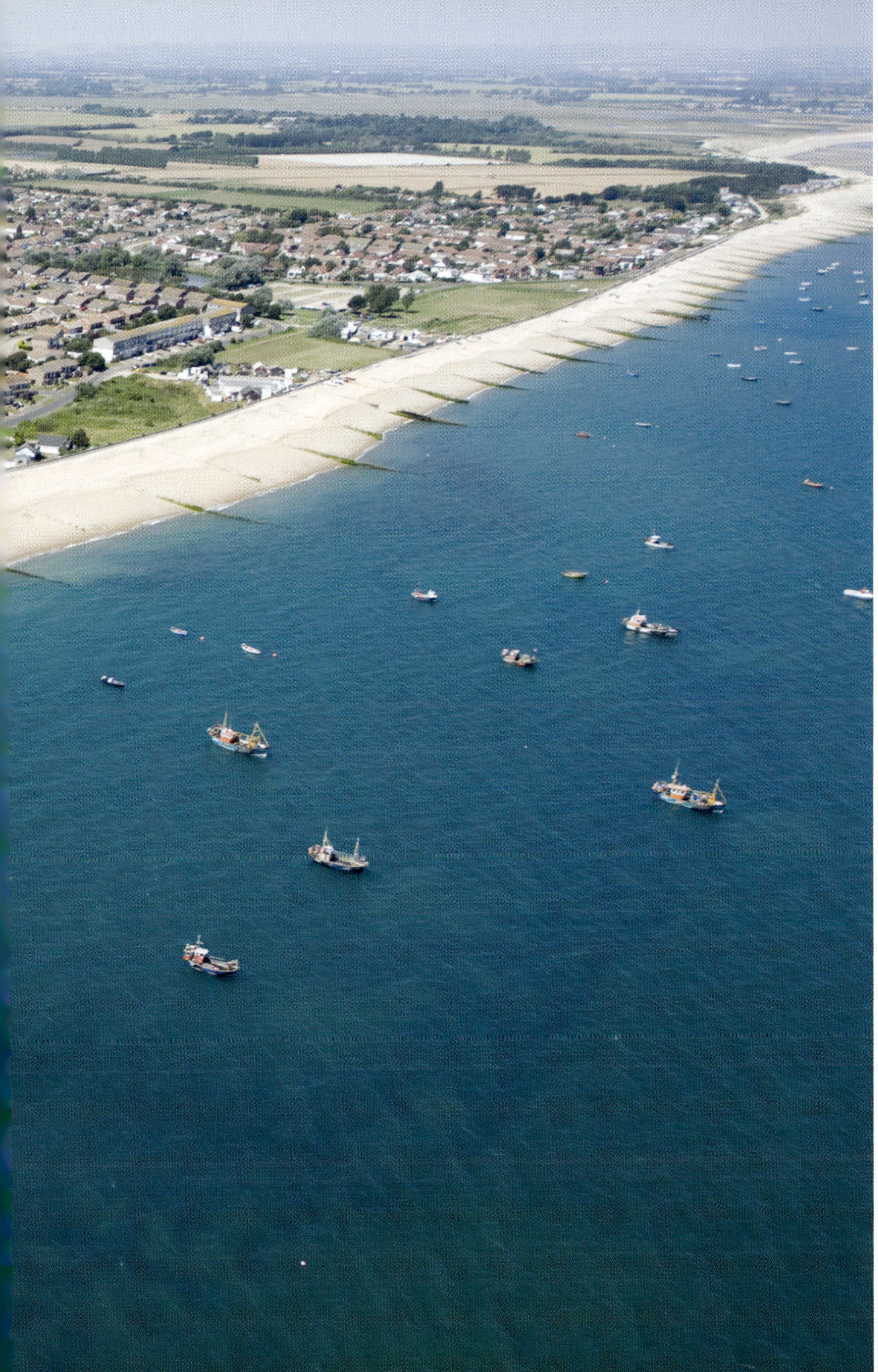

Its relatively low lying position has left Selsey vulnerable to flooding, and erosion on this coast is a constant threat. The lifeboat station with a new approach-way was built in 1960.

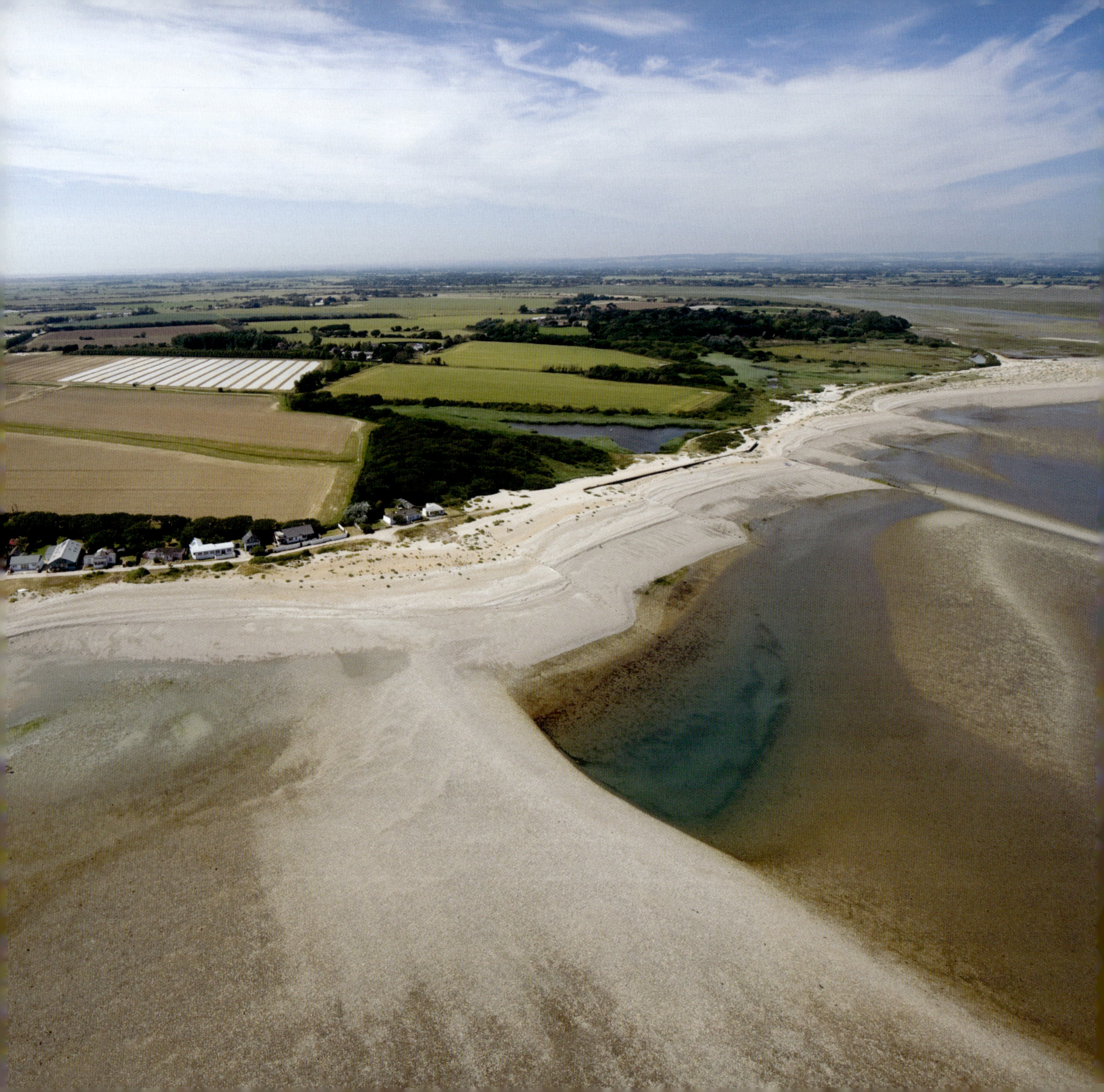

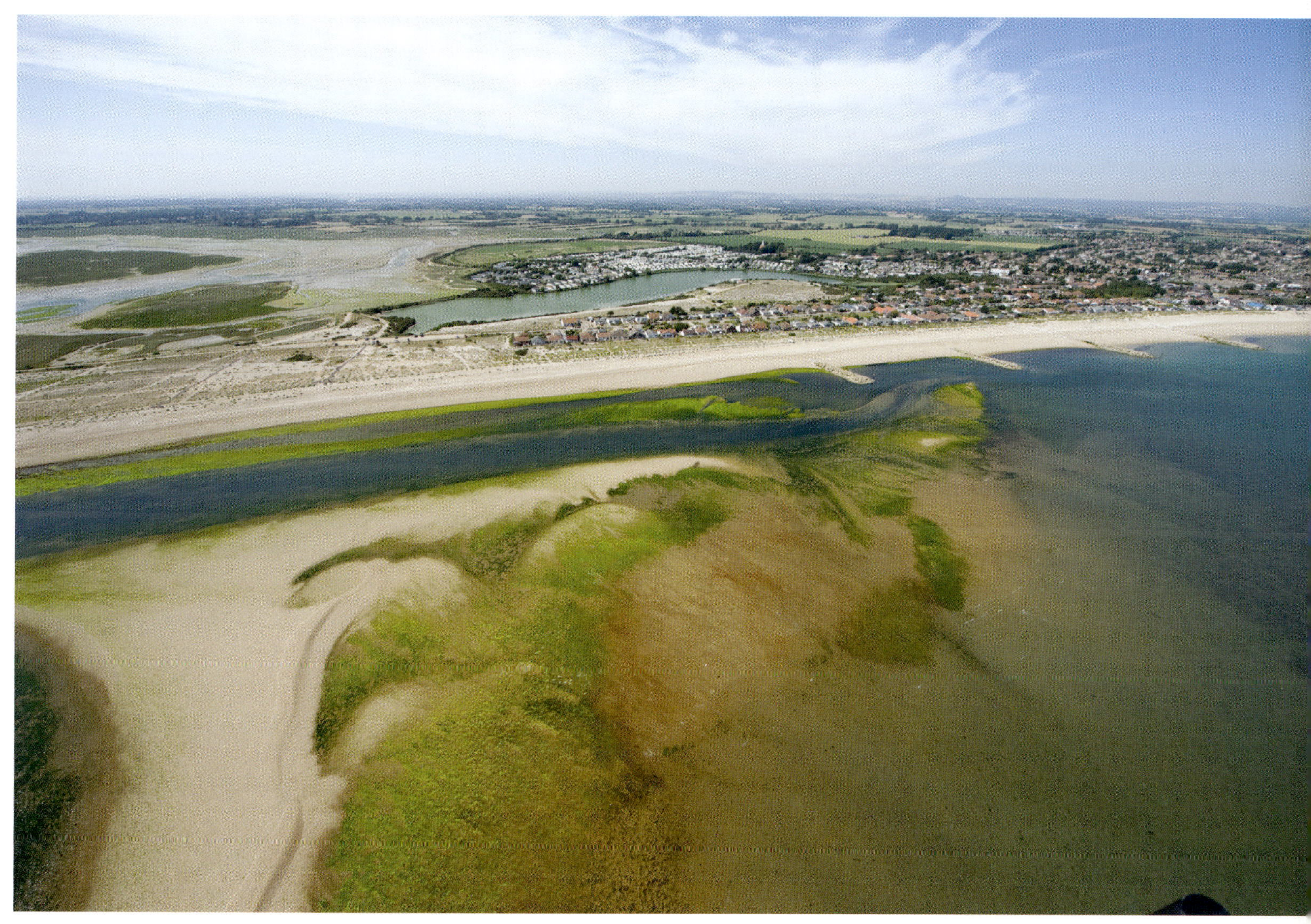

Left: Looking east from Selsey towards Pagham Harbour.

Above: Once a thriving port, and home to smugglers, Pagham Harbour is now a nature reserve. Pagham Lagoon, seen centre, used to be the outlet to Pagham Harbour in the late 1800s.

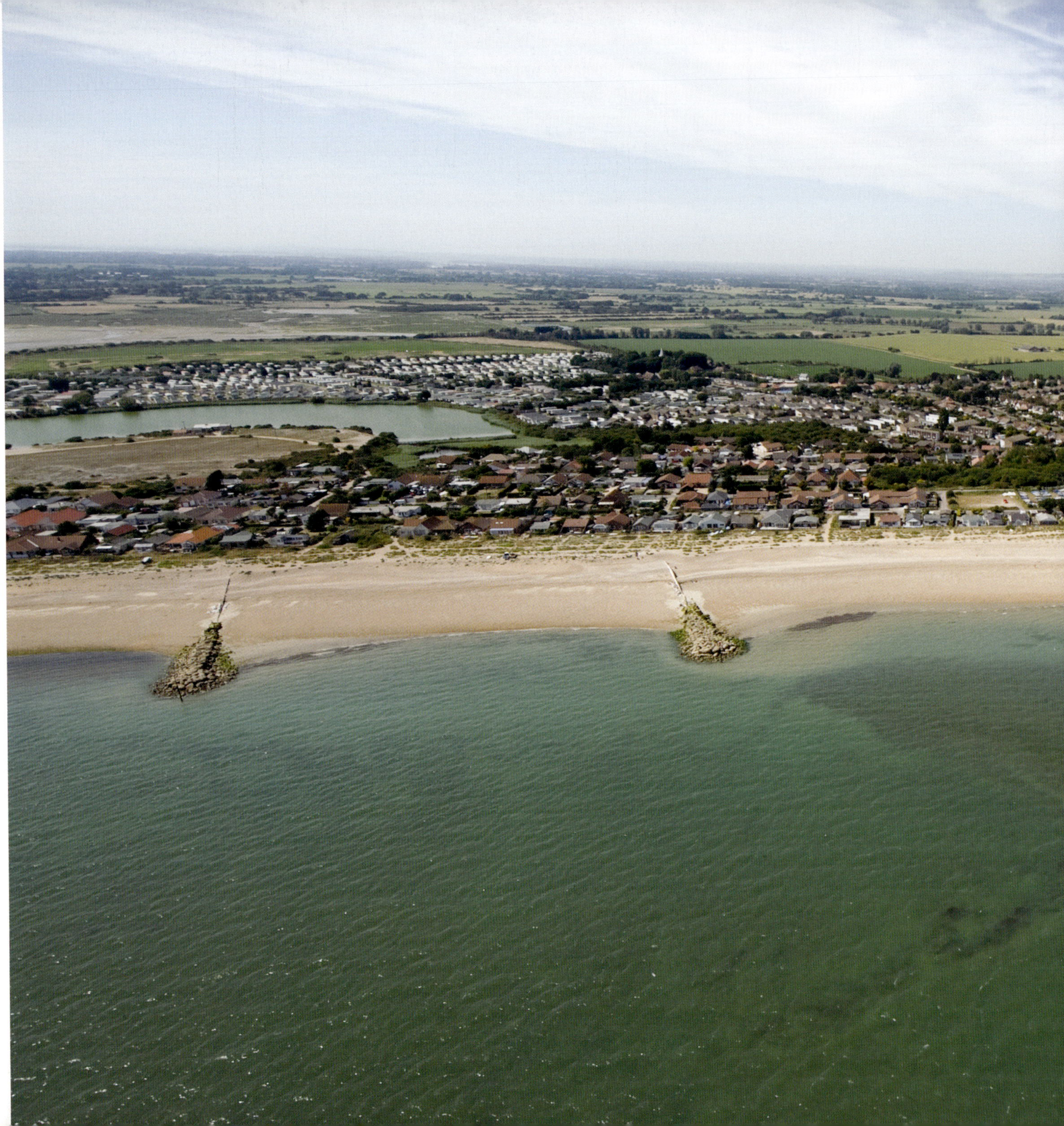

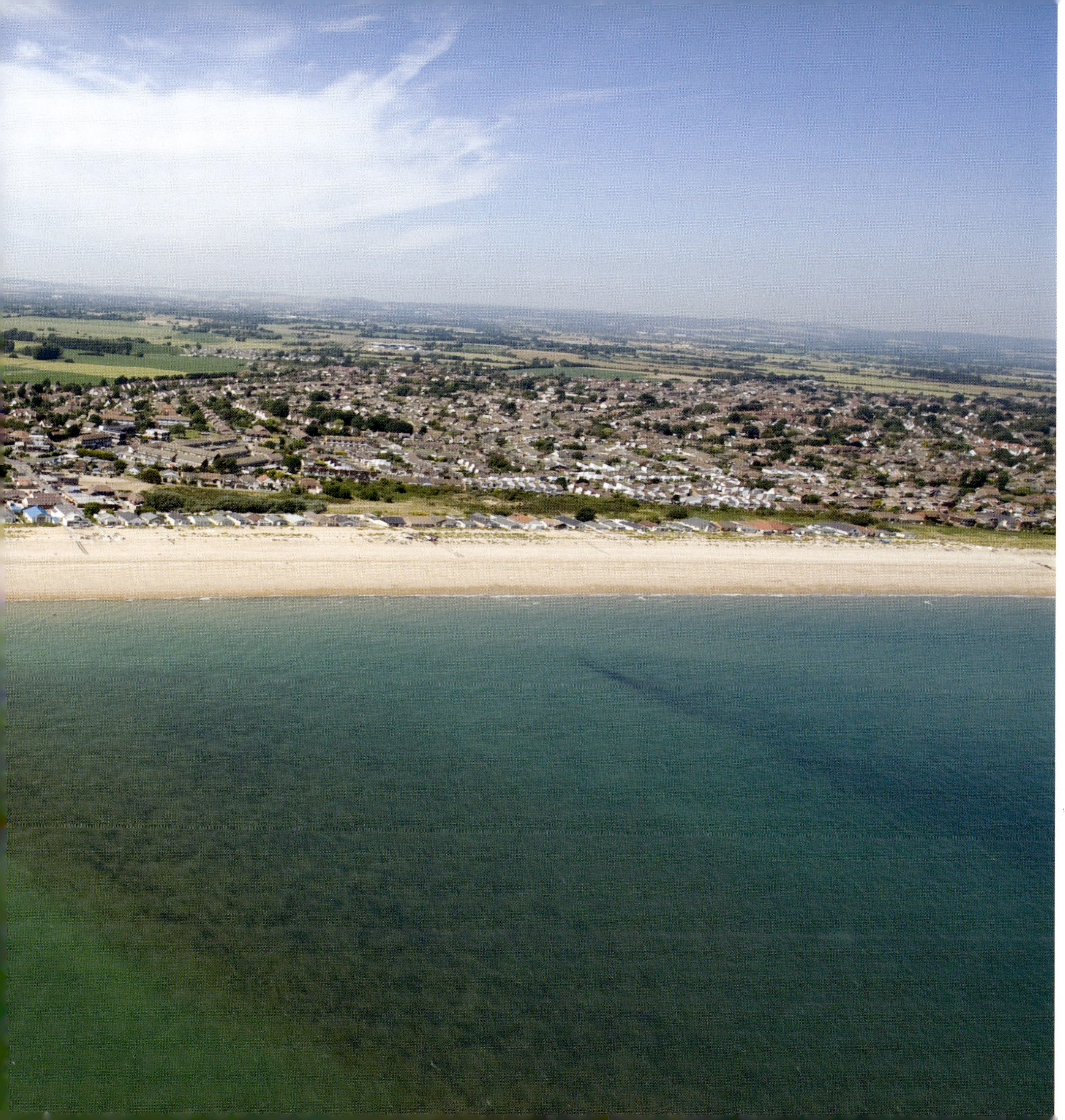

Previous page: A superb view inland over Pagham.

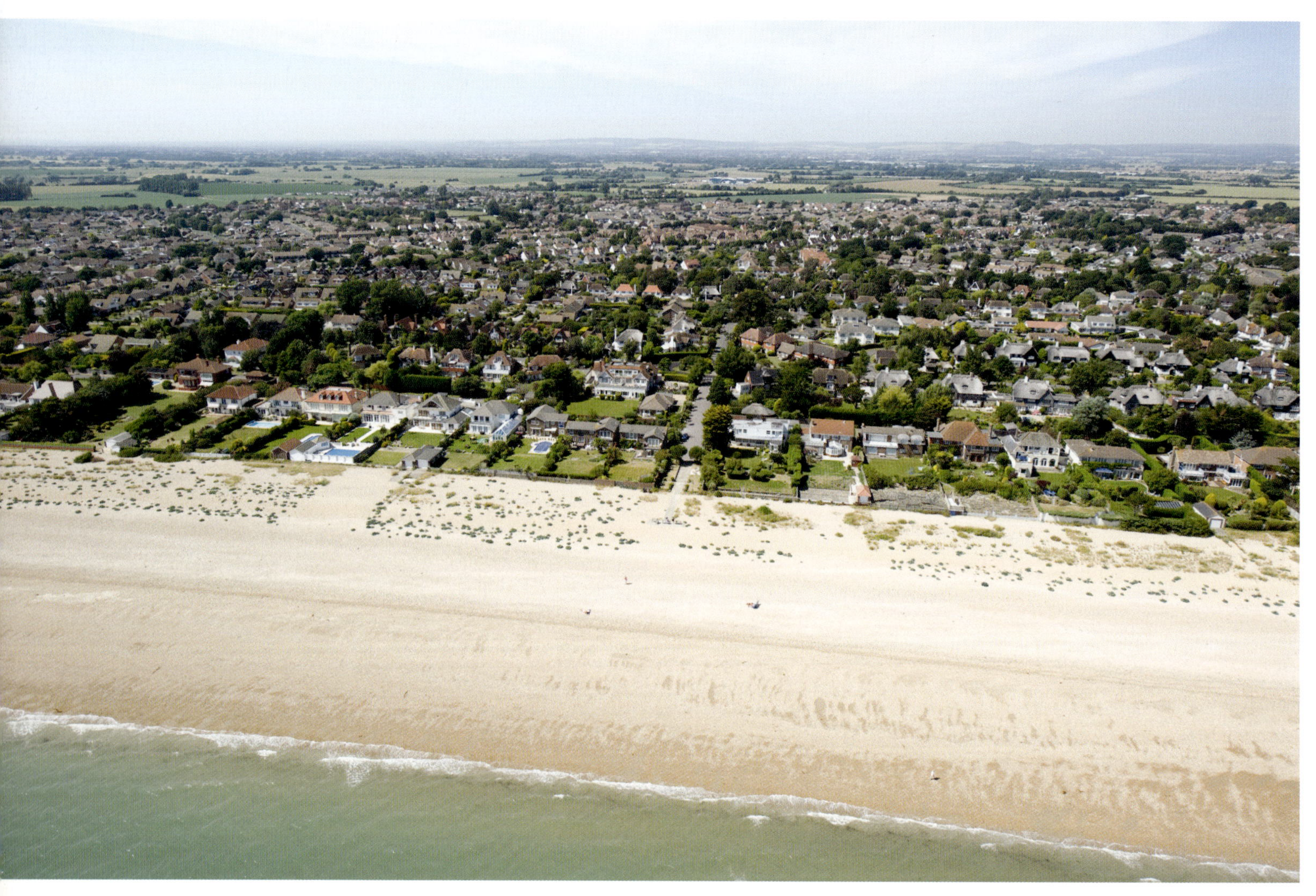

Above: Pagham rubs shoulders with Aldwick to the east.

Above: Beachfront properties in Aldwick which is now part of the built-up area west of Bognor Regis.

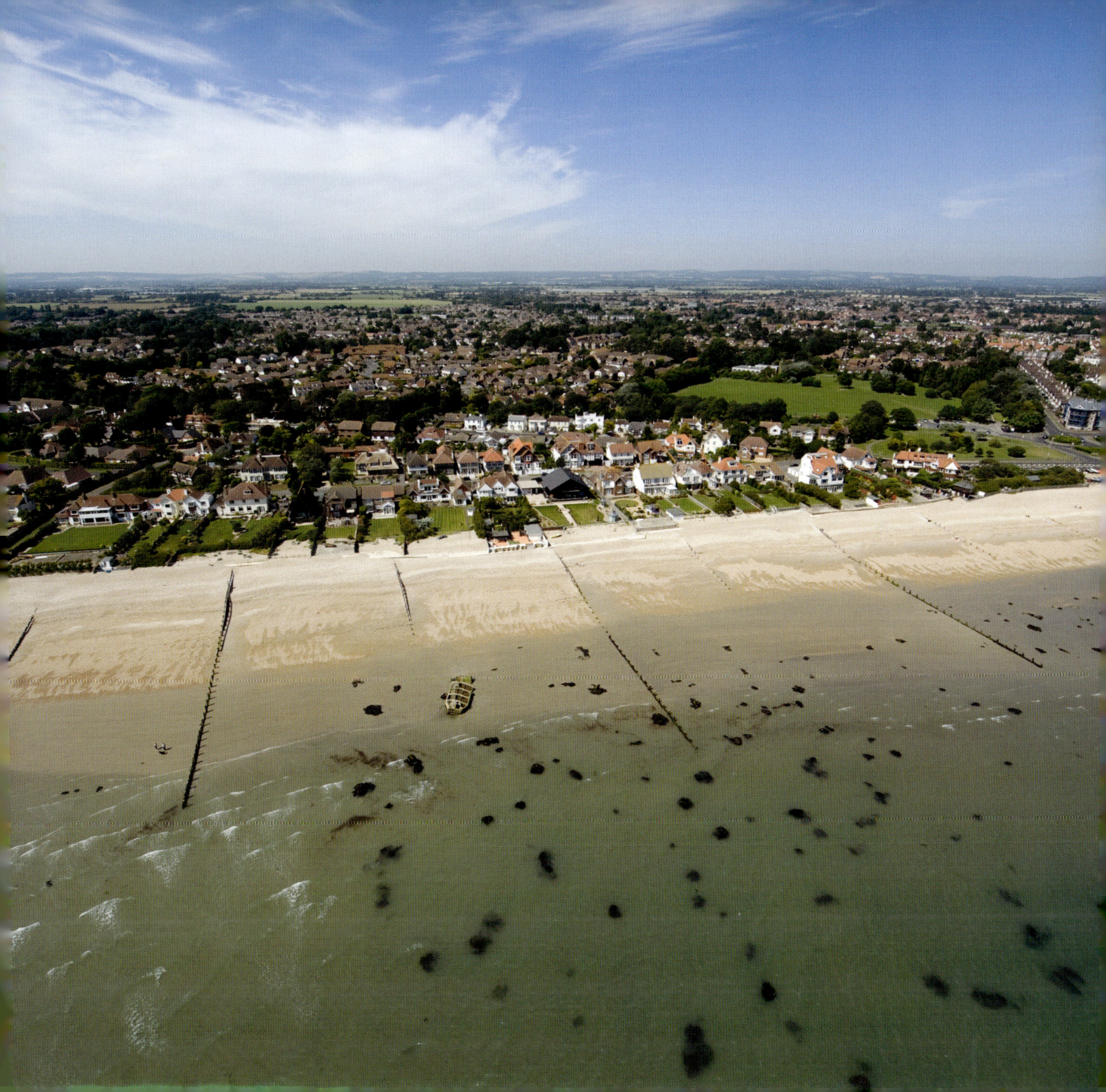

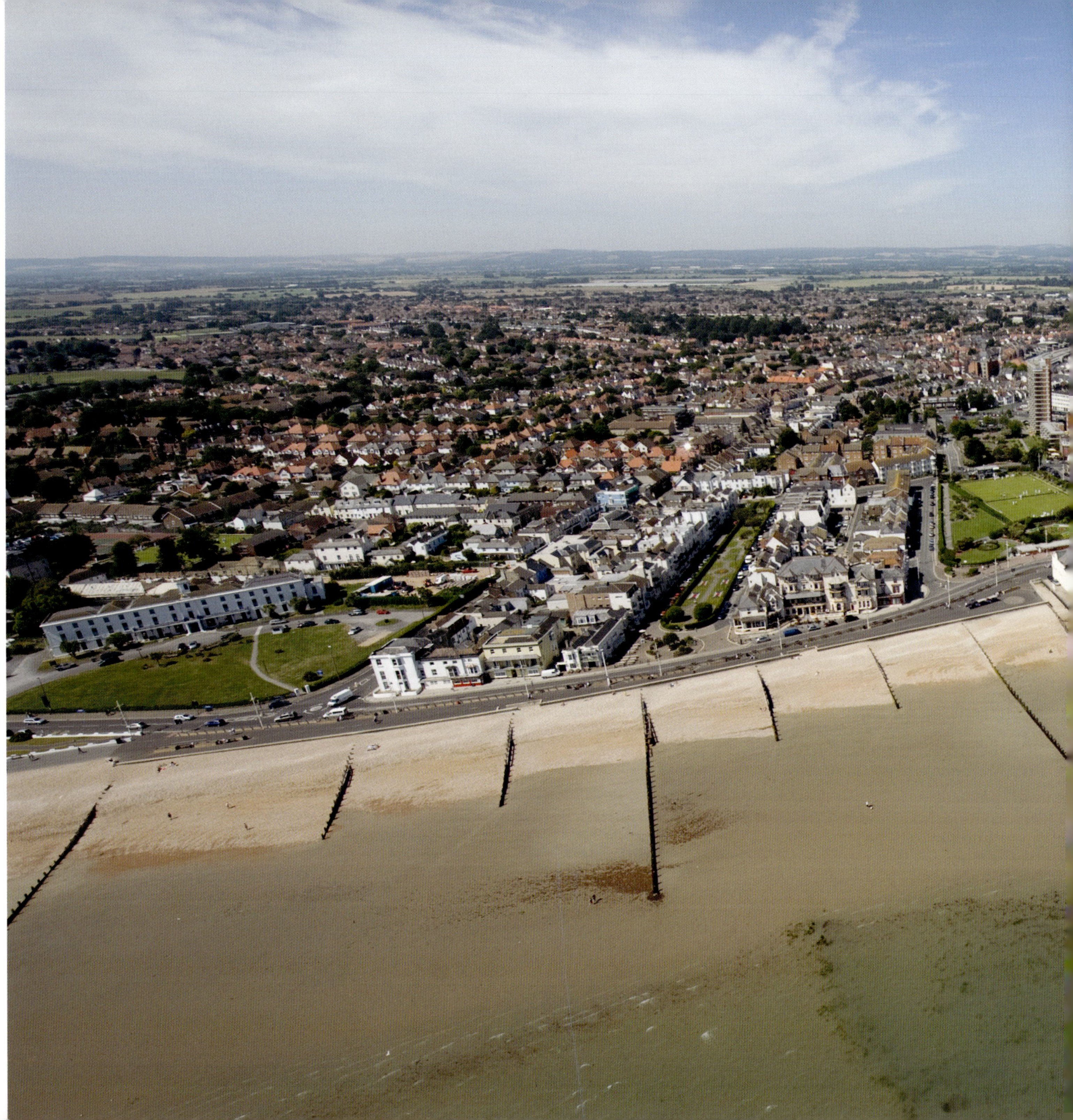

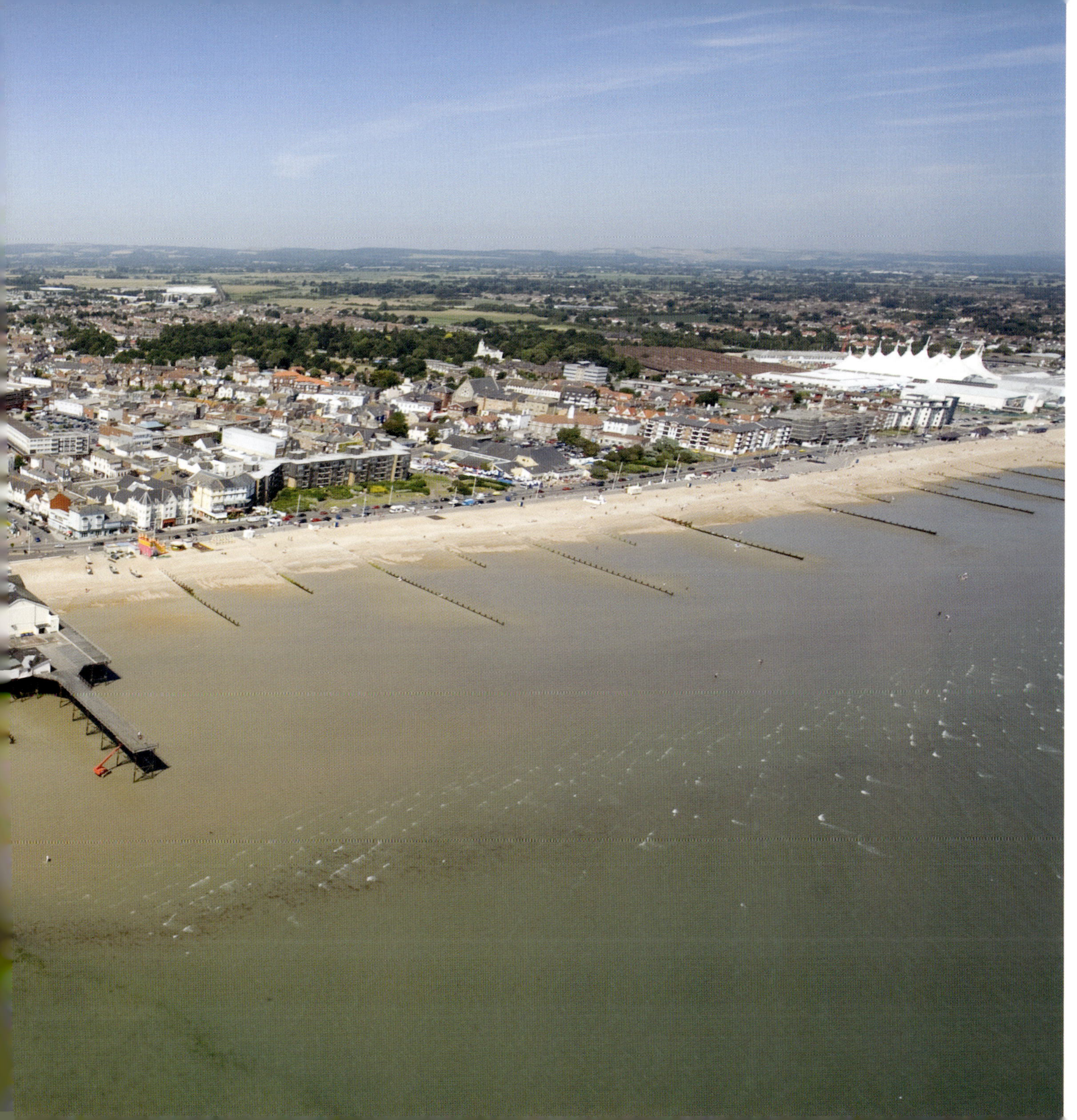

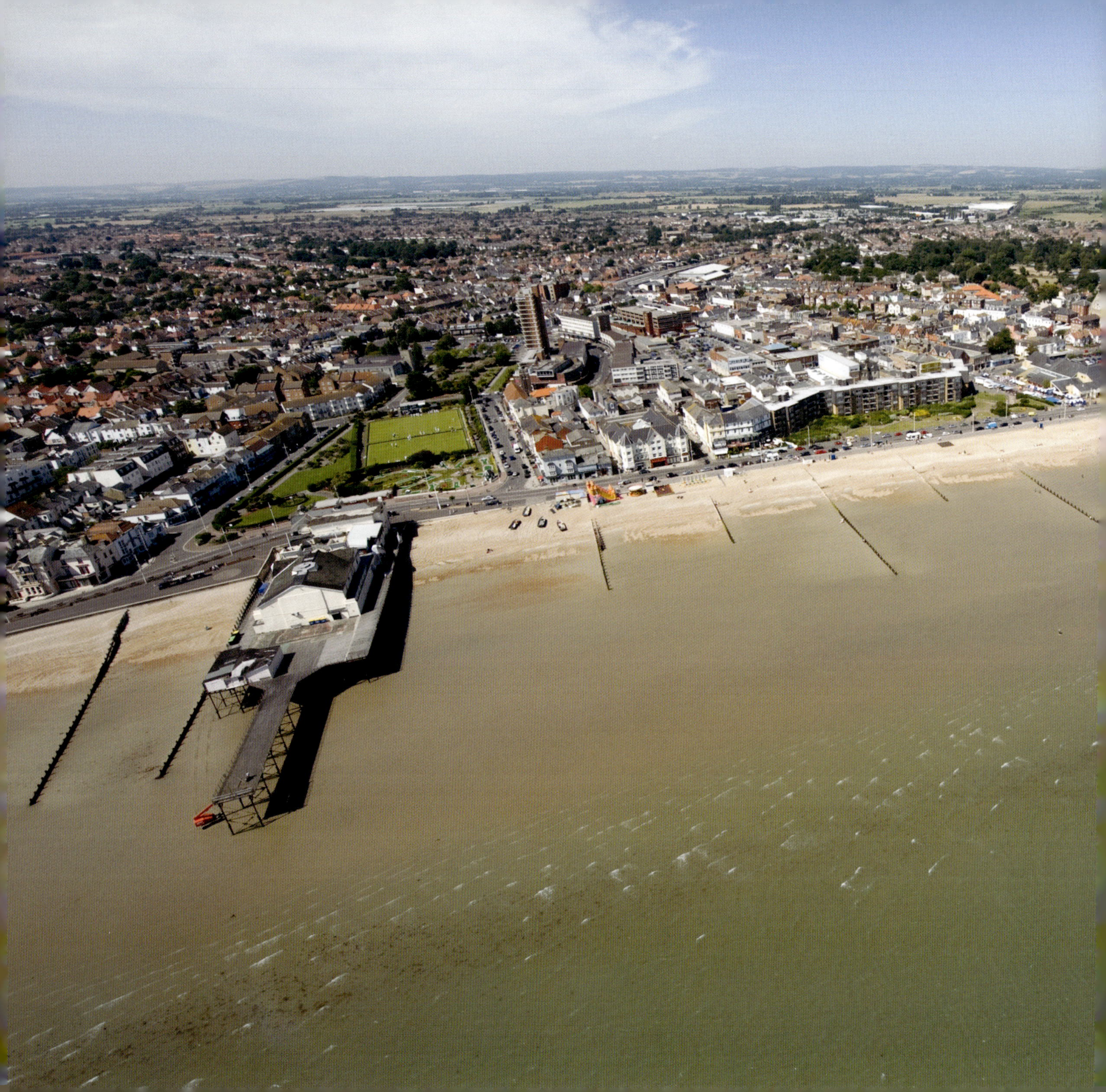

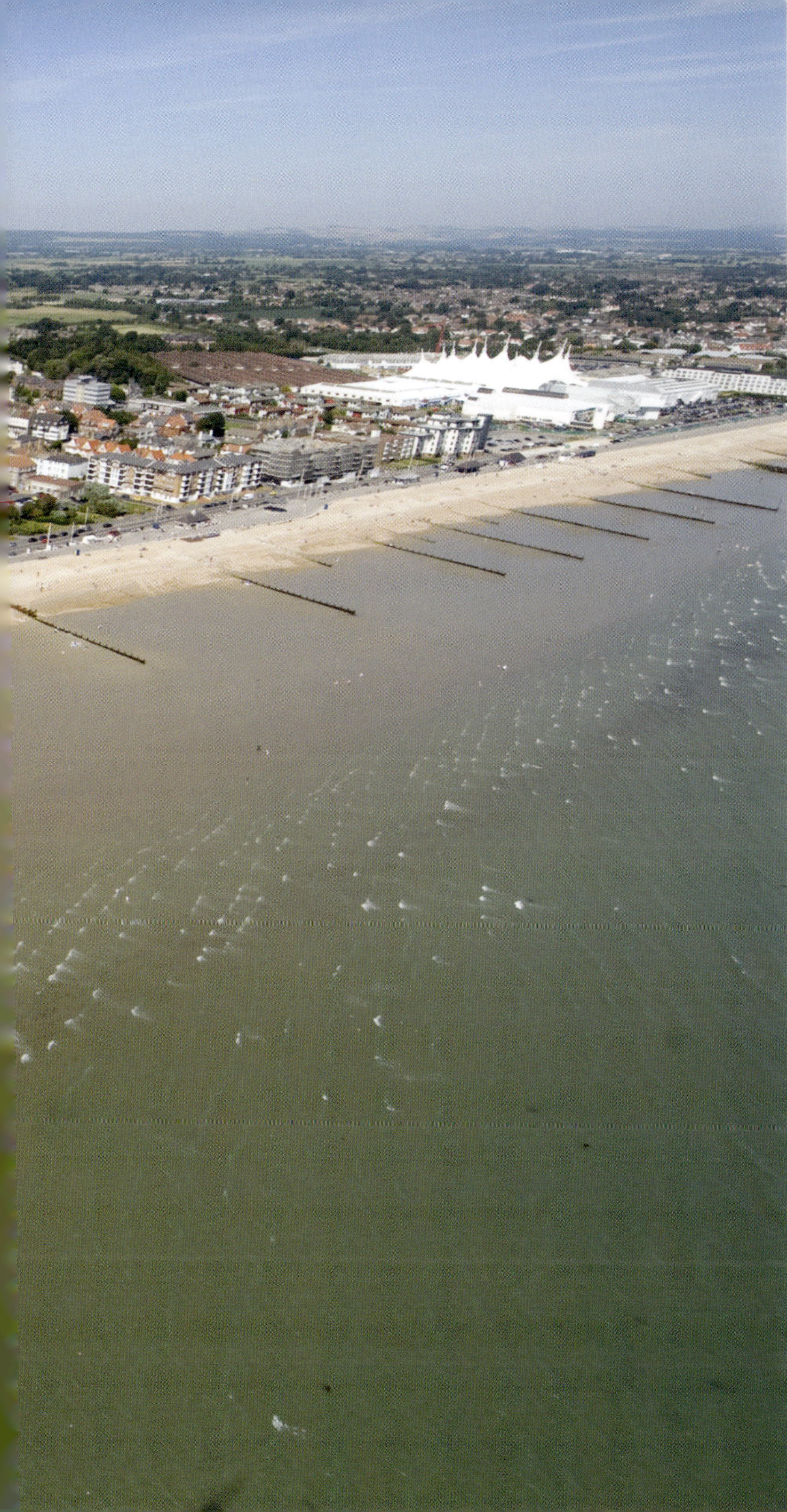

Previous page and left: As a resort, Bognor is firmly linked with royalty, and especially with King George V who convalesced here. A pier was first opened here in 1865.

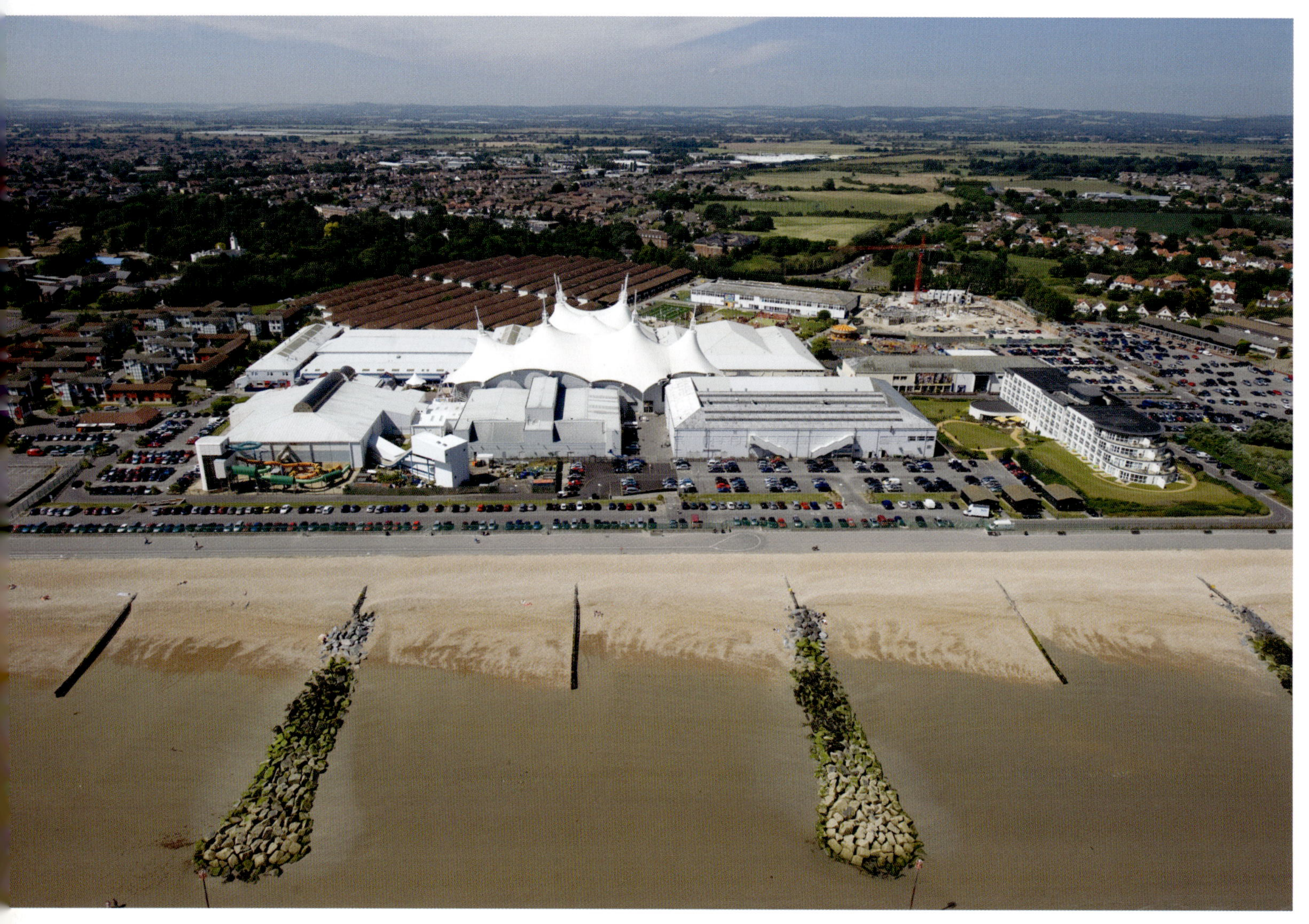

Above: Butlin's famous holiday resort at Bognor Regis was originally opened in 1960.

Right and following page: Felpham, although lying immediately next to Bognor remains a separate community.

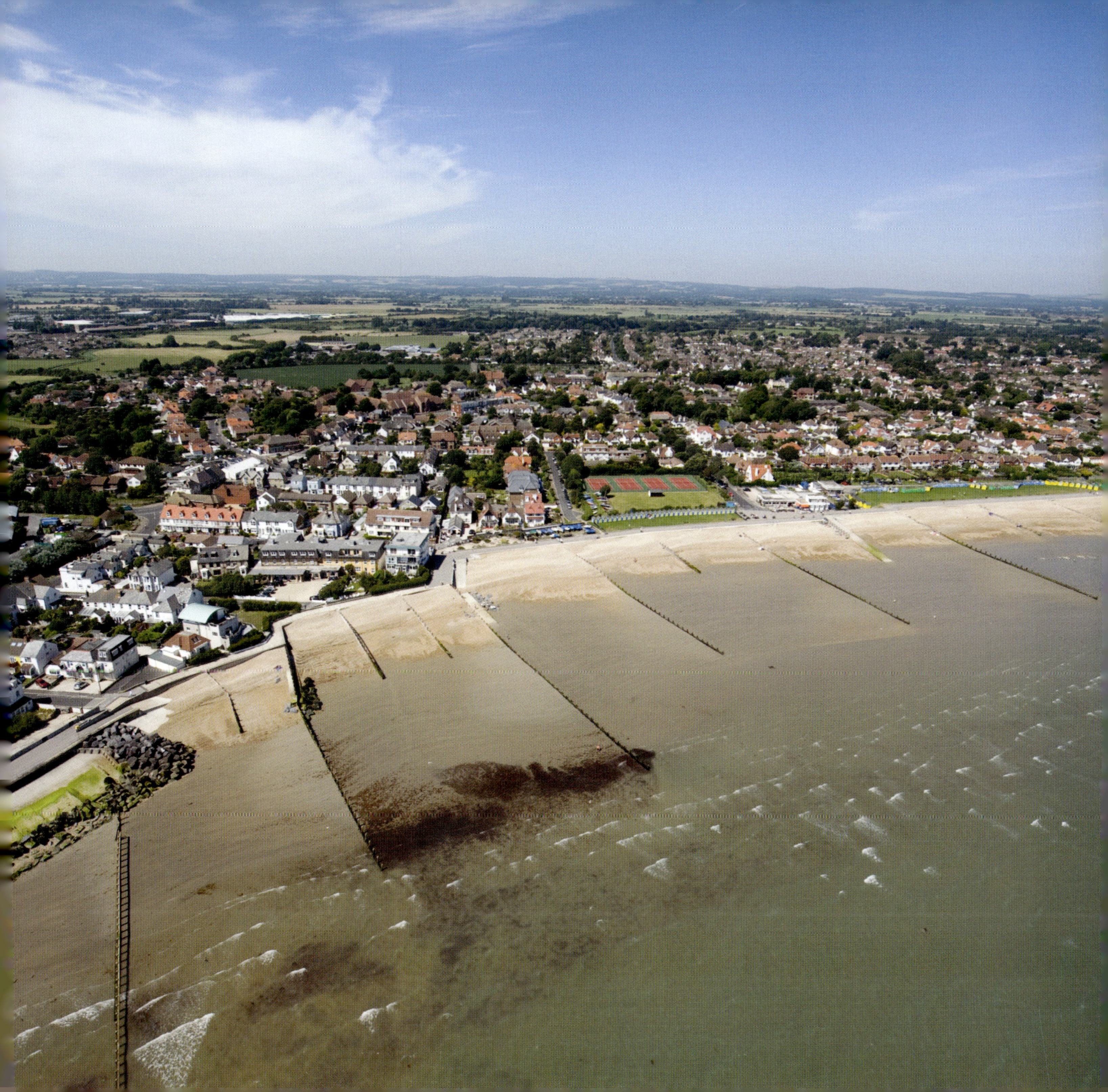

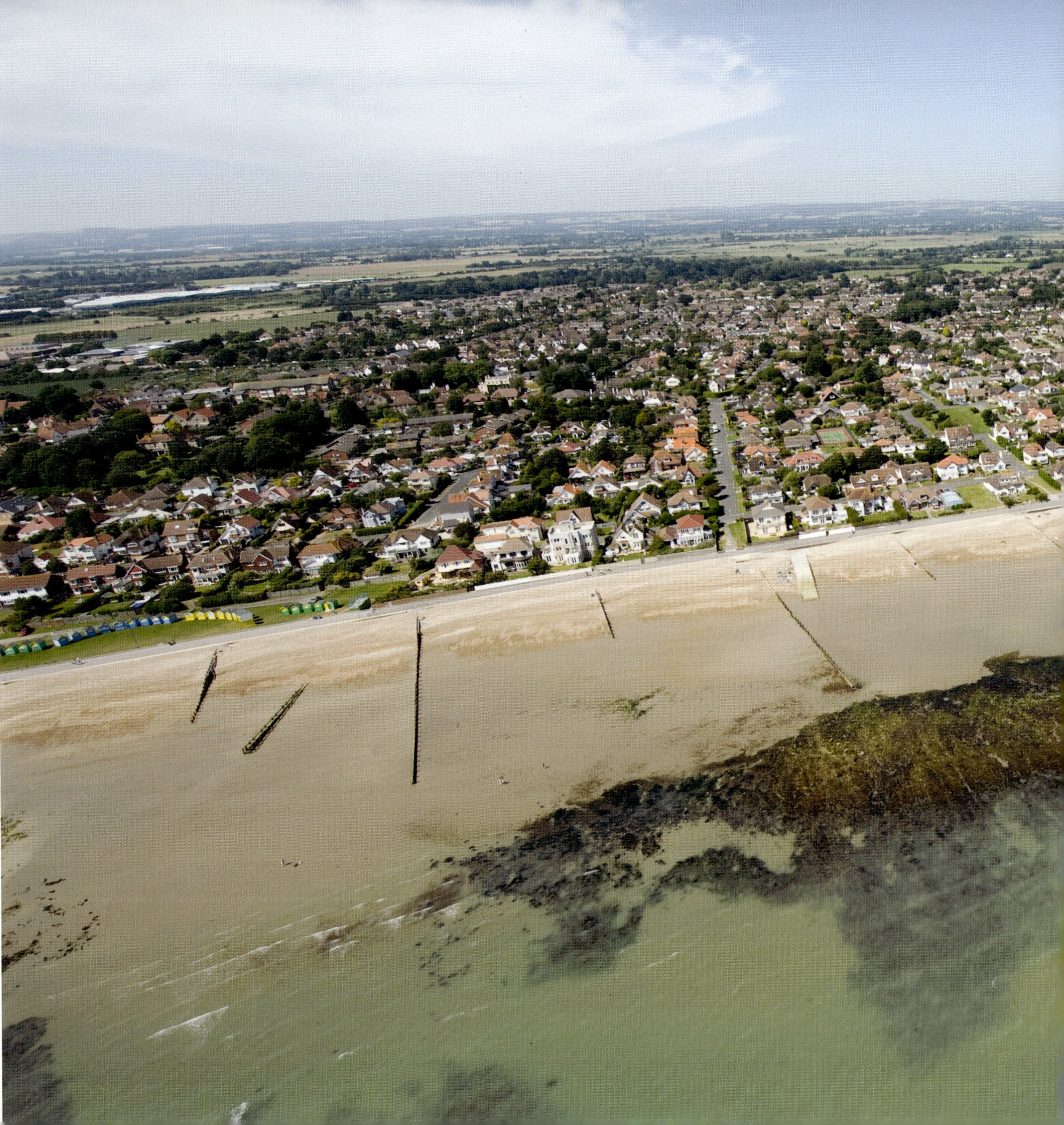

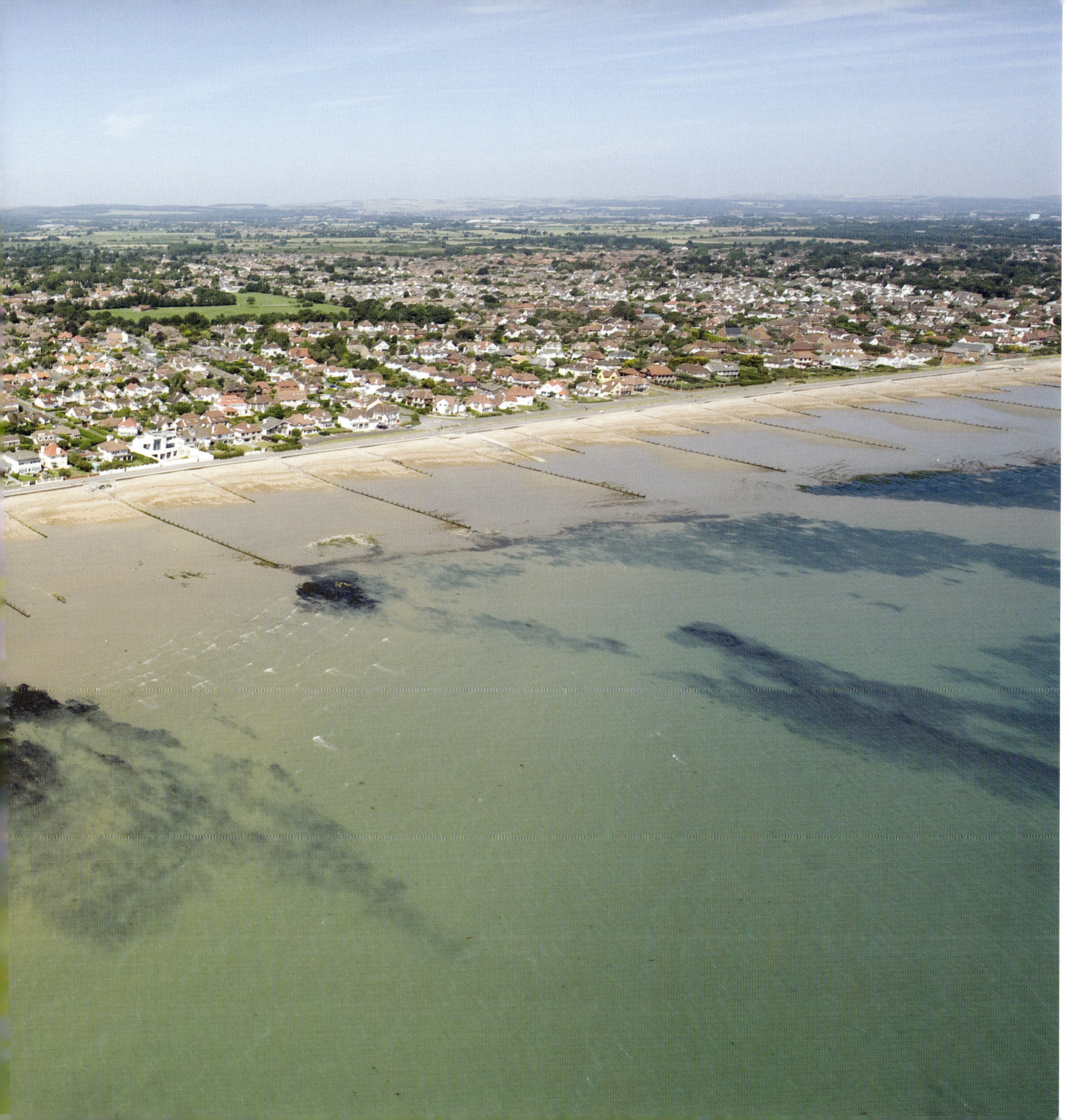

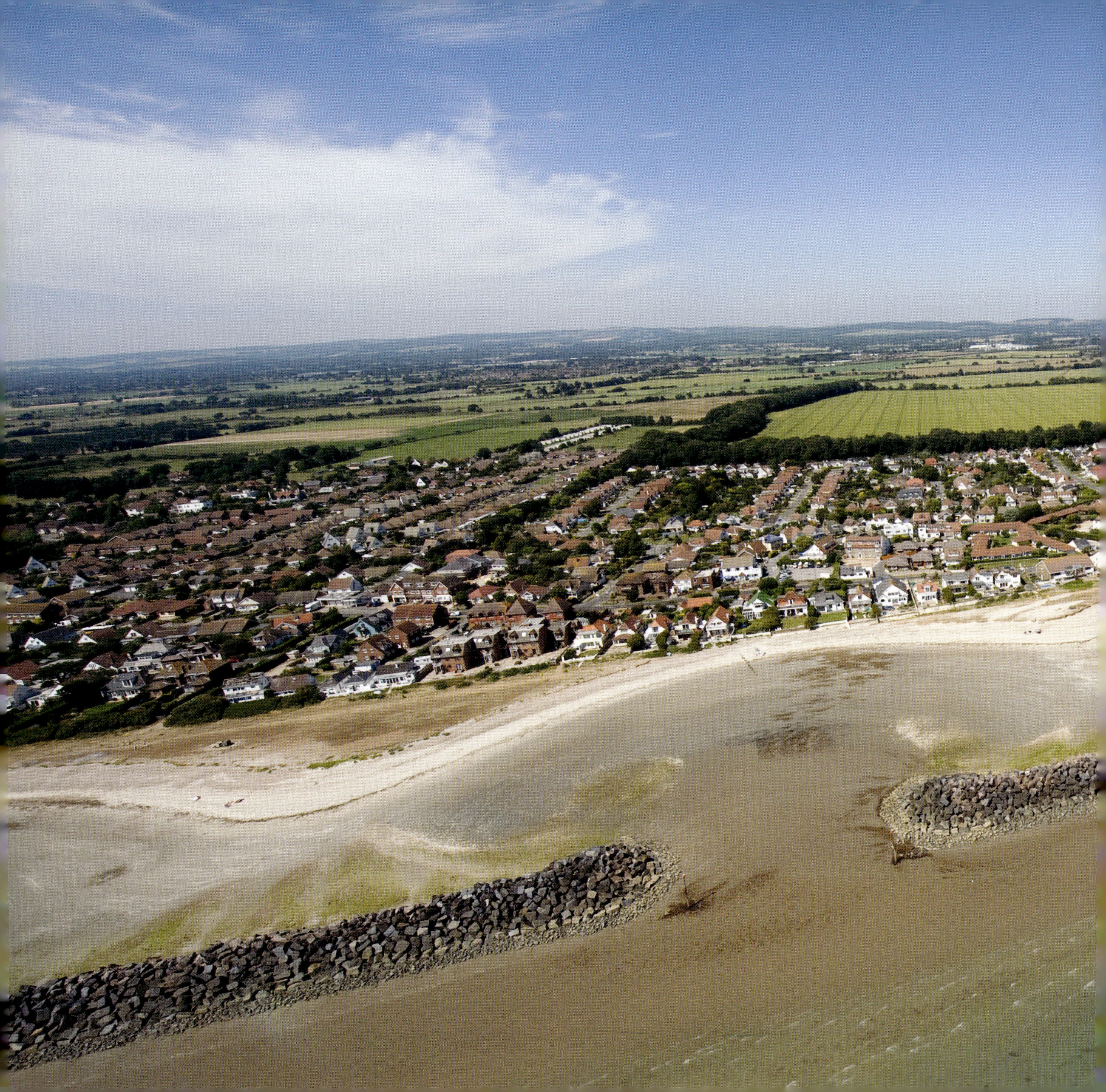

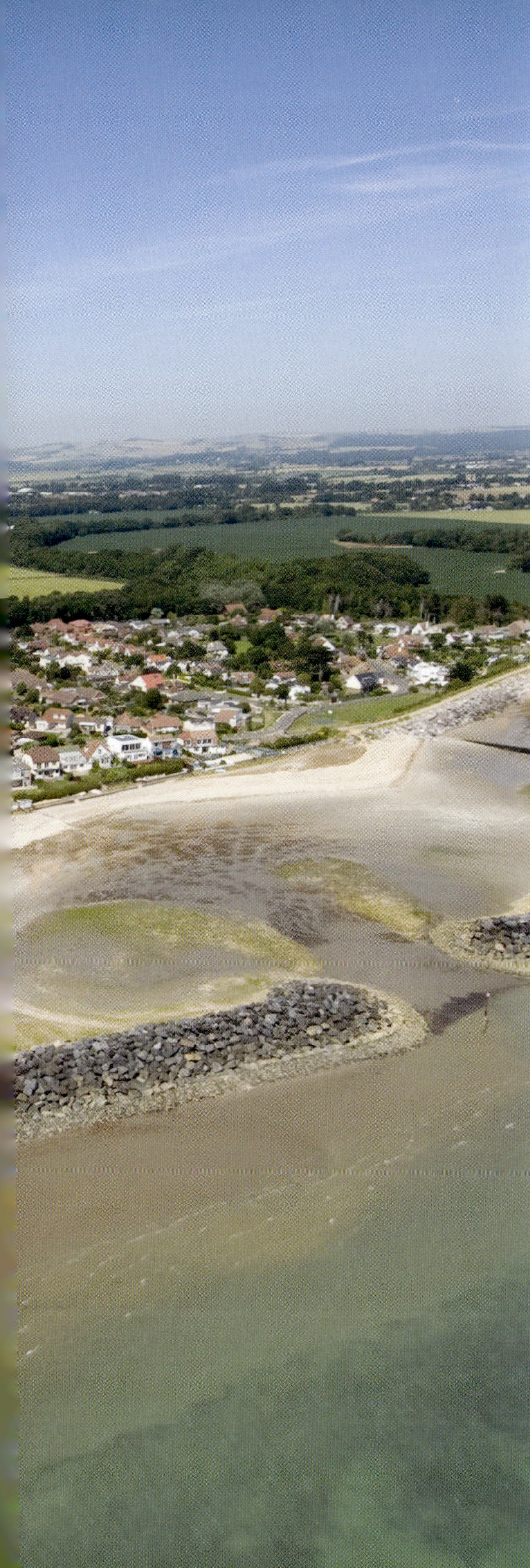

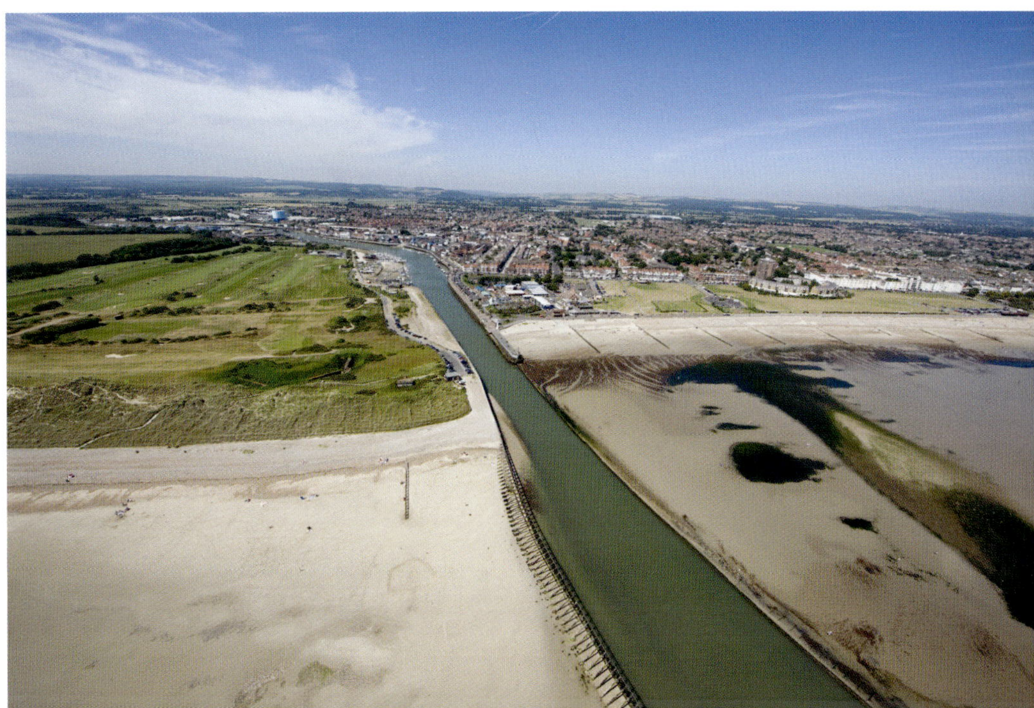

Above: Littlehampton nestles at the foot of the South Downs, at the mouth of the River Arun. The harbour provides a safe haven for all leisure craft as well as being a small commercial port.

Left: Elmer lies adjacent to Middleton-on-Sea to the west of Littlehampton. The scouring action of the sea, in part reduced by the offshore defenses seen here, has created scallop-shaped crescents of beach along the shoreline.

Right: A spectacular view looking inland over Littlehampton.

Following page: Rustington is one the county's fastest growing coastal towns, many new homes mixing with traditional Sussex flint buildings.

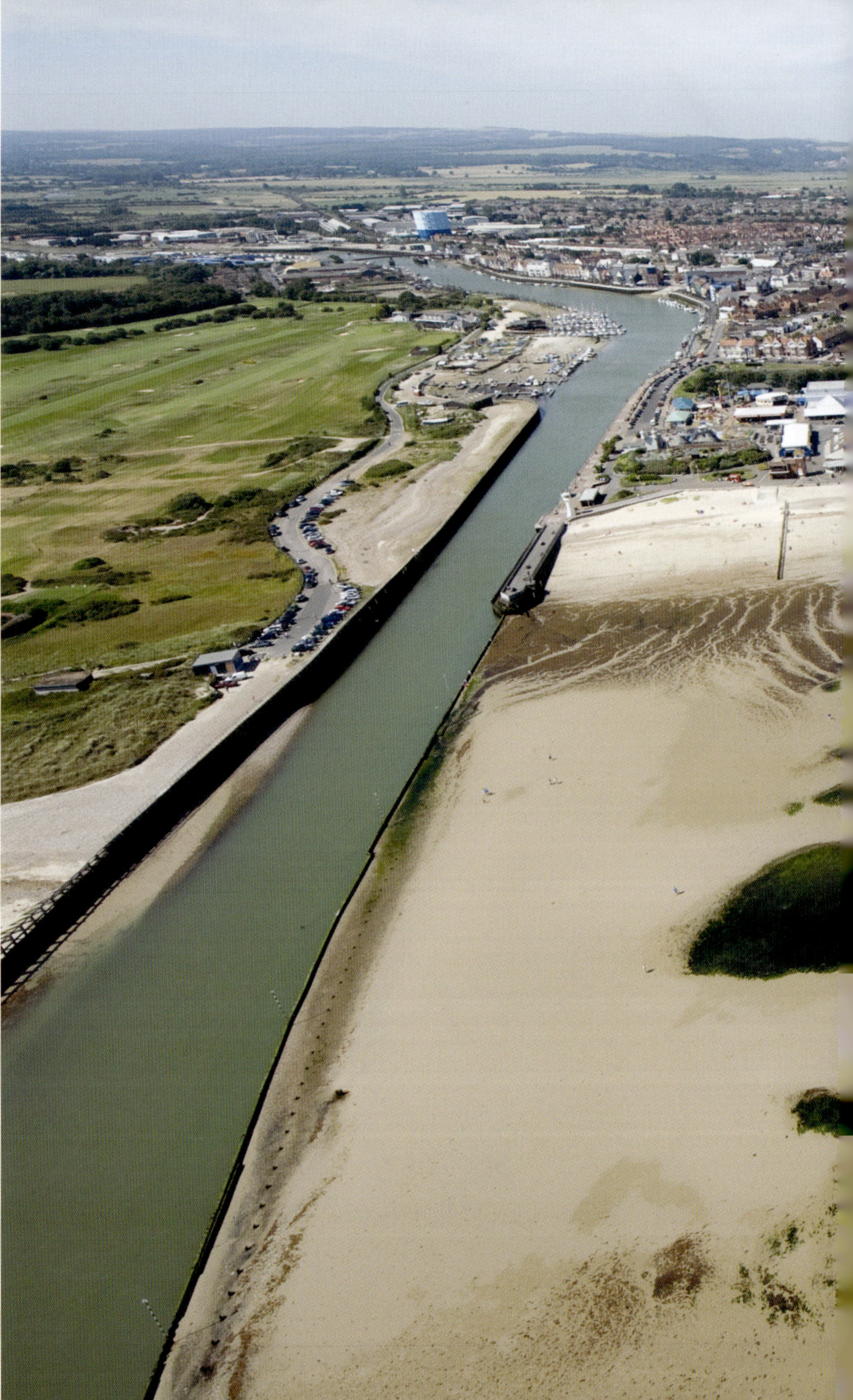

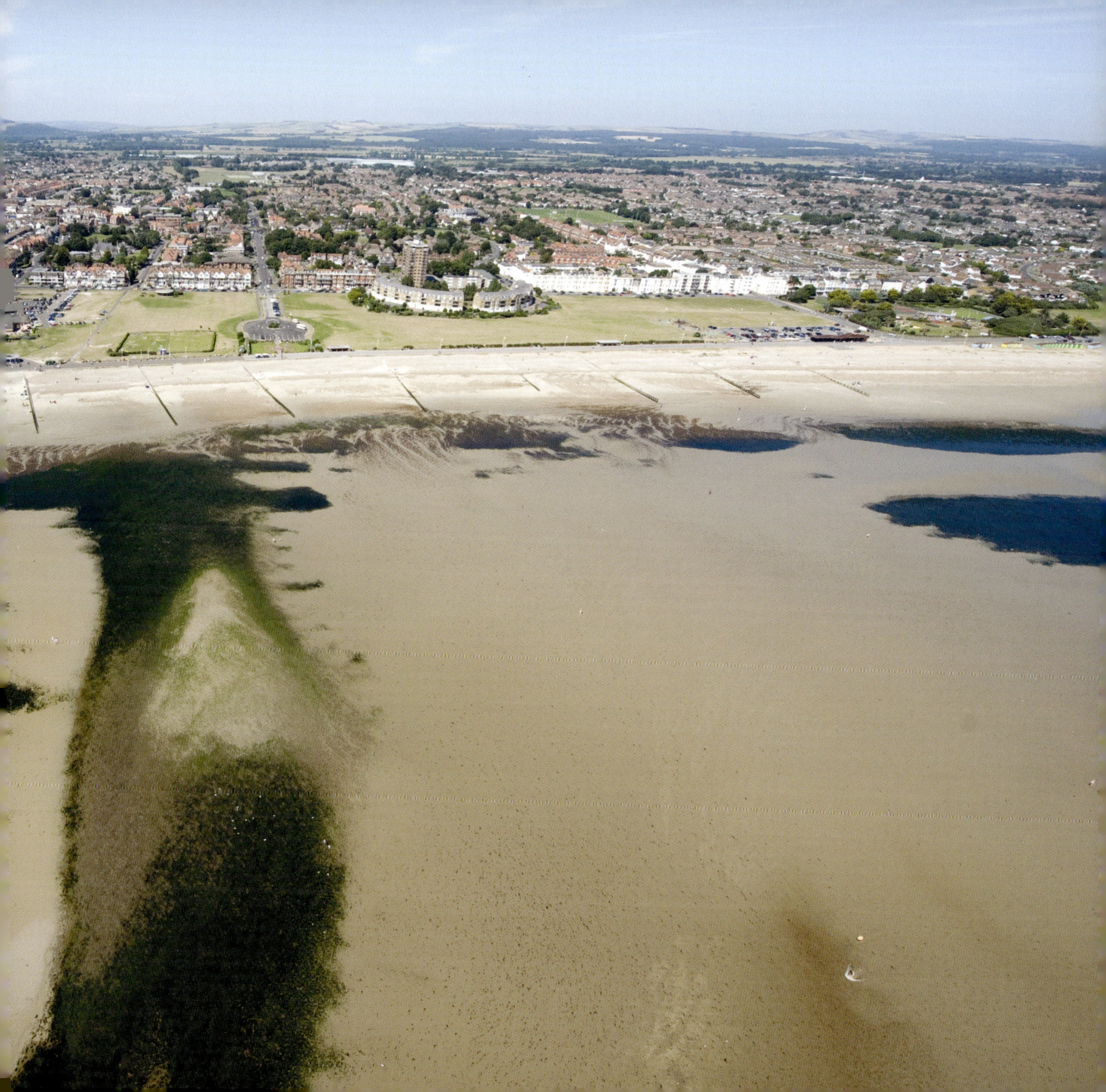

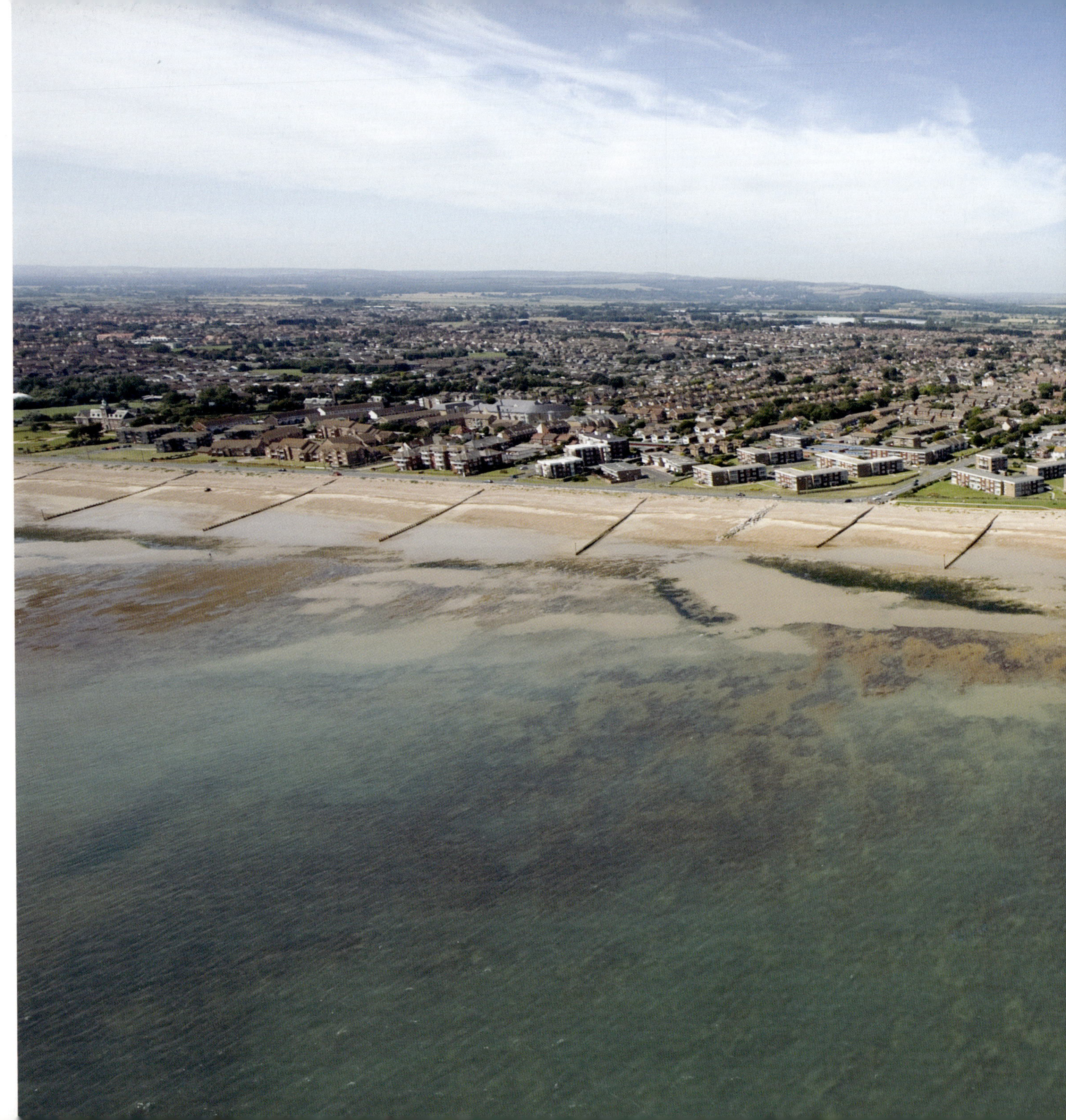

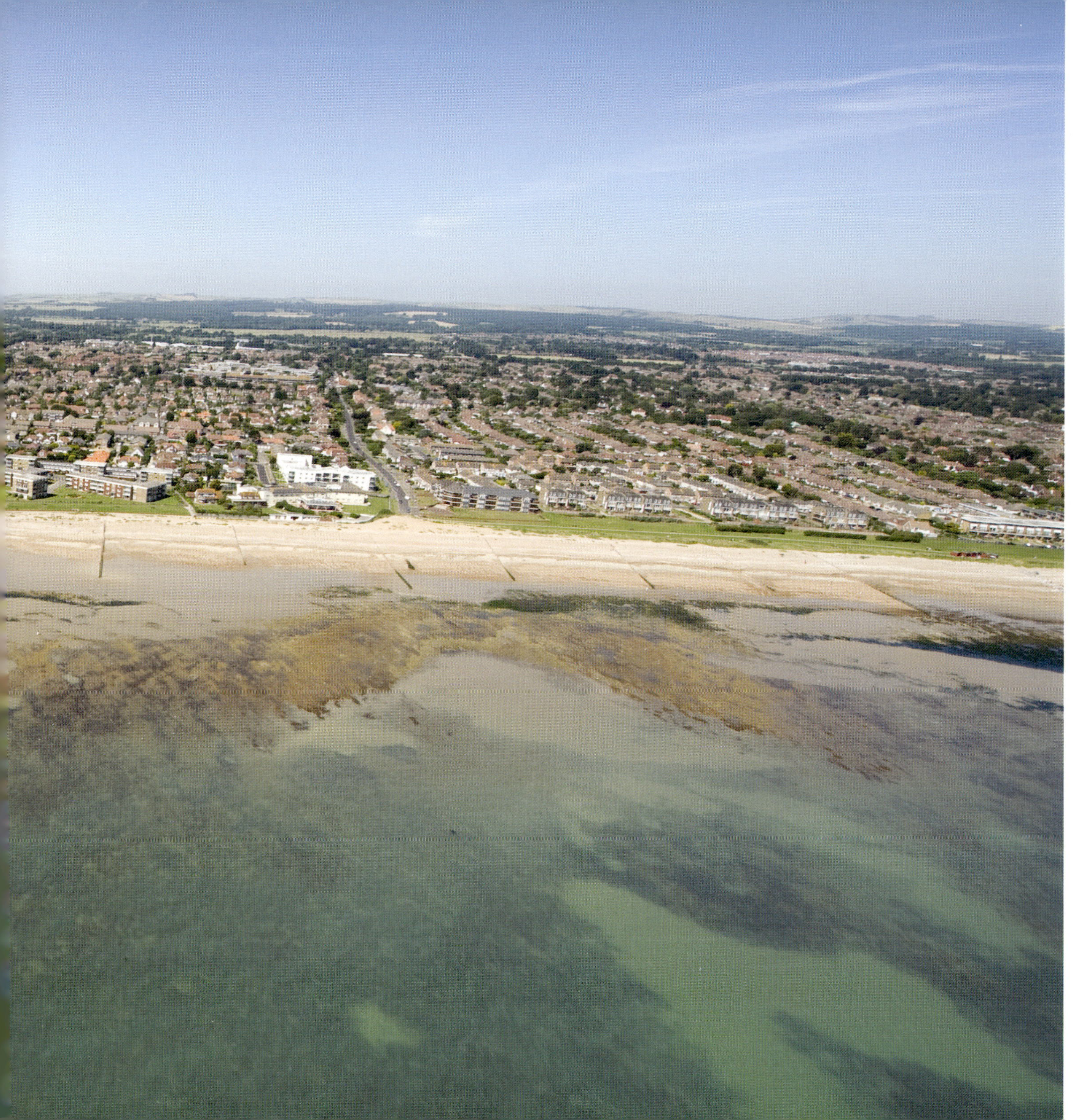

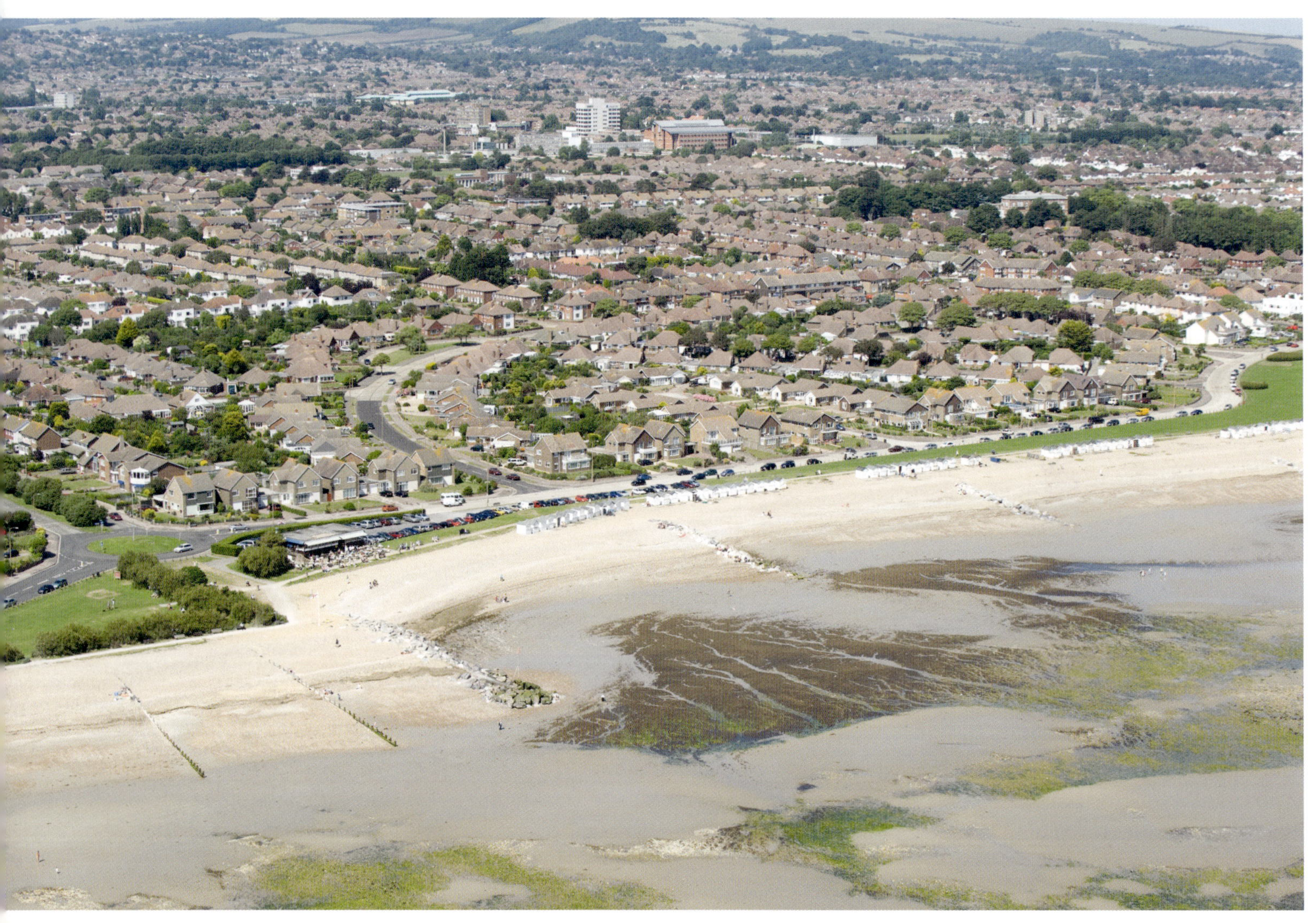

Above: Goring, seen from the western end of Marine Crescent.

Right: A view north along Grand Avenue, Worthing.

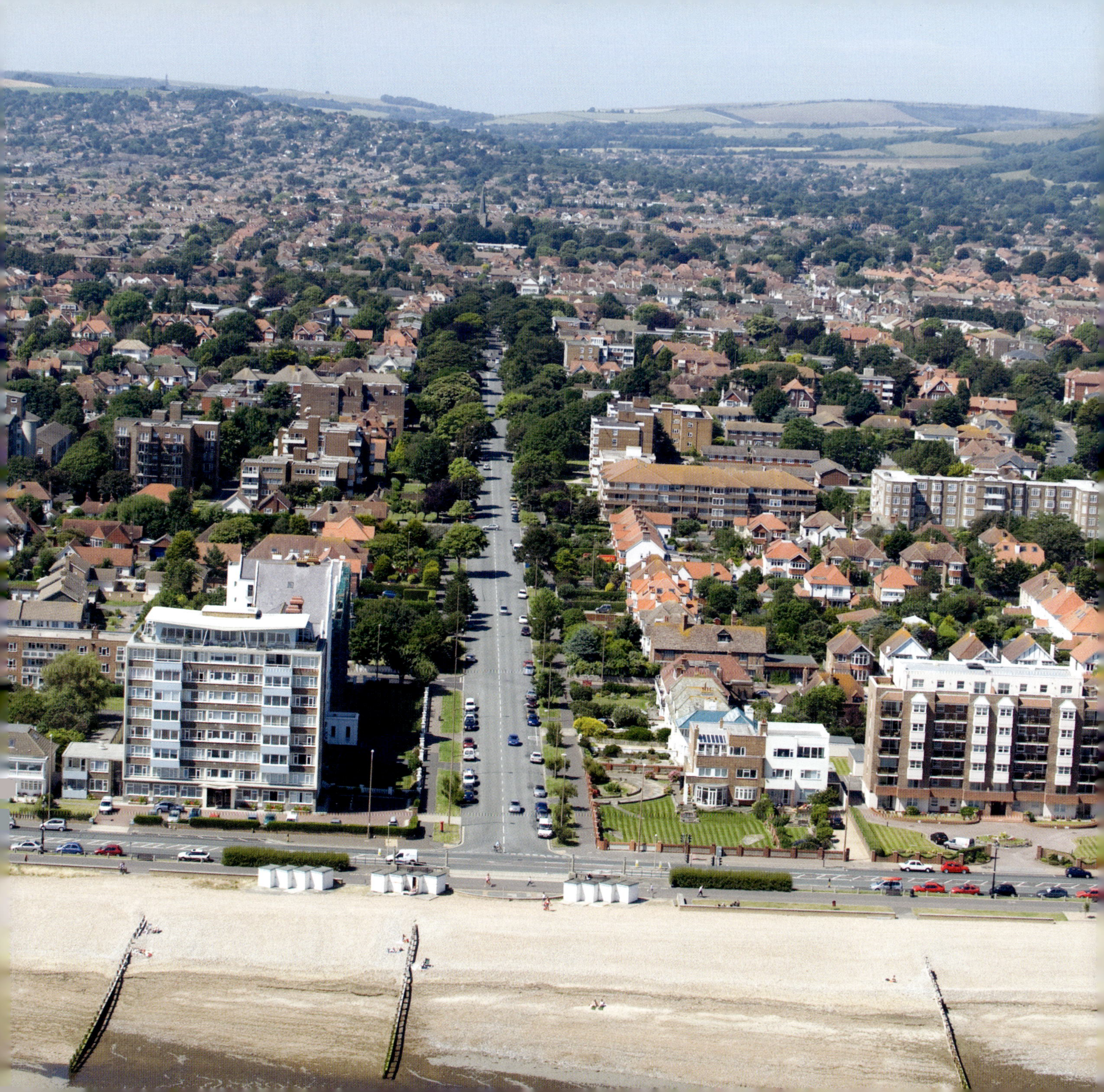

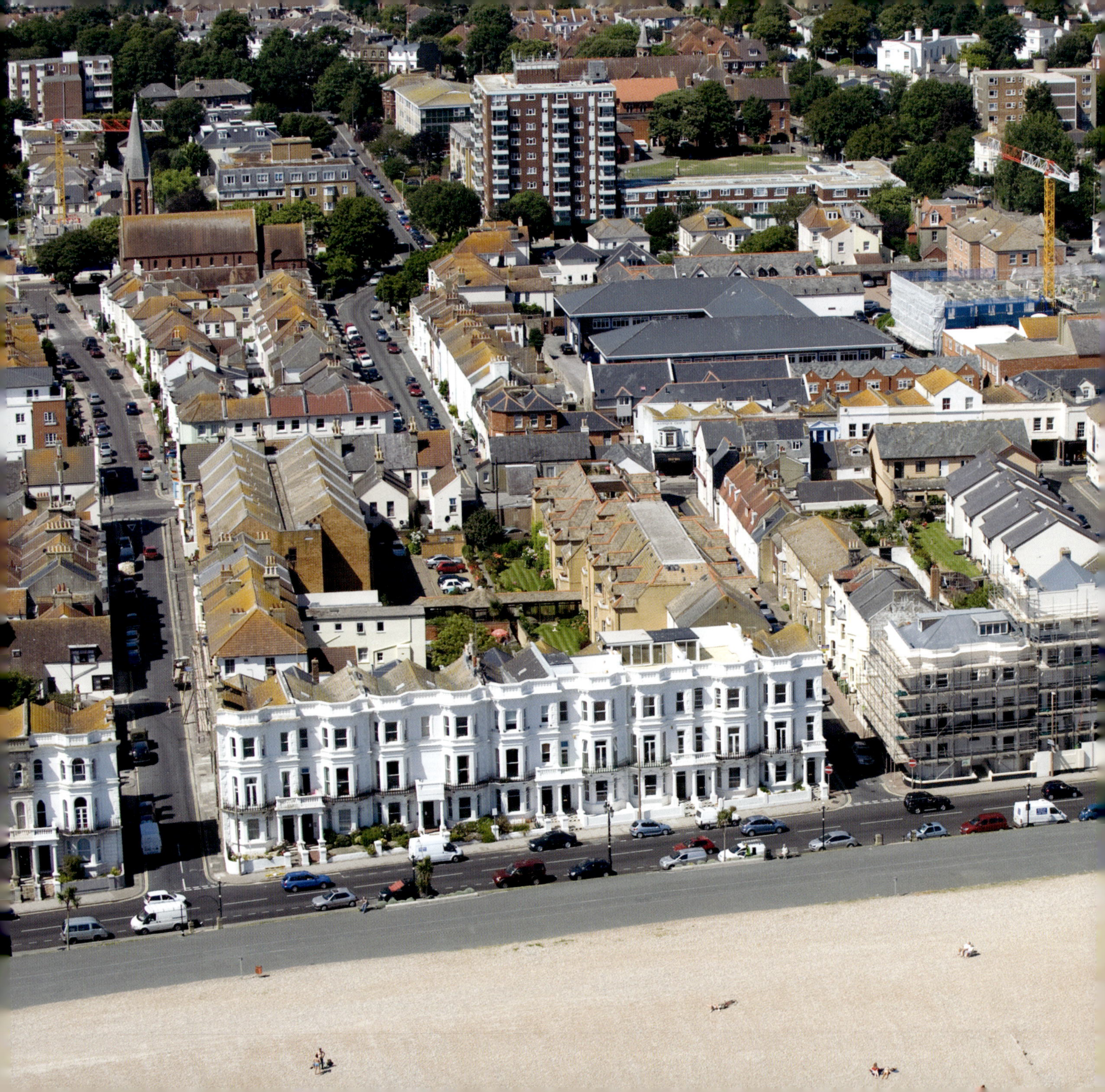

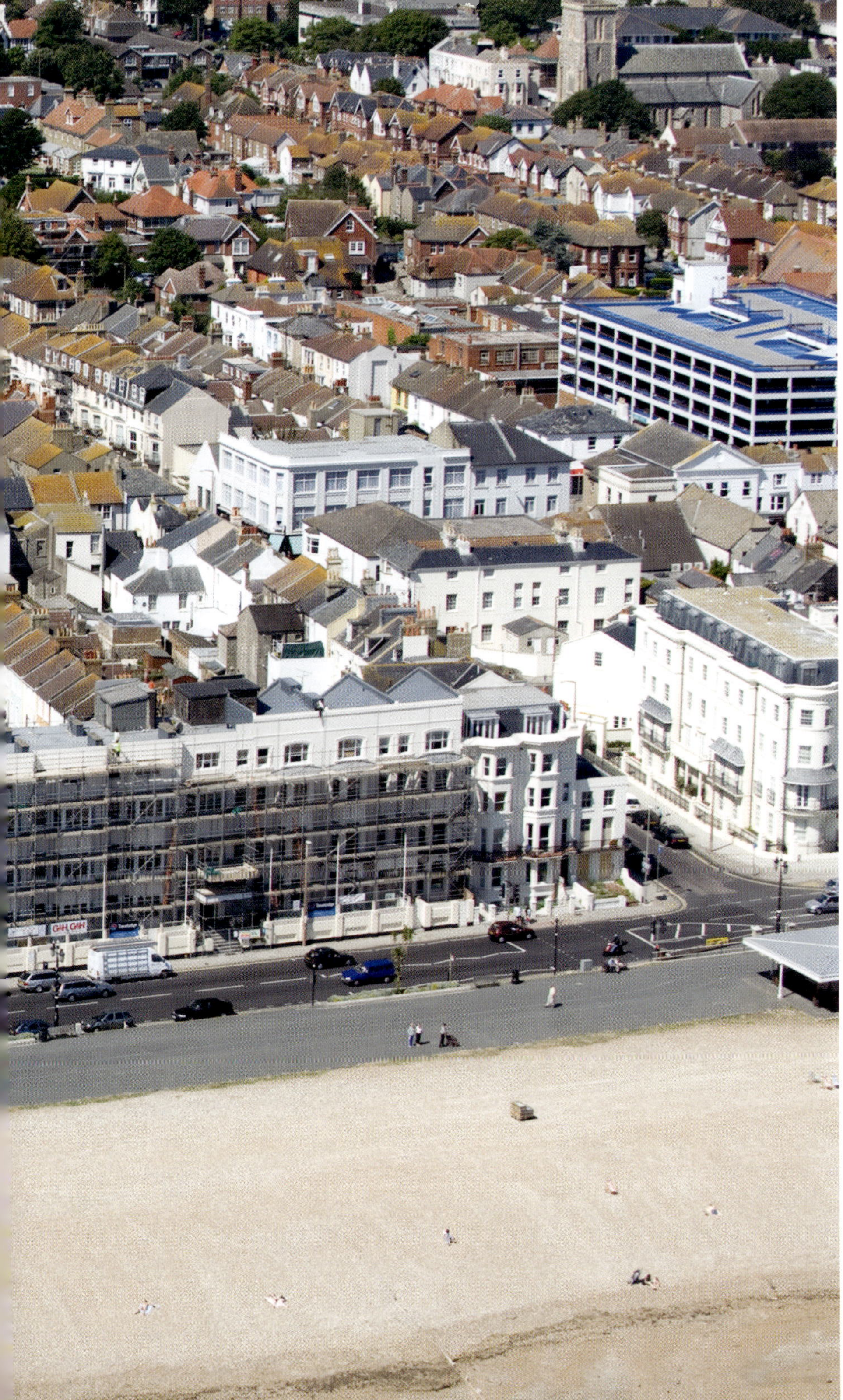

Marine Parade, Worthing

Marine Parade, near Augusta Place, Worthing.

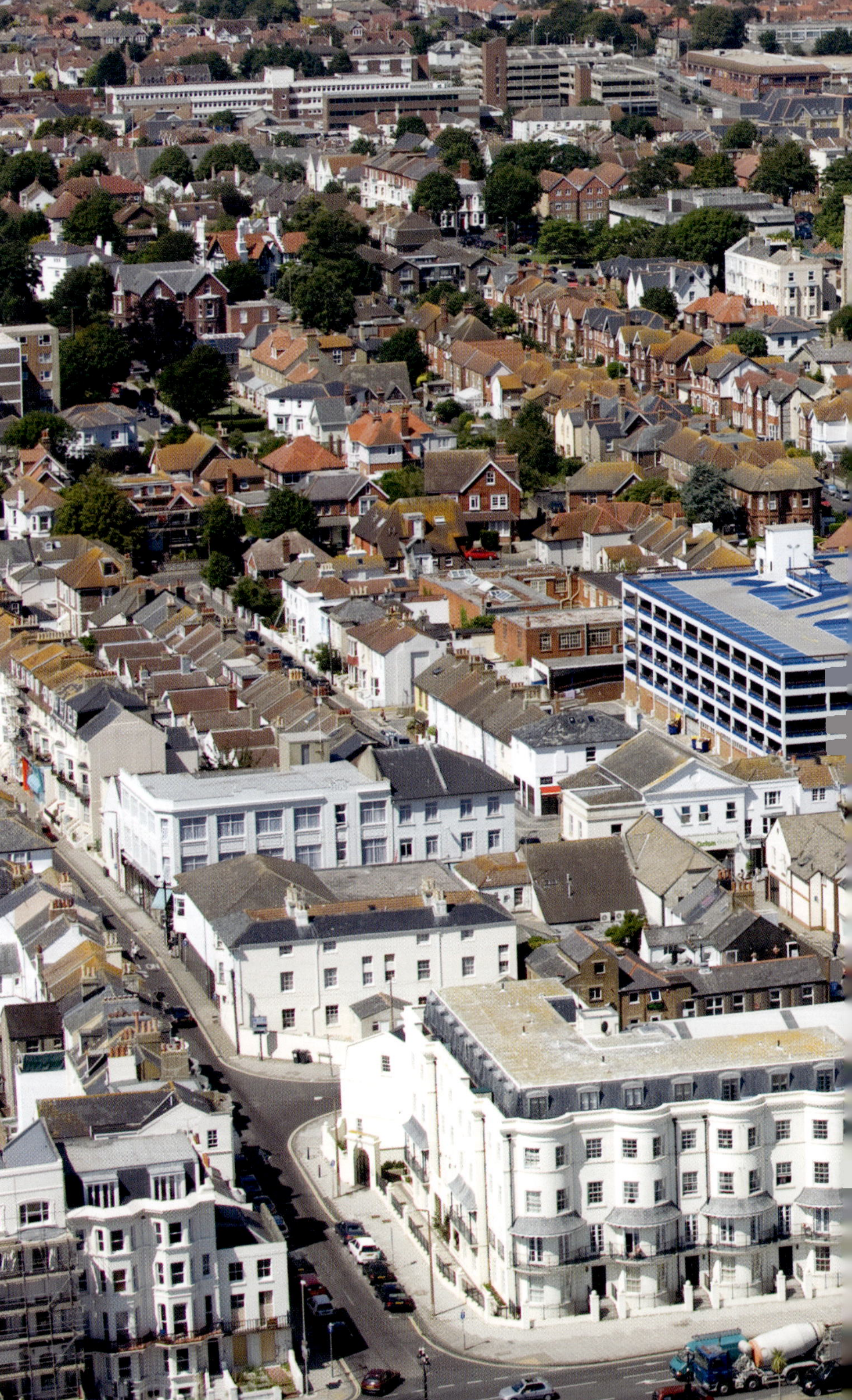

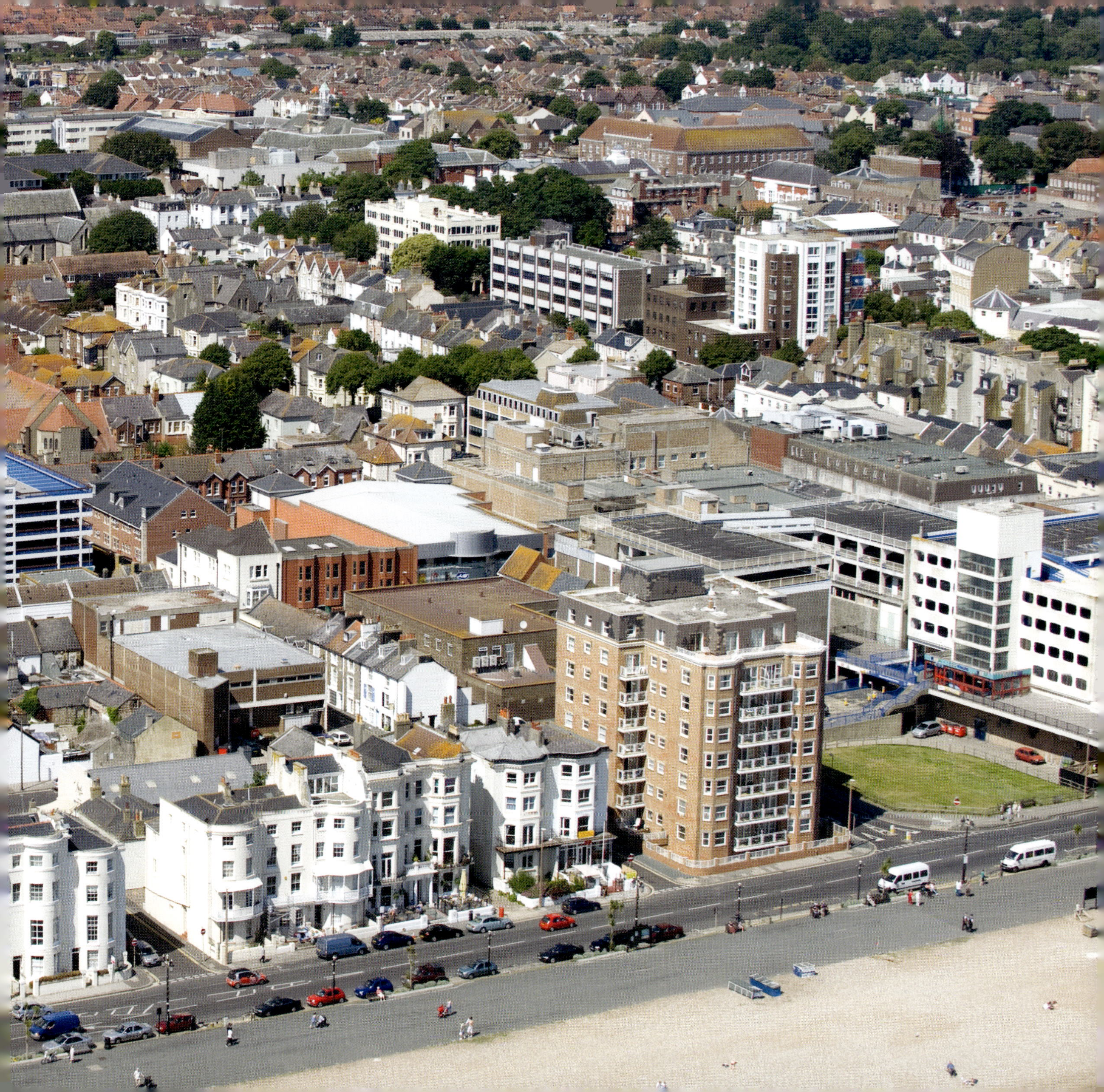

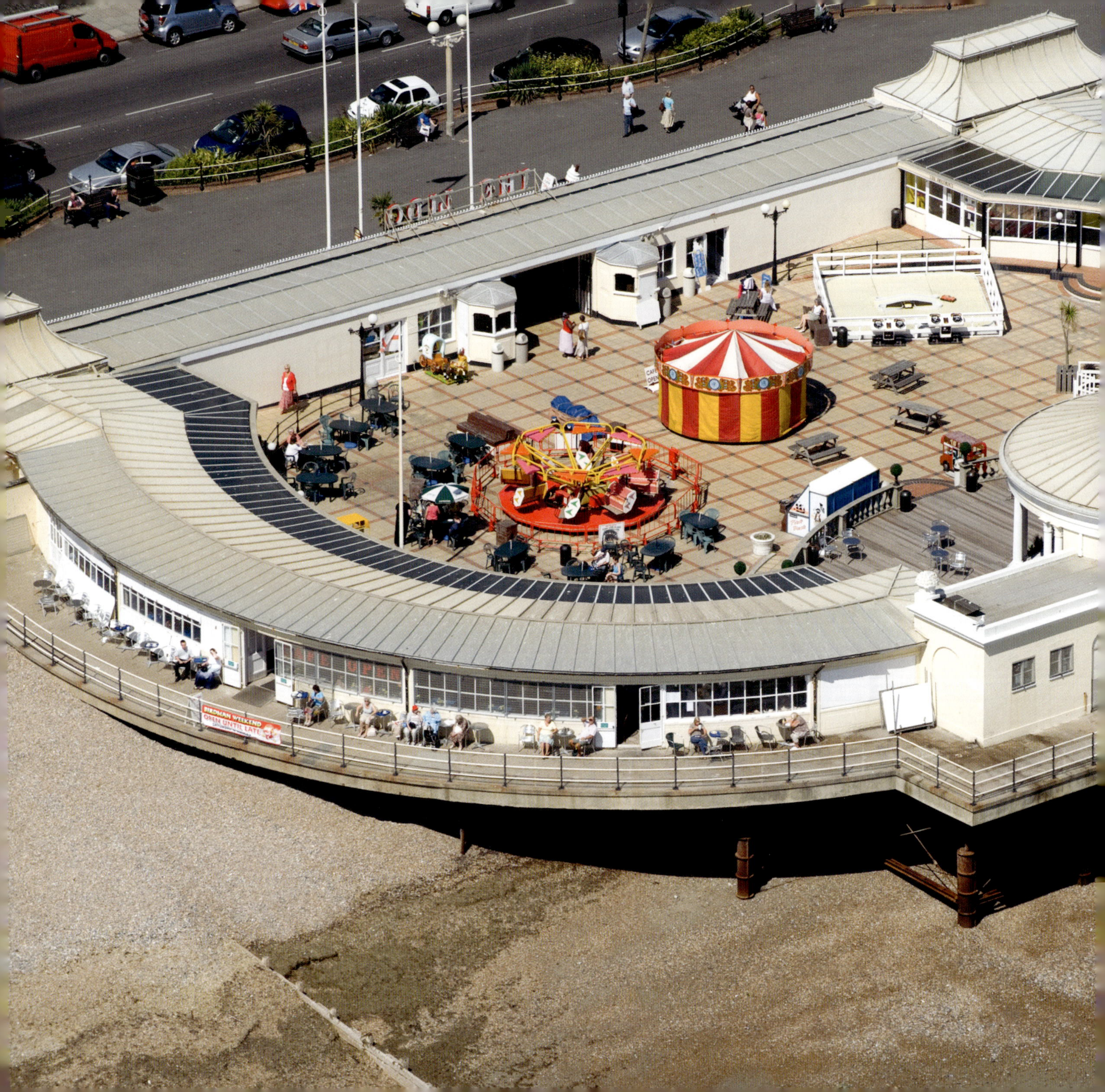
BIRDMAN WEEKEND
OPEN UNTIL LATE

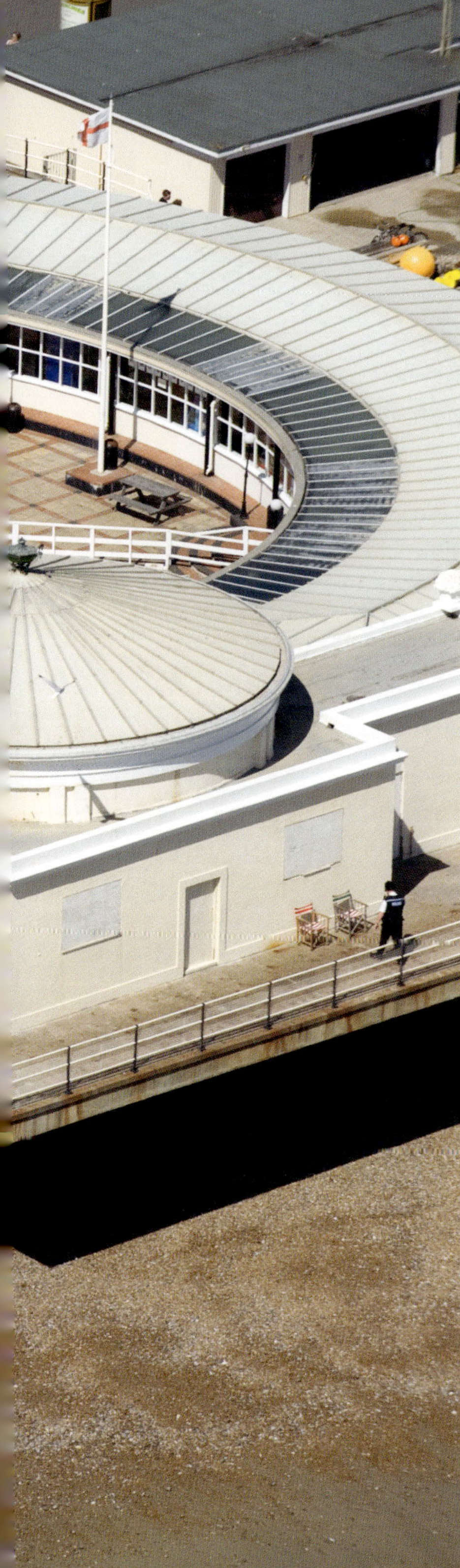

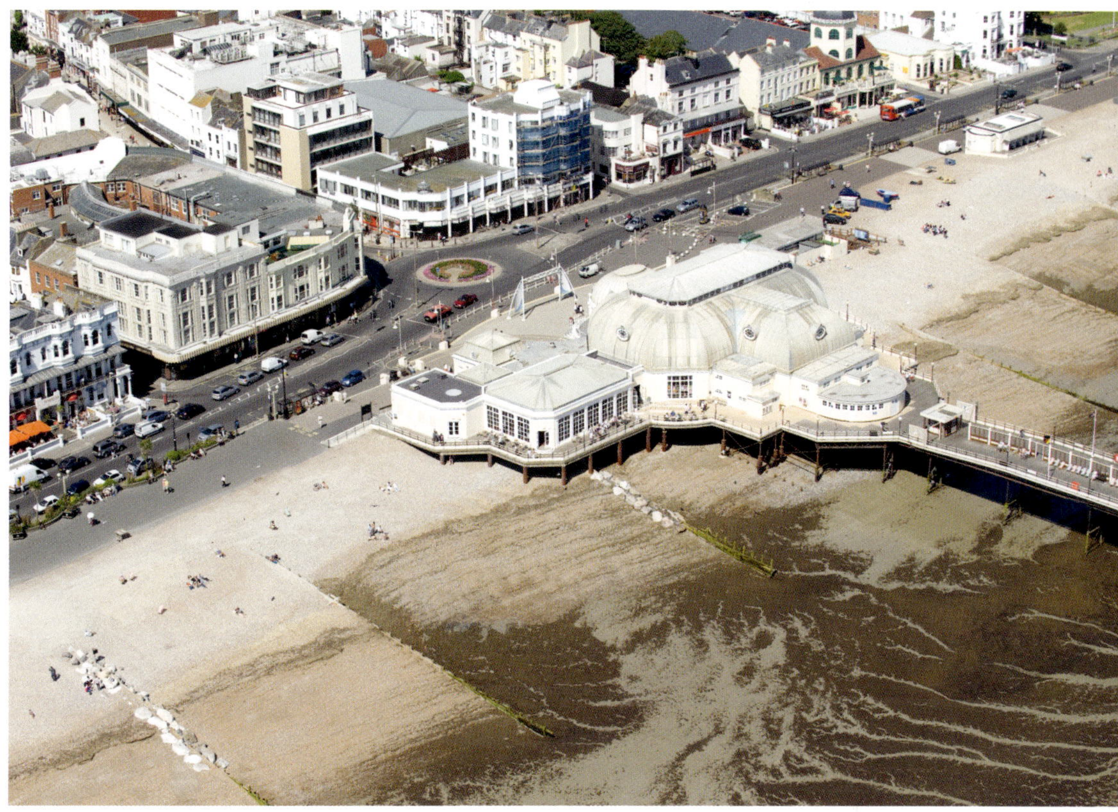

Above: Looking down on to Marine Parade and the shoreward end of Worthing pier.

Left: The Lido, Worthing, is a family entertainment centre offering children's rides, amusement arcades, and shops.

Following page: Part of the Aquarena centre, Beach Parade, Worthing.

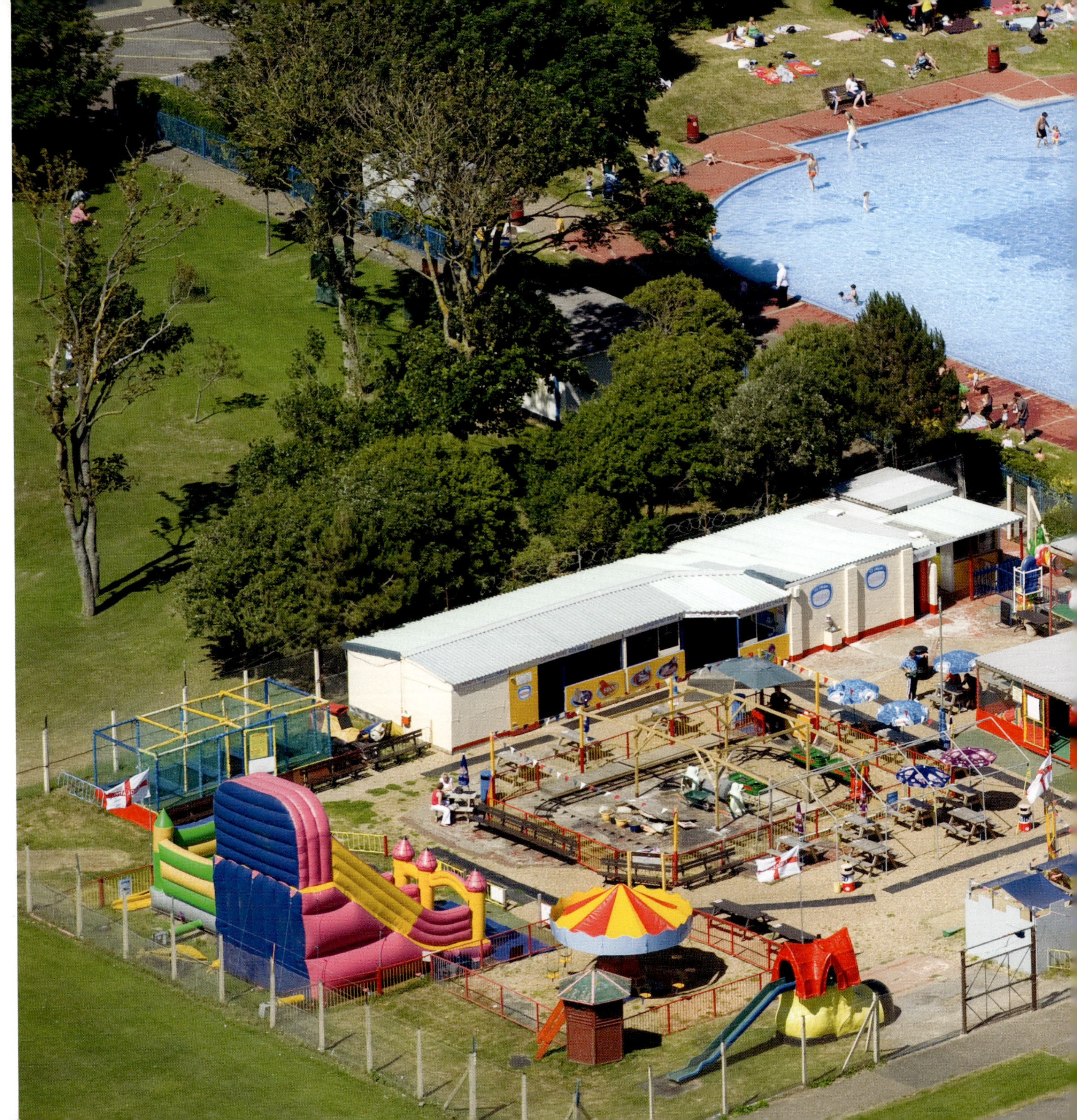

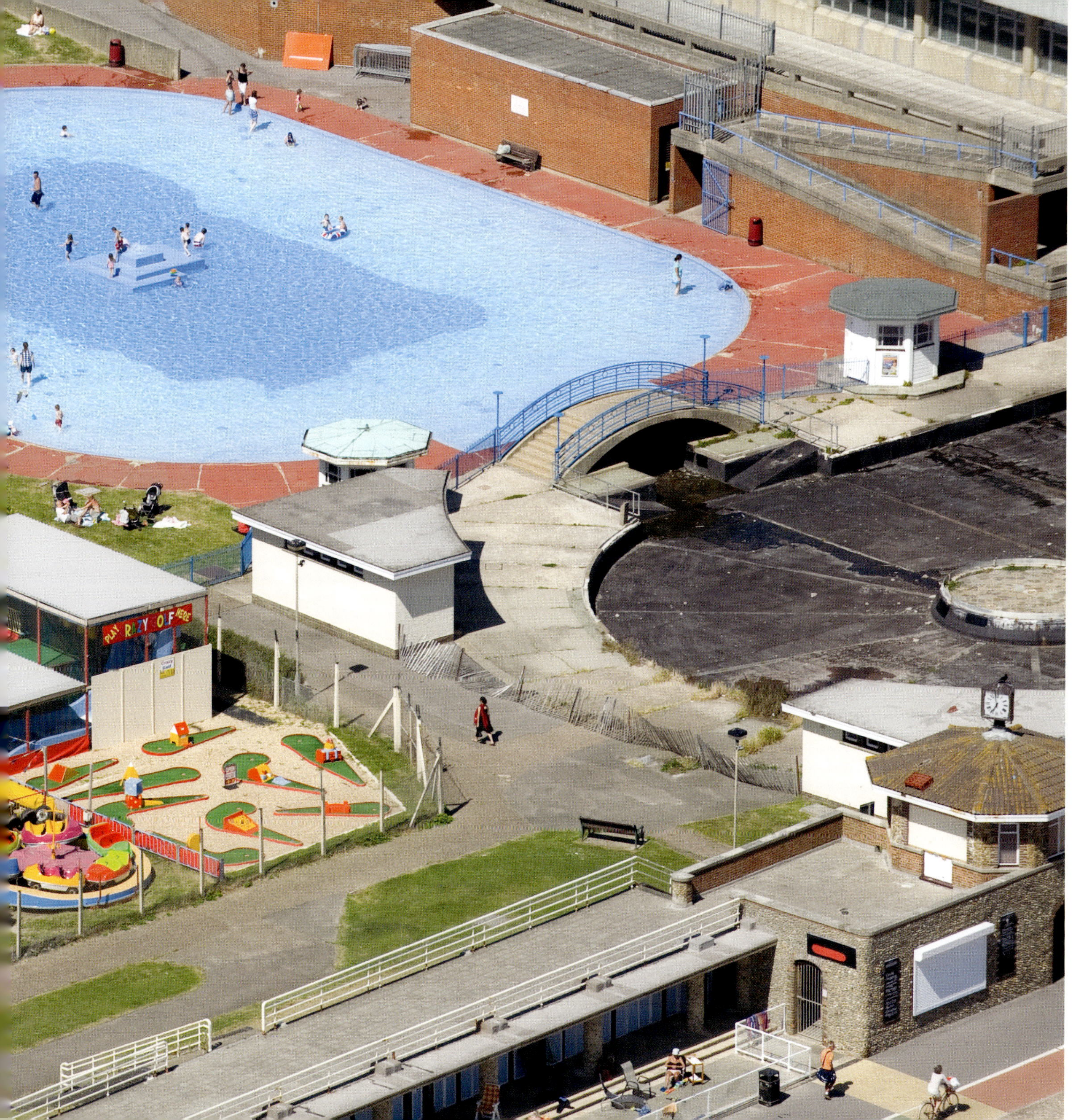
PLAY RAZY OLF HERE

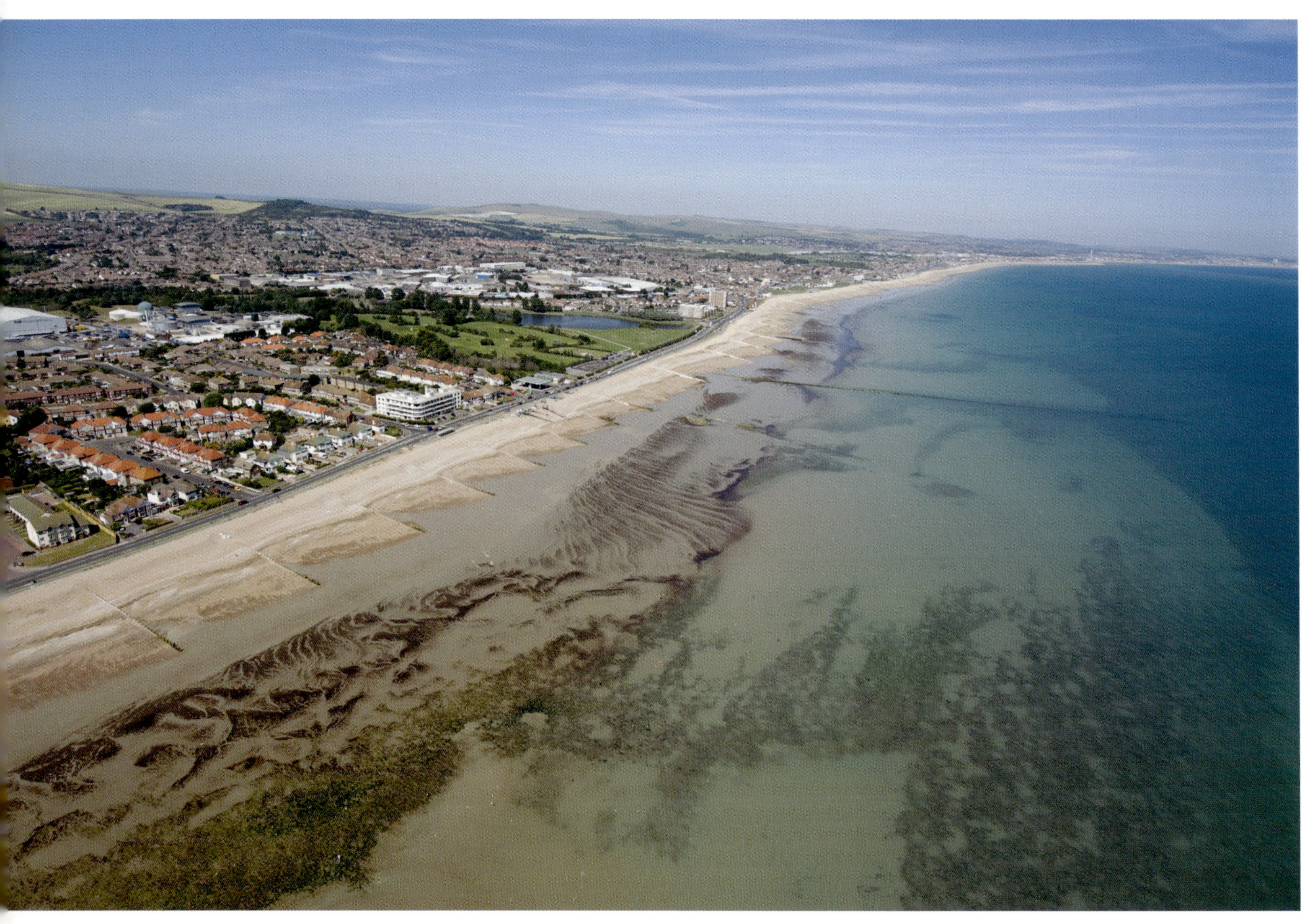

Above: A magnificent view eastwards over Worthing towards Lancing, with Shoreham far distant.

Right: Looking inland over the golf course, with Worthing on the left and Lancing on the right.

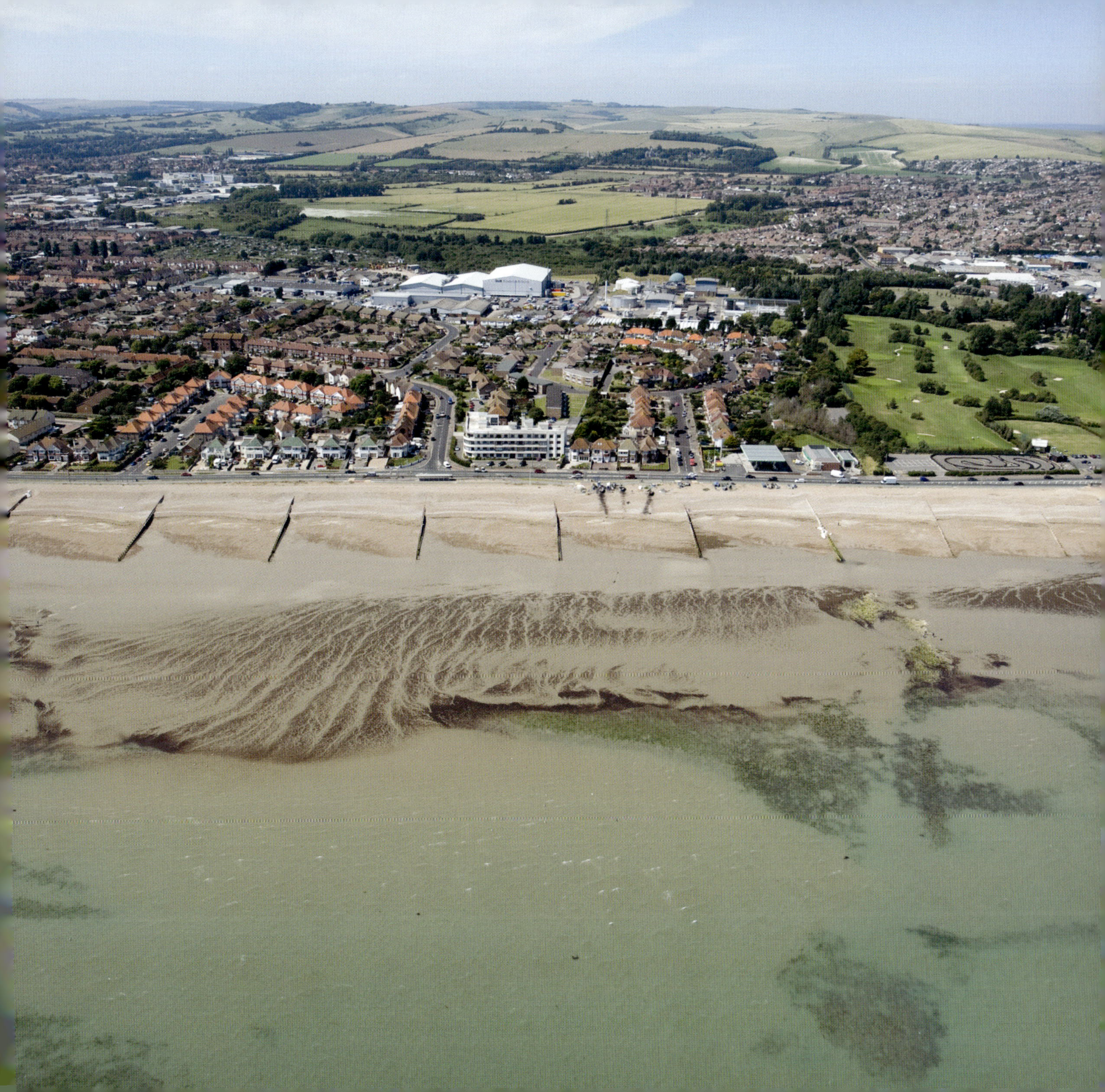

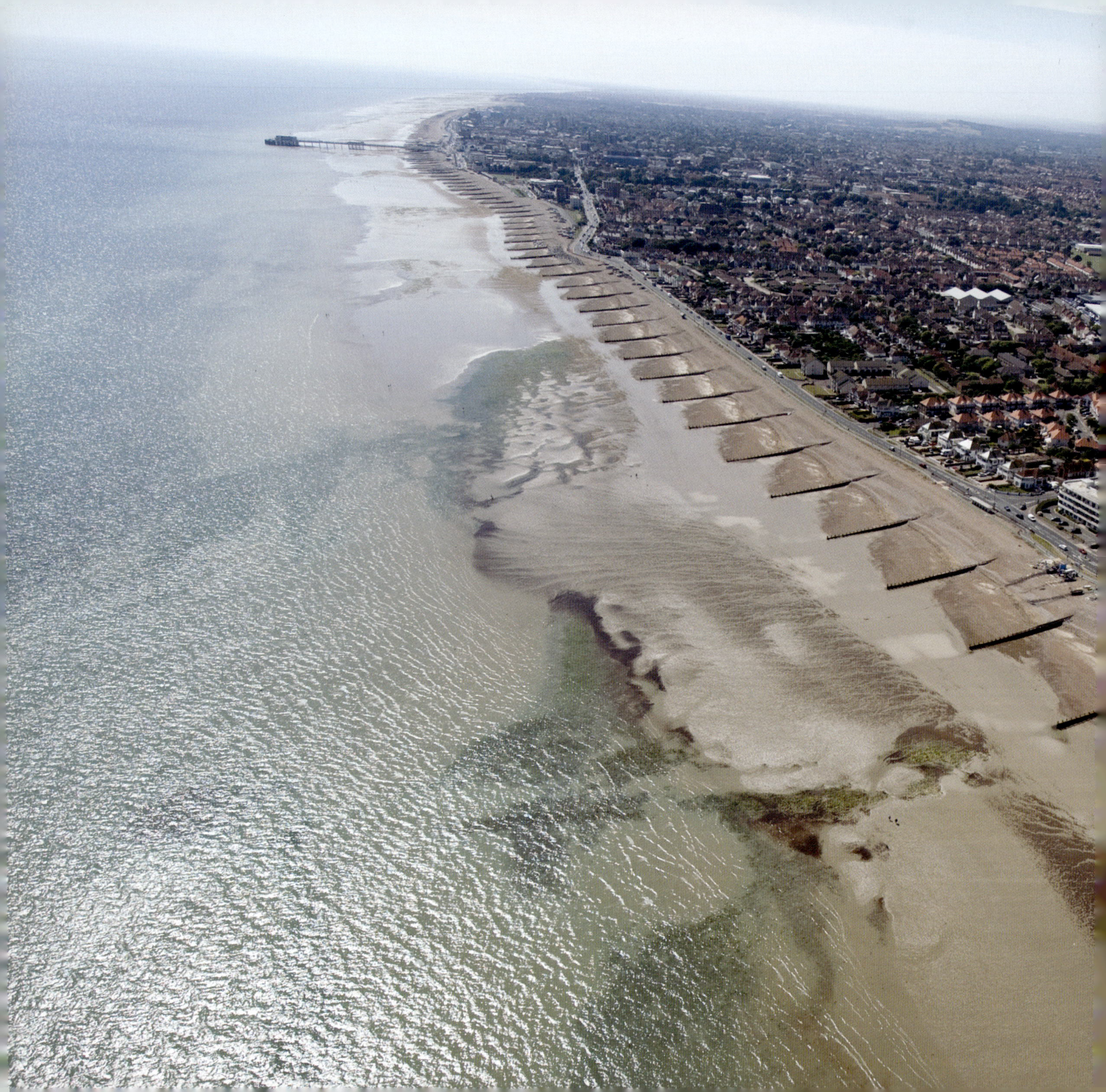

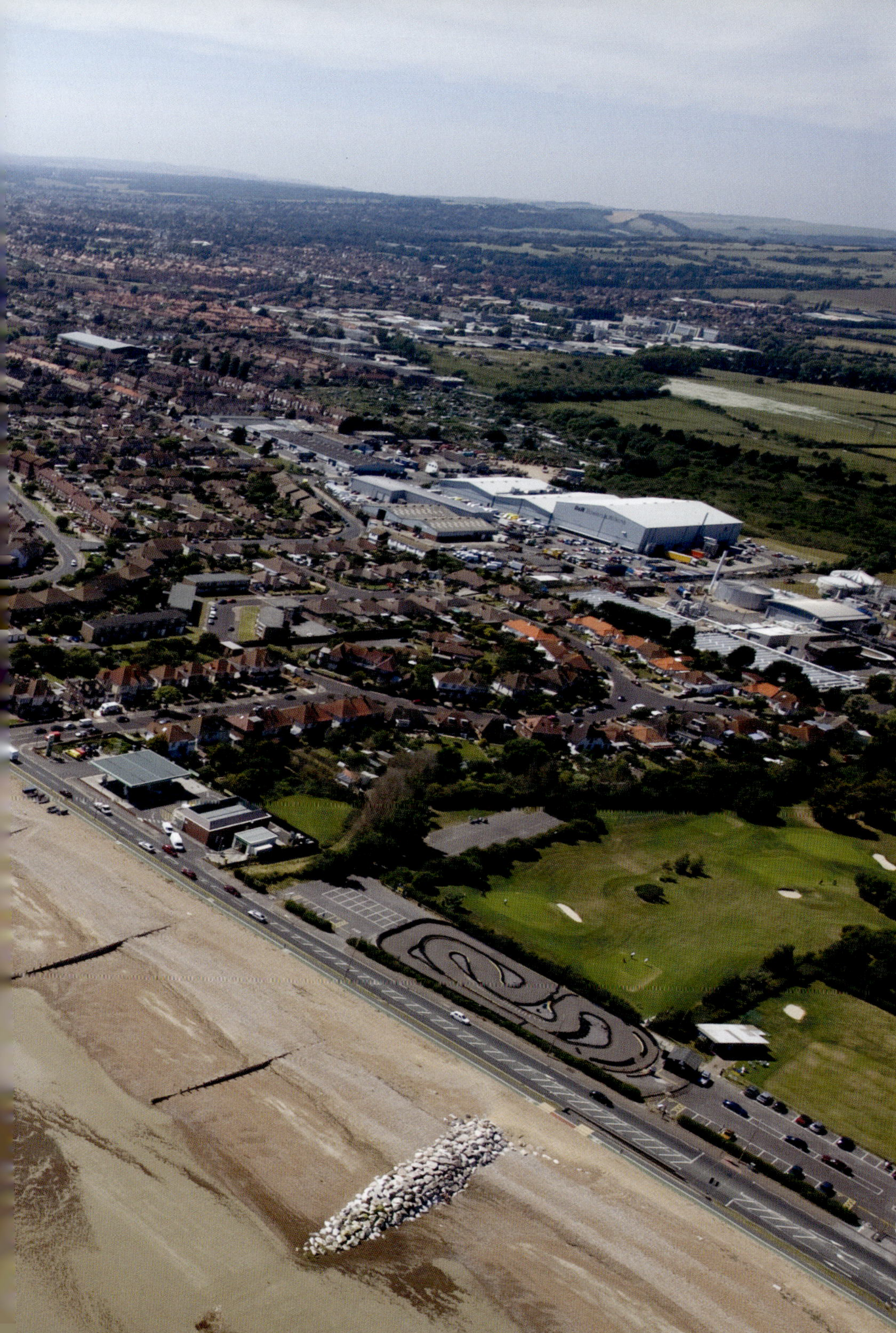

The view westward down the coast, taking in most of Worthing.

The Brighton Road runs parallel to the coast through South Lancing, with the Downs rising in the distance.

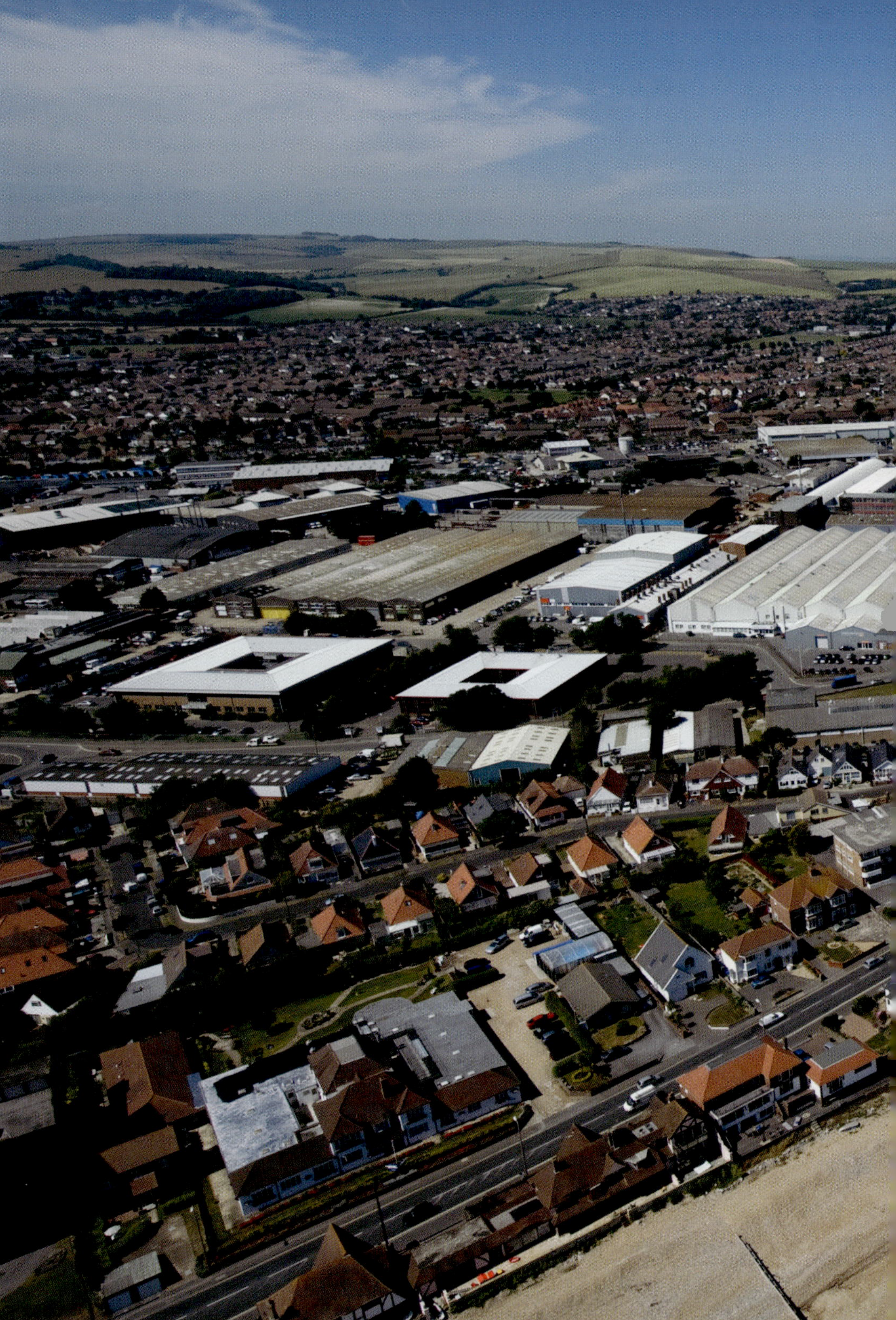

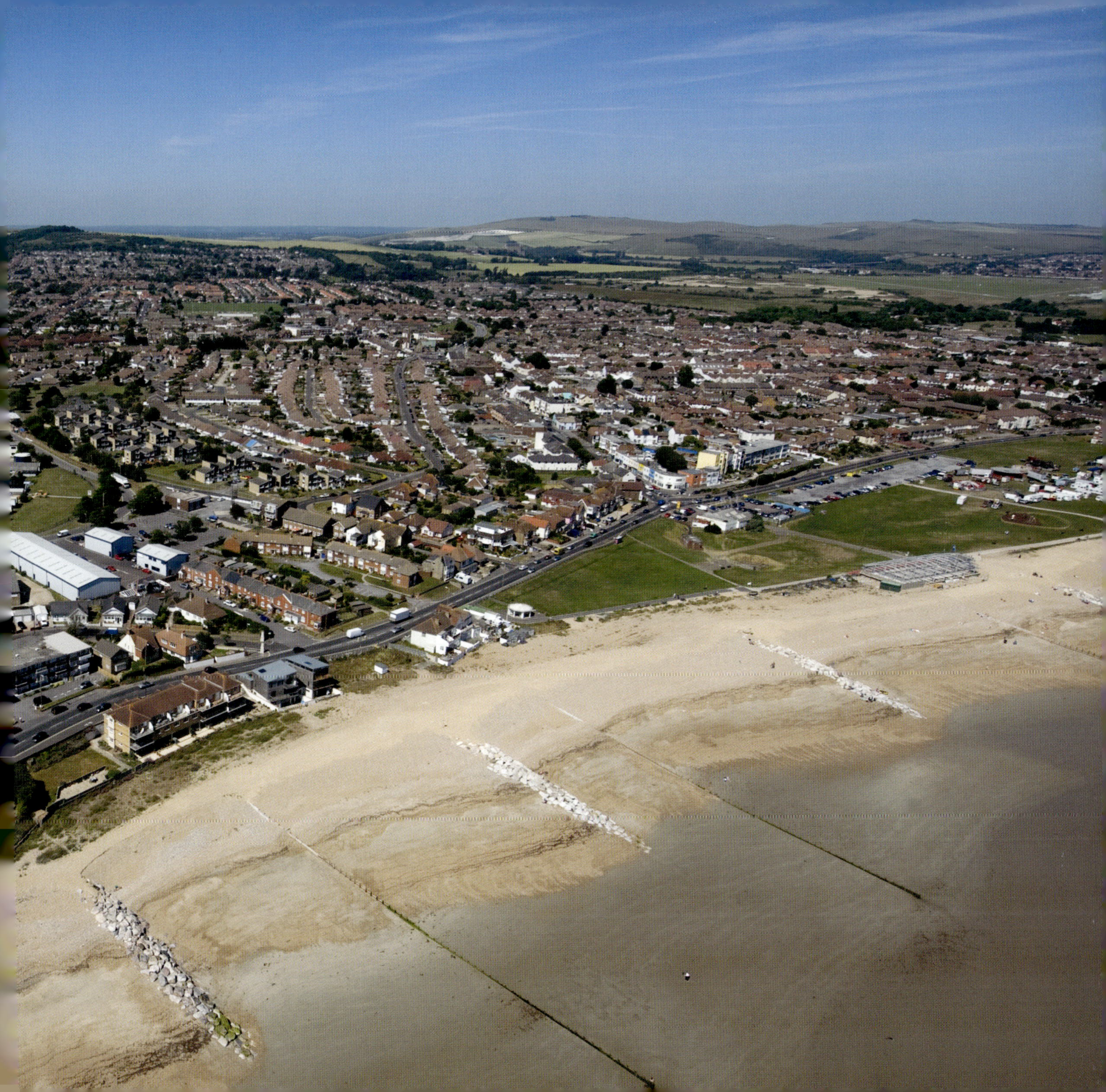

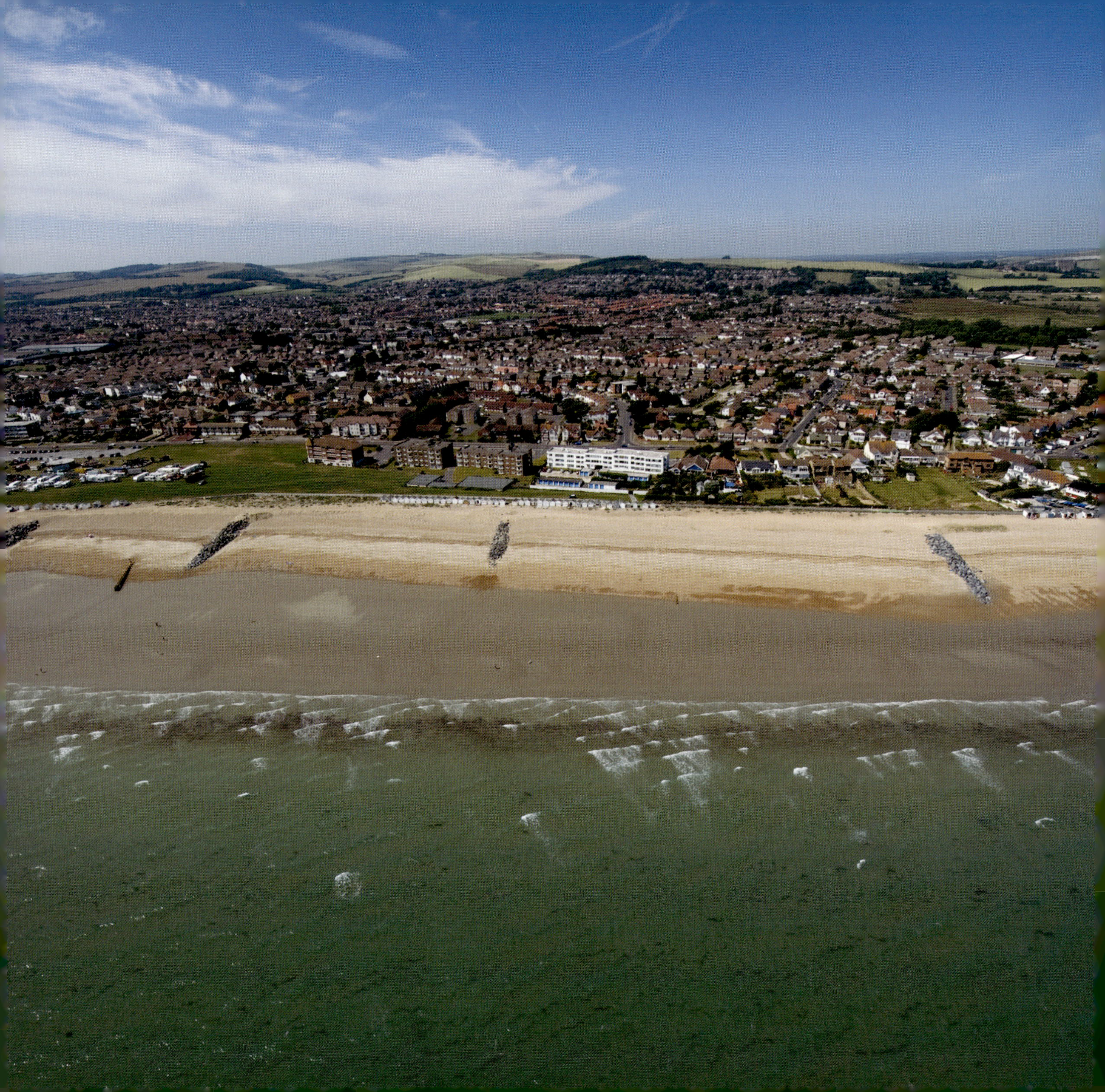

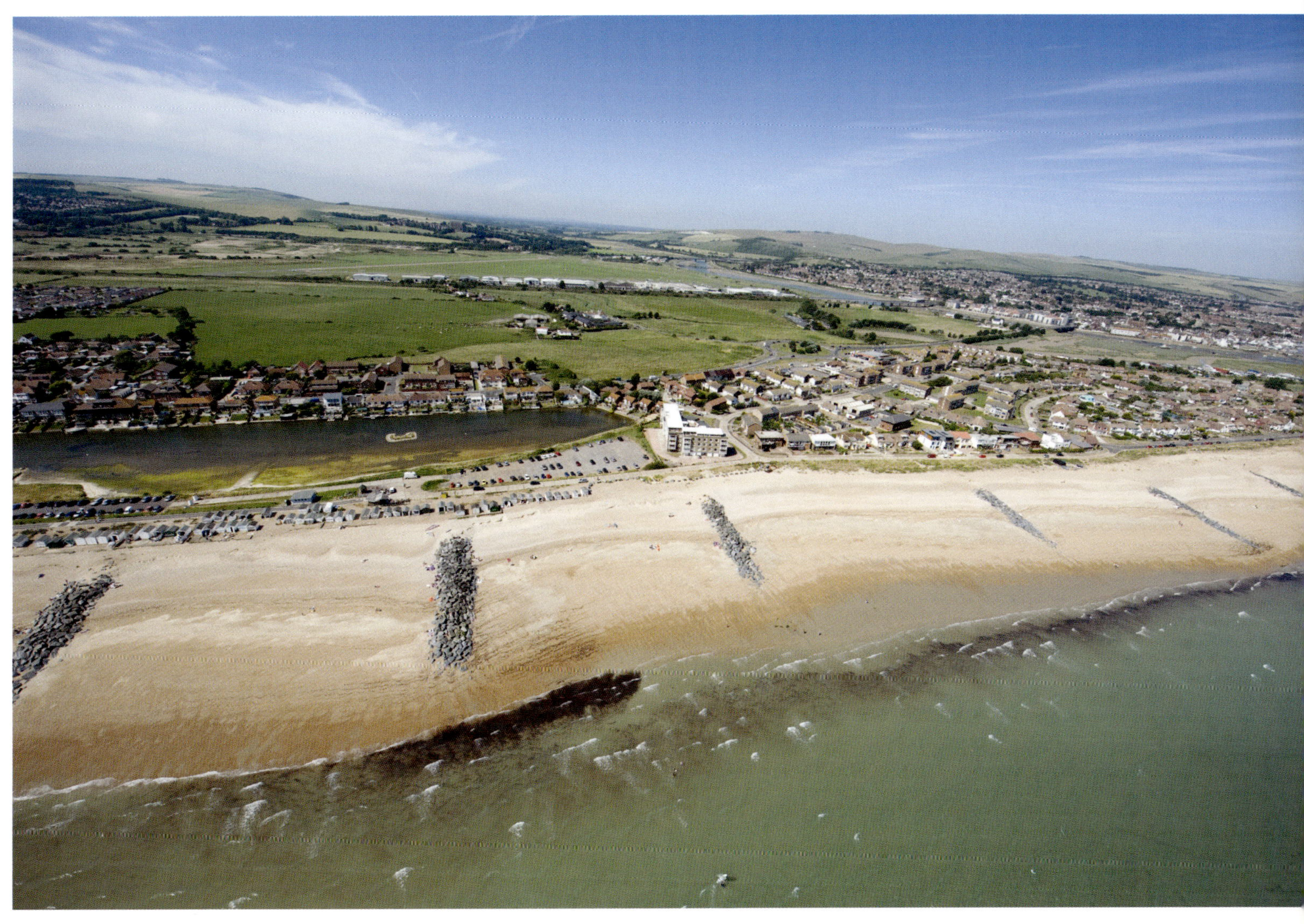

Left: Lancing and Sompting, looking north.

Above: Shoreham-by-the-Sea. Shoreham Beach extends to the right of this photograph, separated from the town by the River Adur.

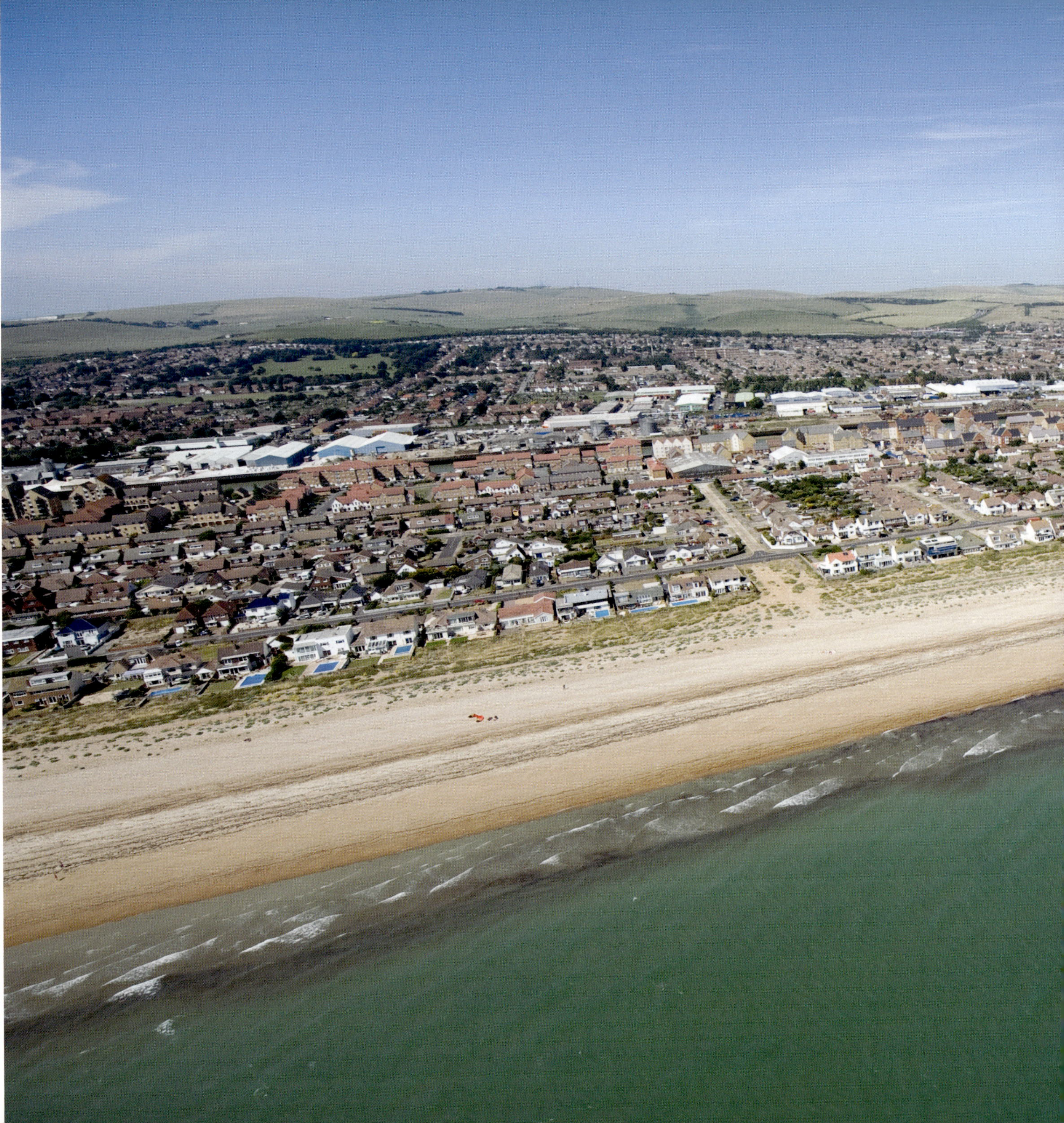

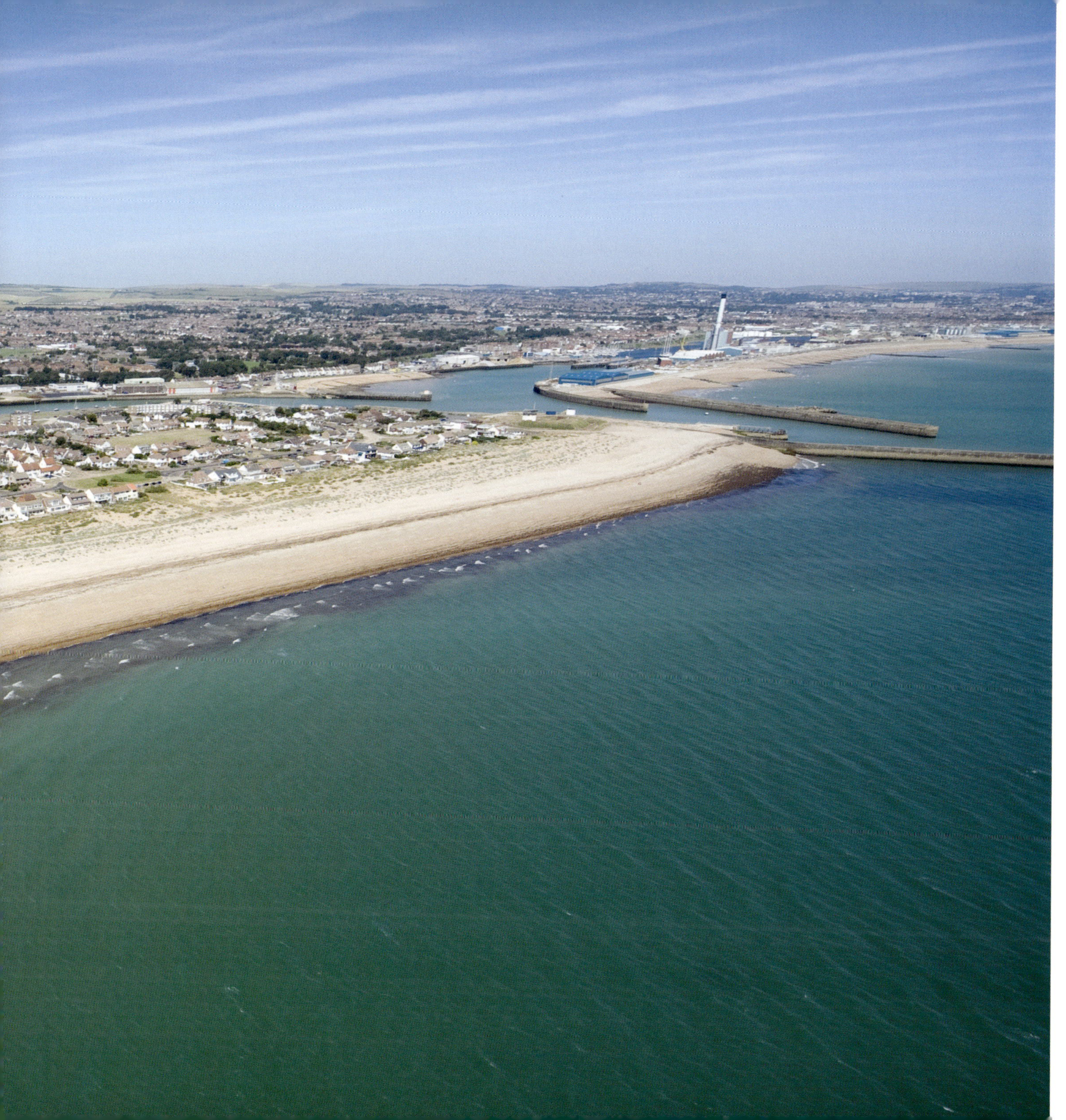

Previous page: A stunning view of Shoreham looking over Shoreham Beach.

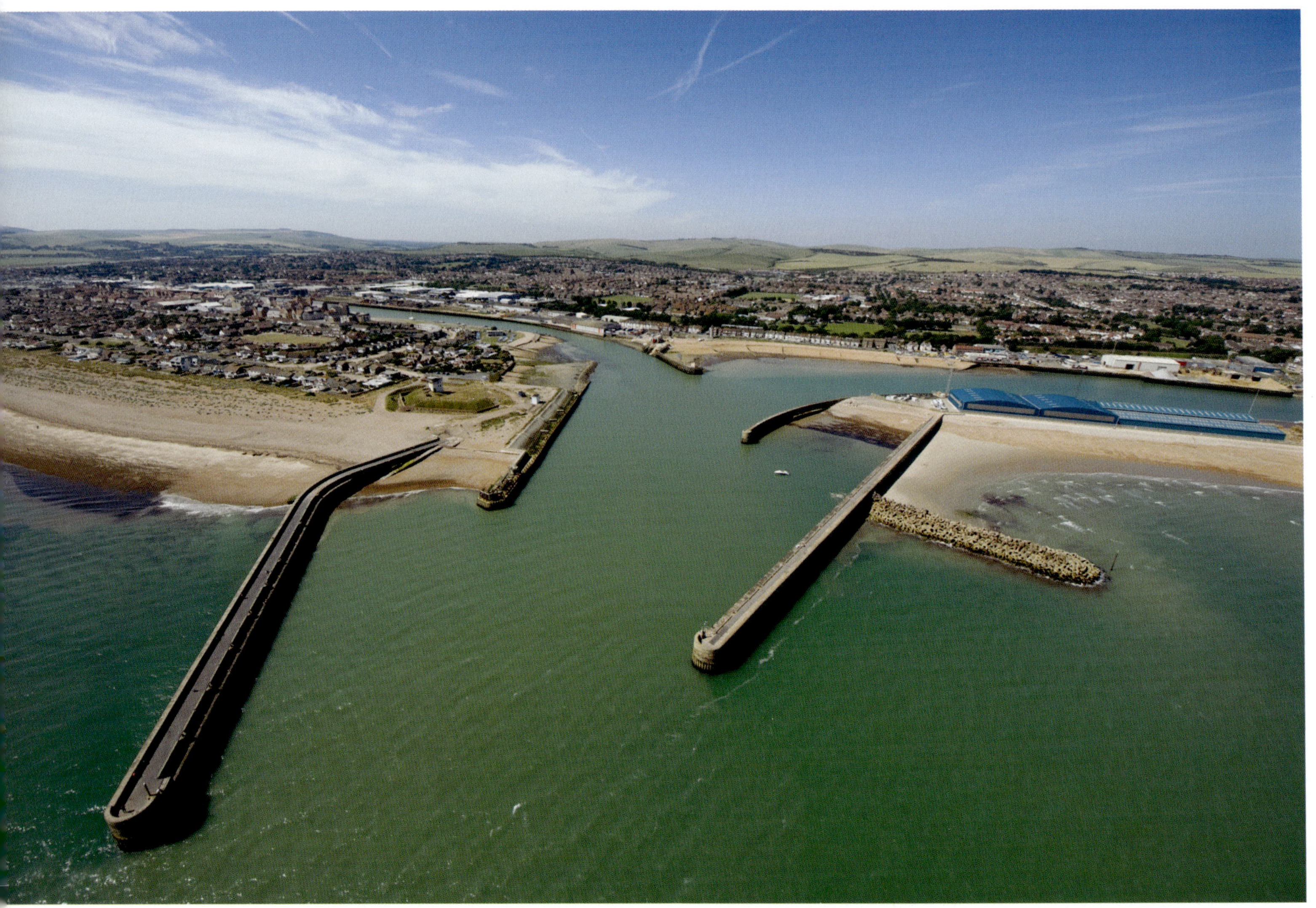

Above: Shoreham Harbour is the principal port of Sussex.

Right: Looking down on King's Esplanade and the seafront of Hove, Portslade on the left.

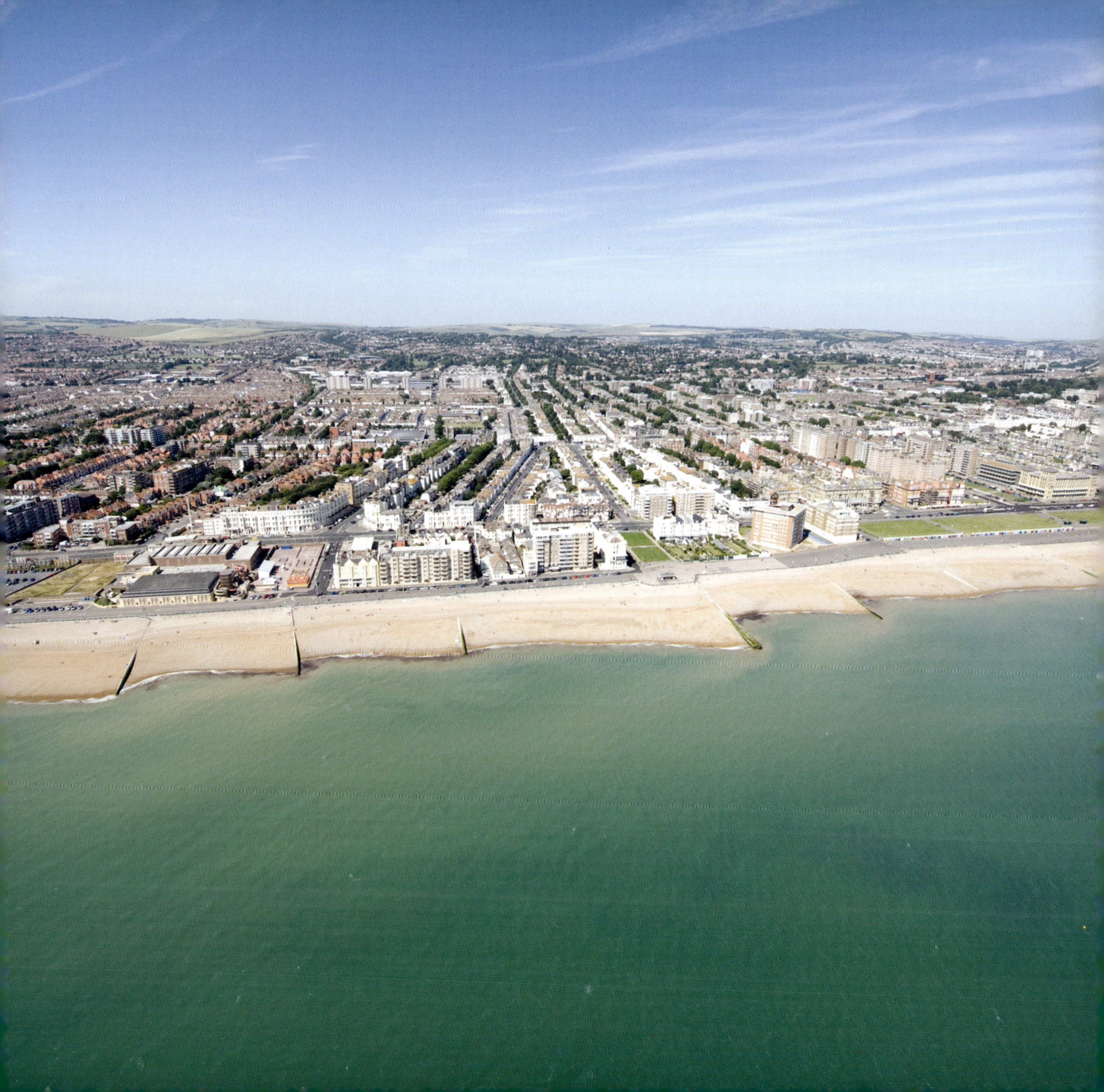

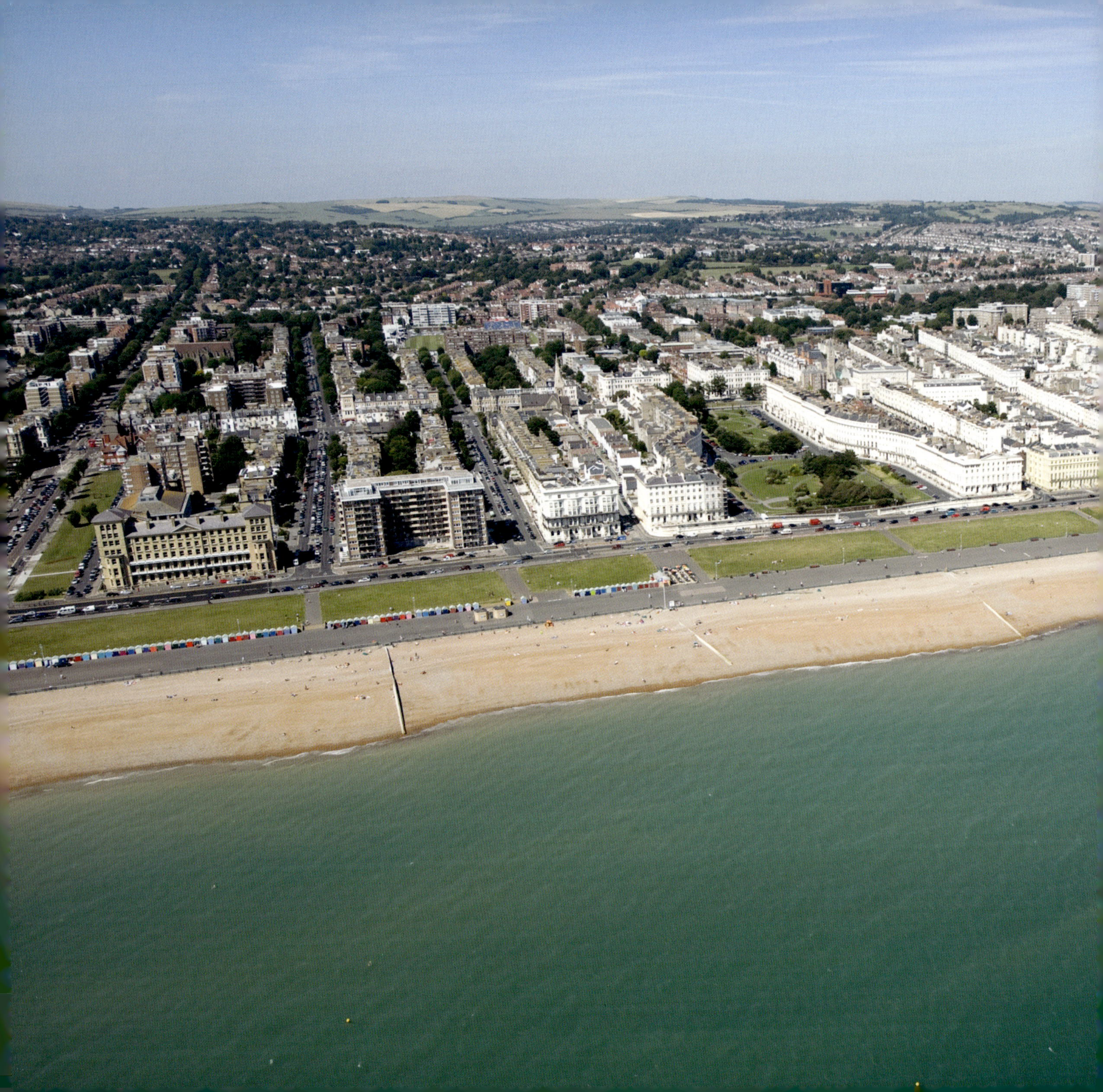

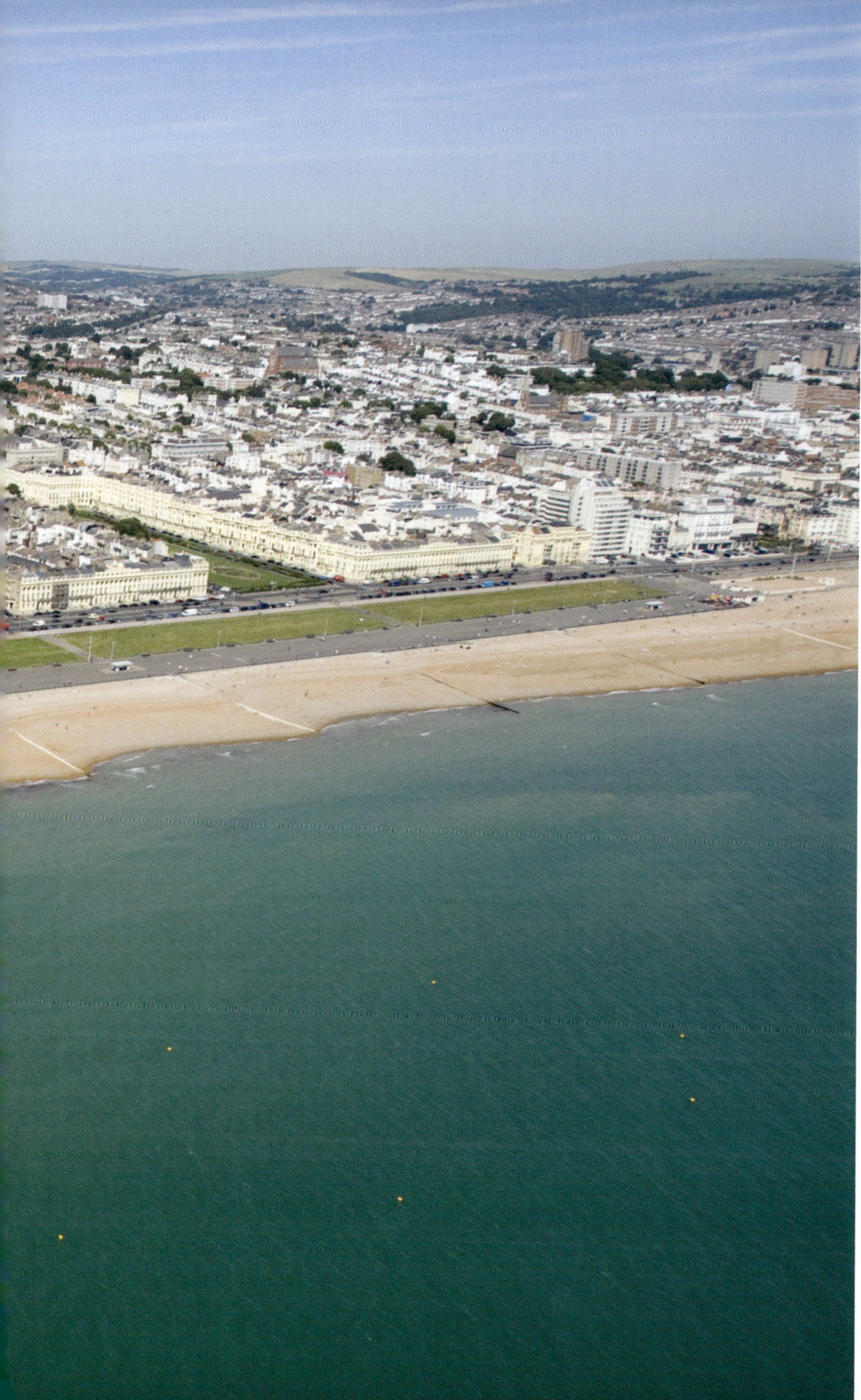

Whilst now forming a single conurbation with Brighton, Hove retains much of its grand distinctiveness, not least through the Regency architecture on and around Brunswick Terrace. Central in the foreground of the photograph is Adelaide Crescent, named after Queen Adelaide, wife of William IV.

Where Hove meets Brighton. One of the most famous seafronts in the world remains a popular summer destination. The old West Pier has suffered many indignities. Severely damaged by storms in 2002 and 2003, fires finally put paid to the remaining structure, although all hope of a rebuild is not yet lost.

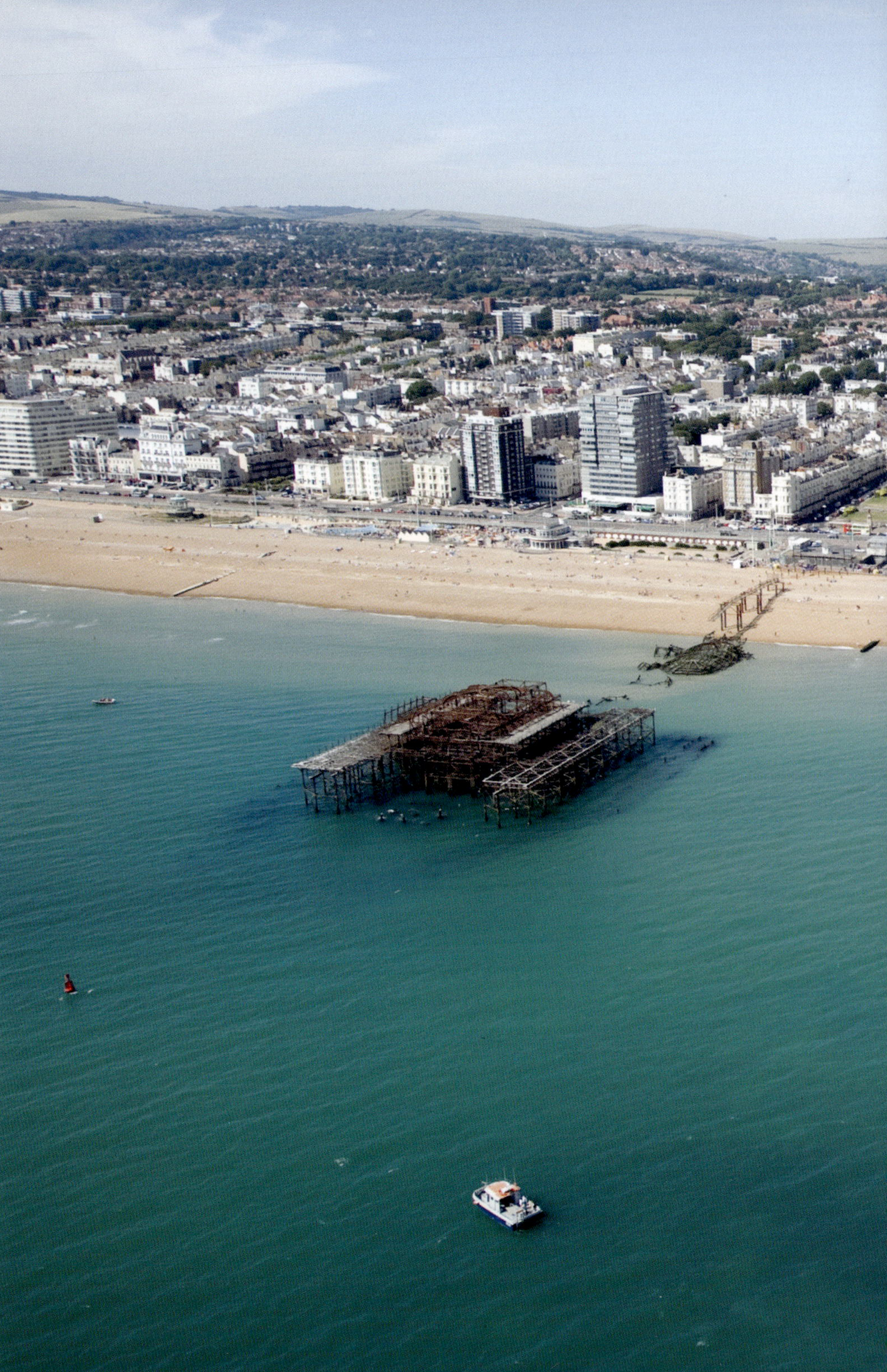

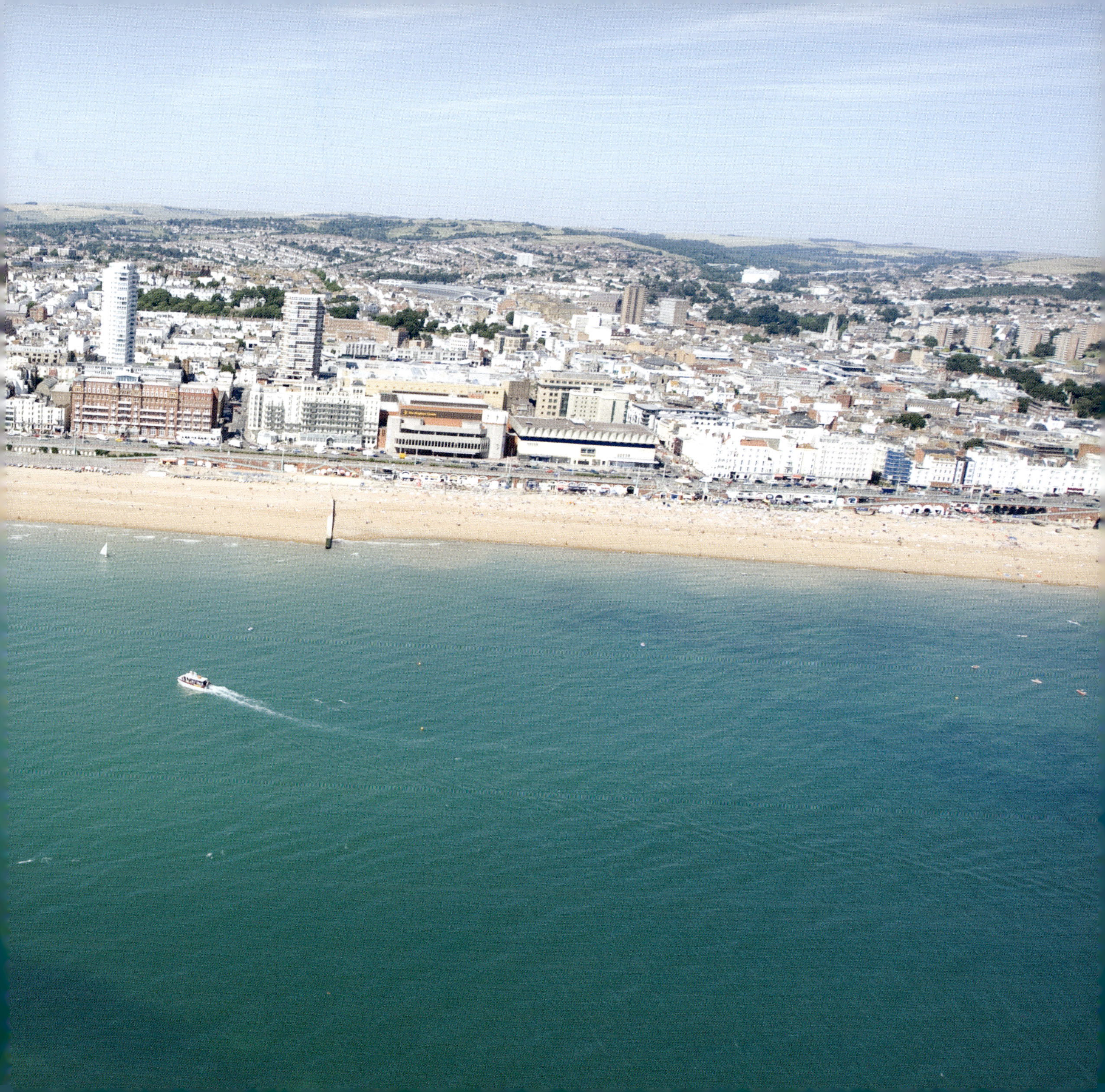

Cool pool, Brighton.

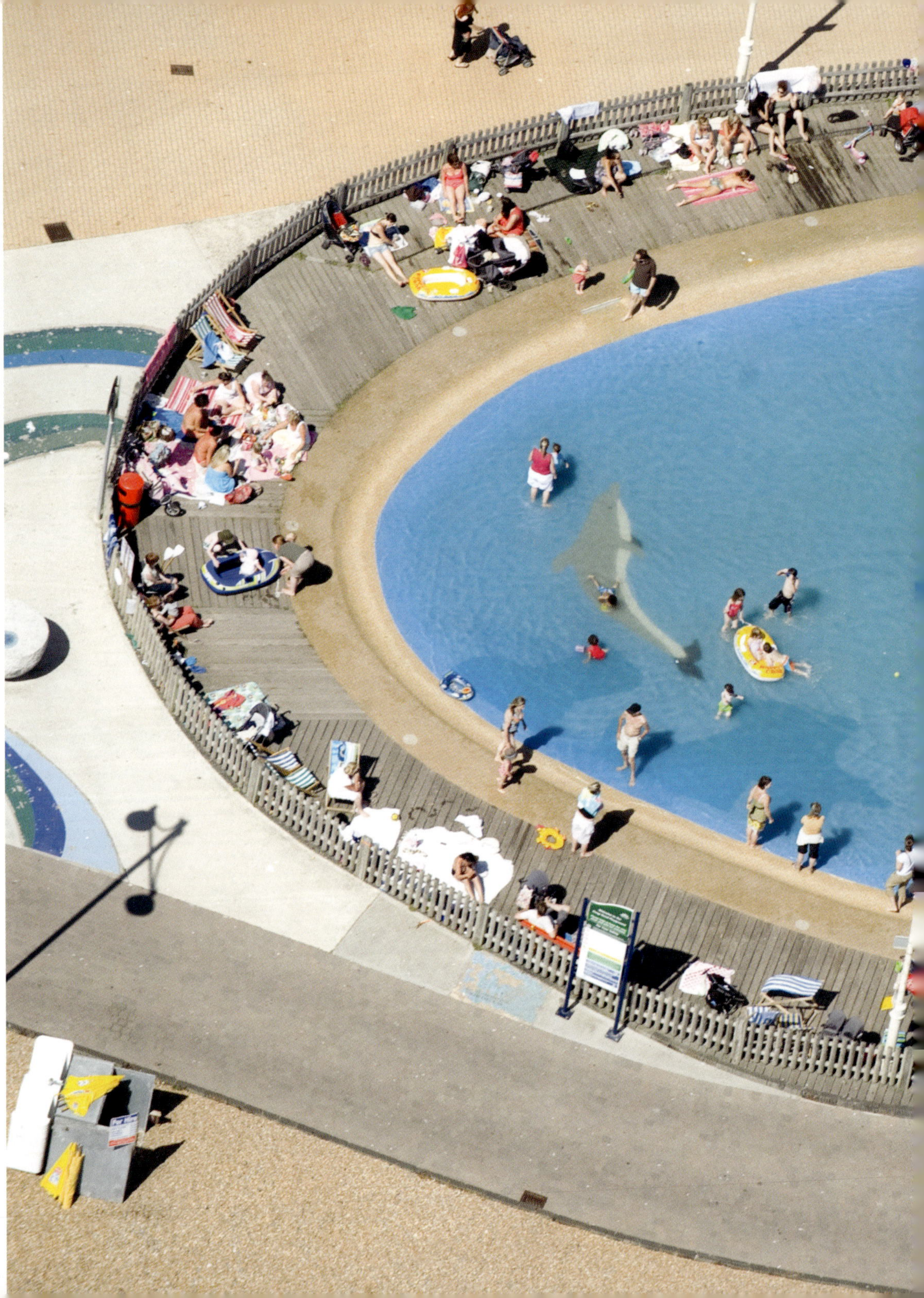

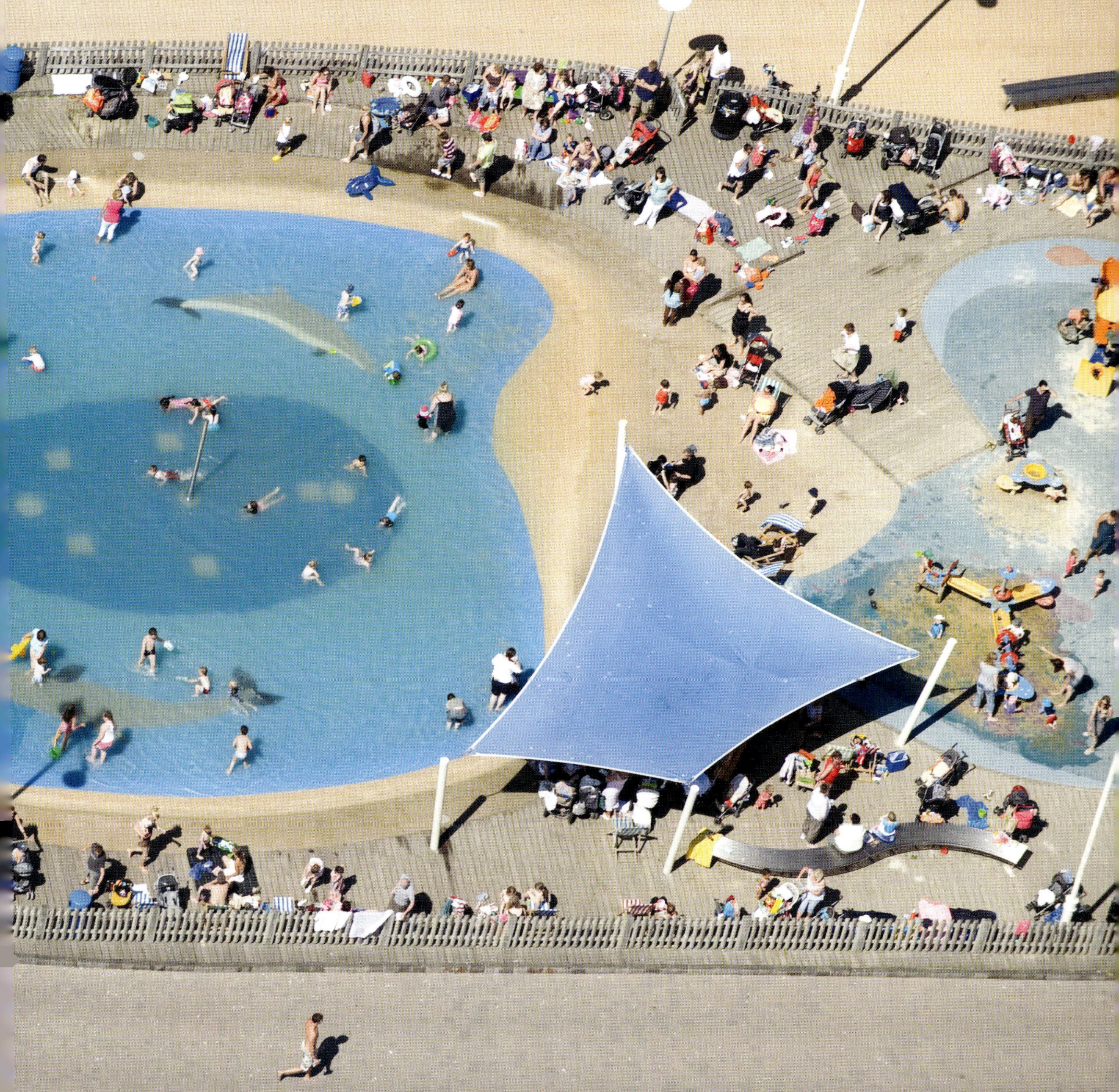

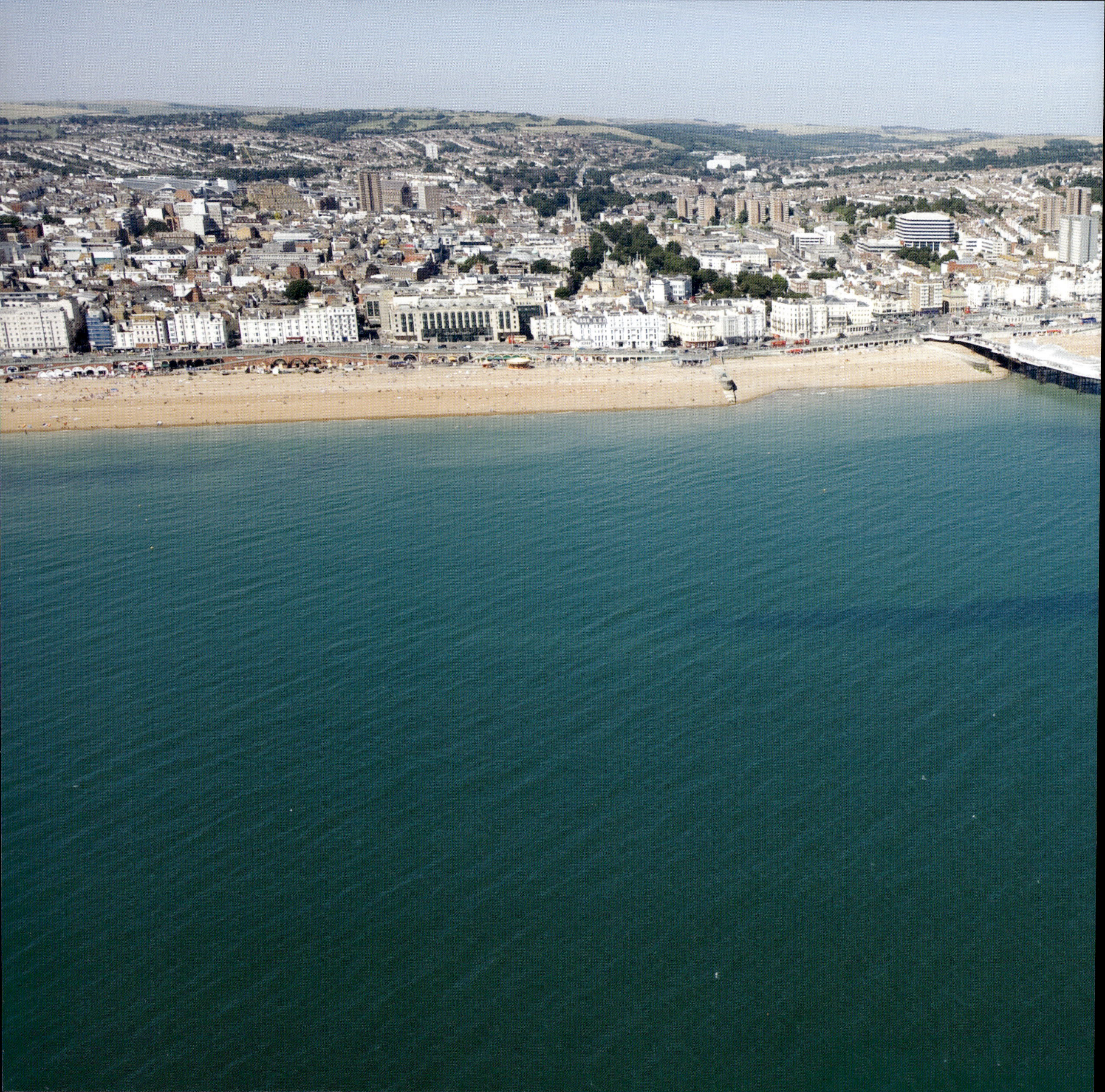

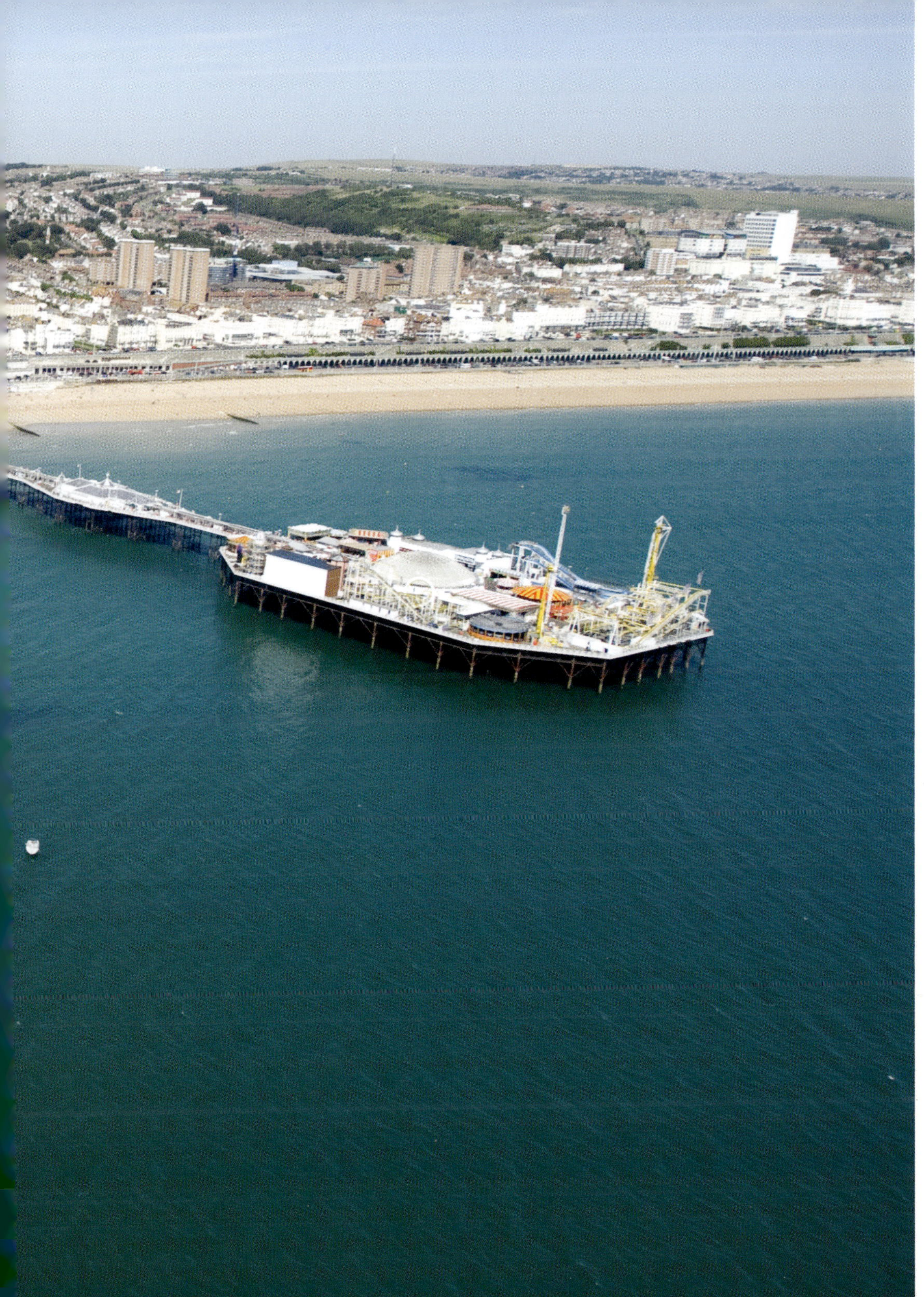

Many of Brighton's famous landmarks can be seen in this photograph including The Royal Pavilion and, of course, the pier.

Following page: Cooking on the beach, Brighton.

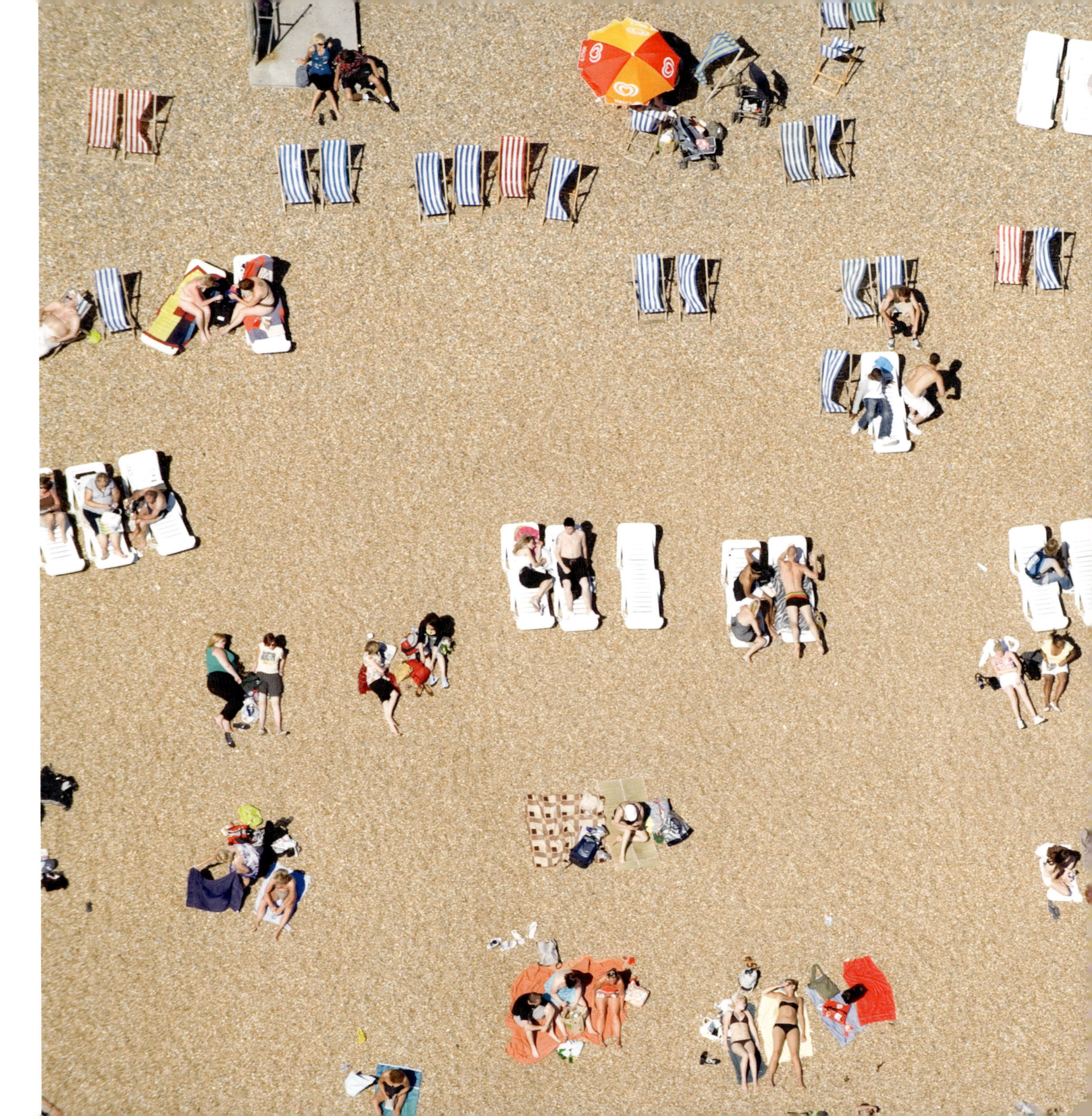

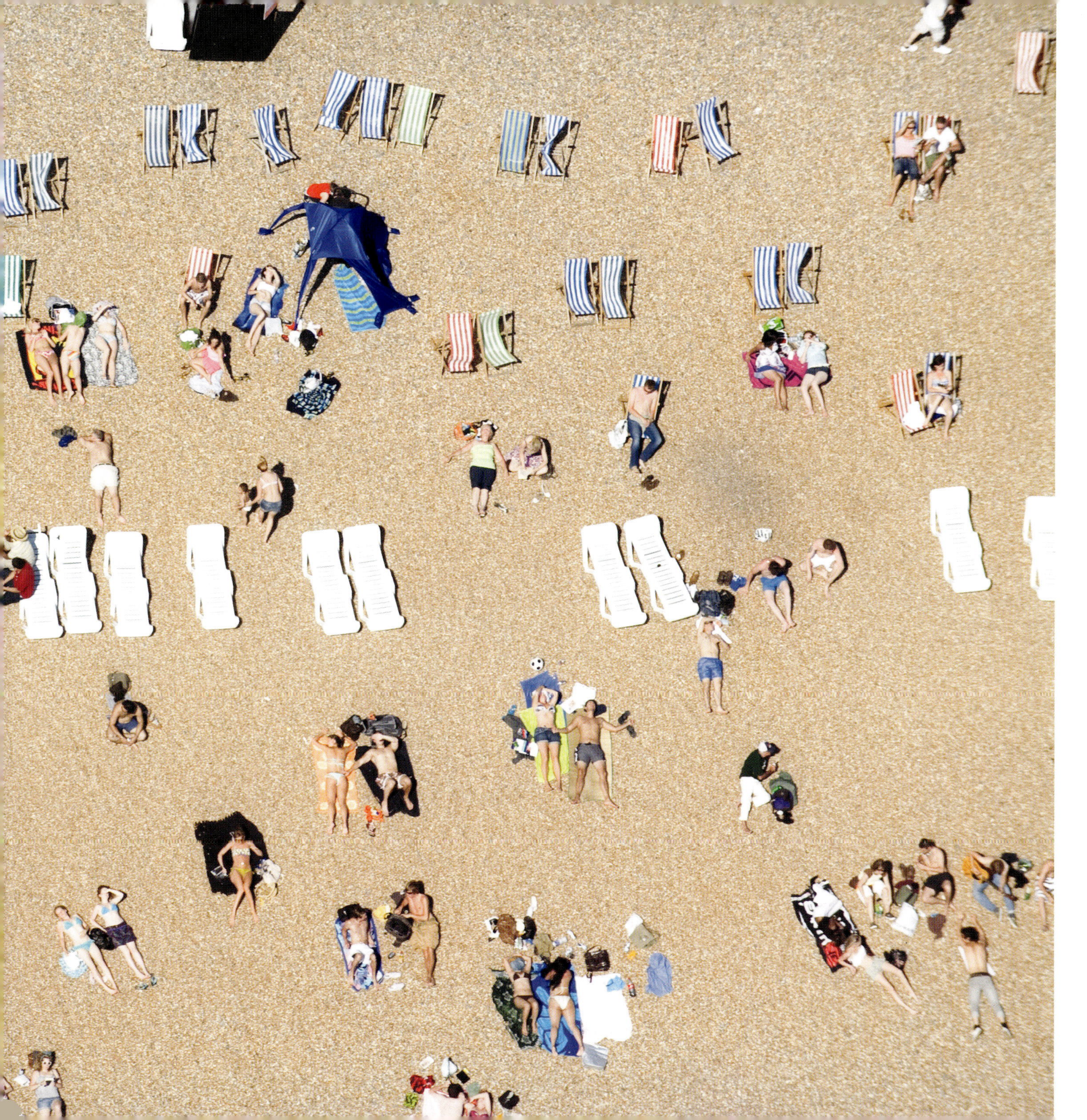

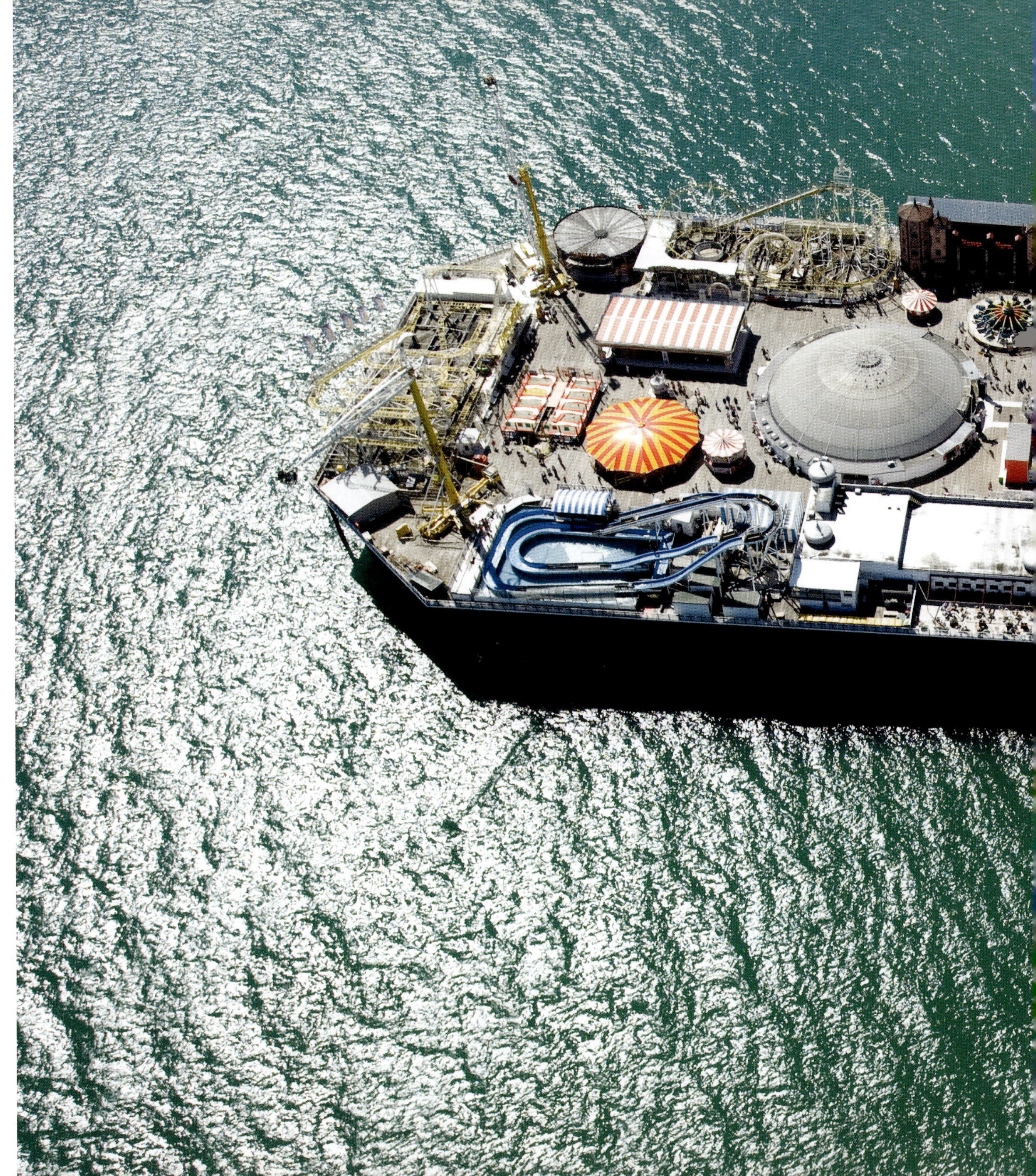

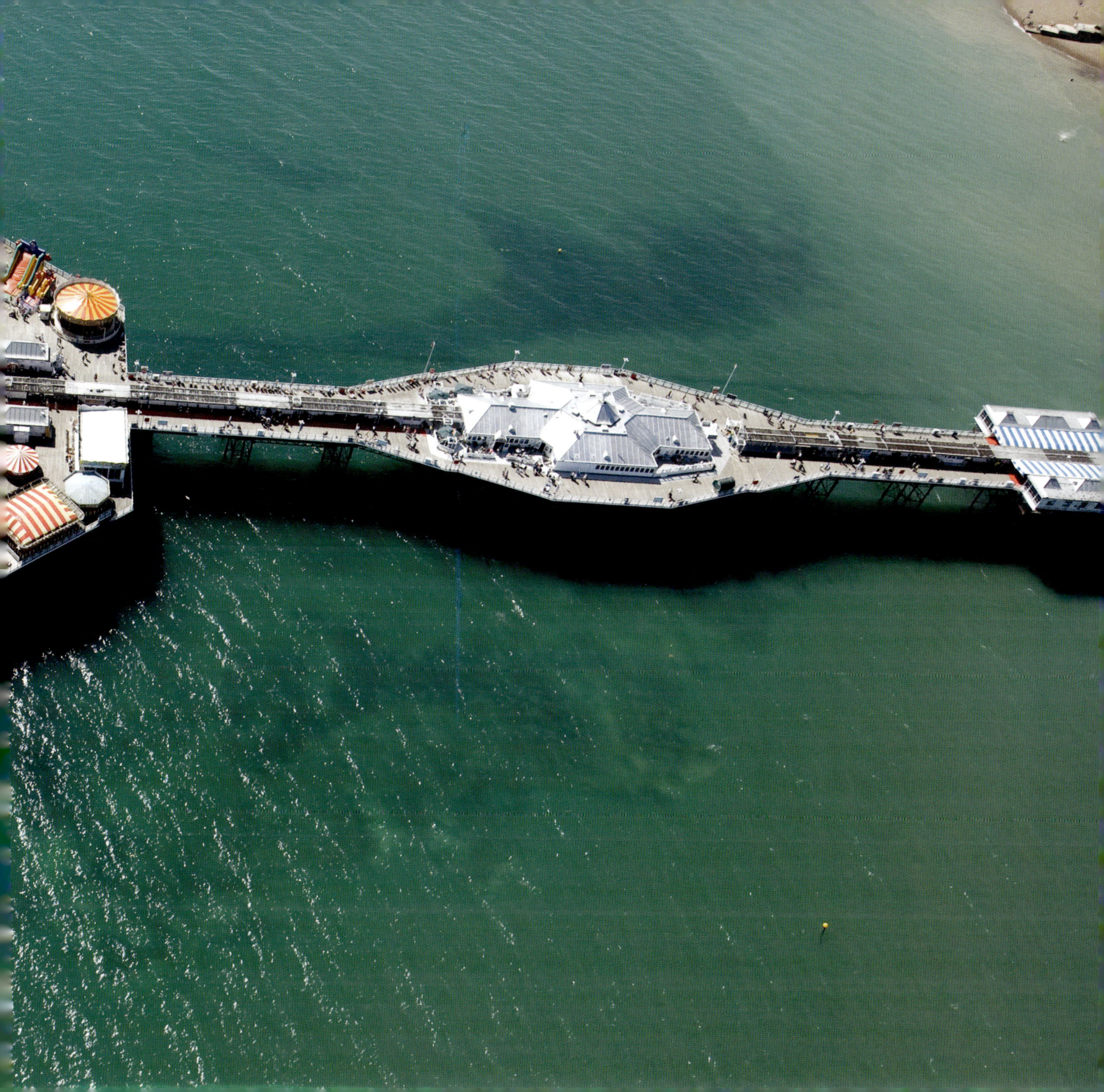

Previous page: Brighton Pier dominates this photograph.

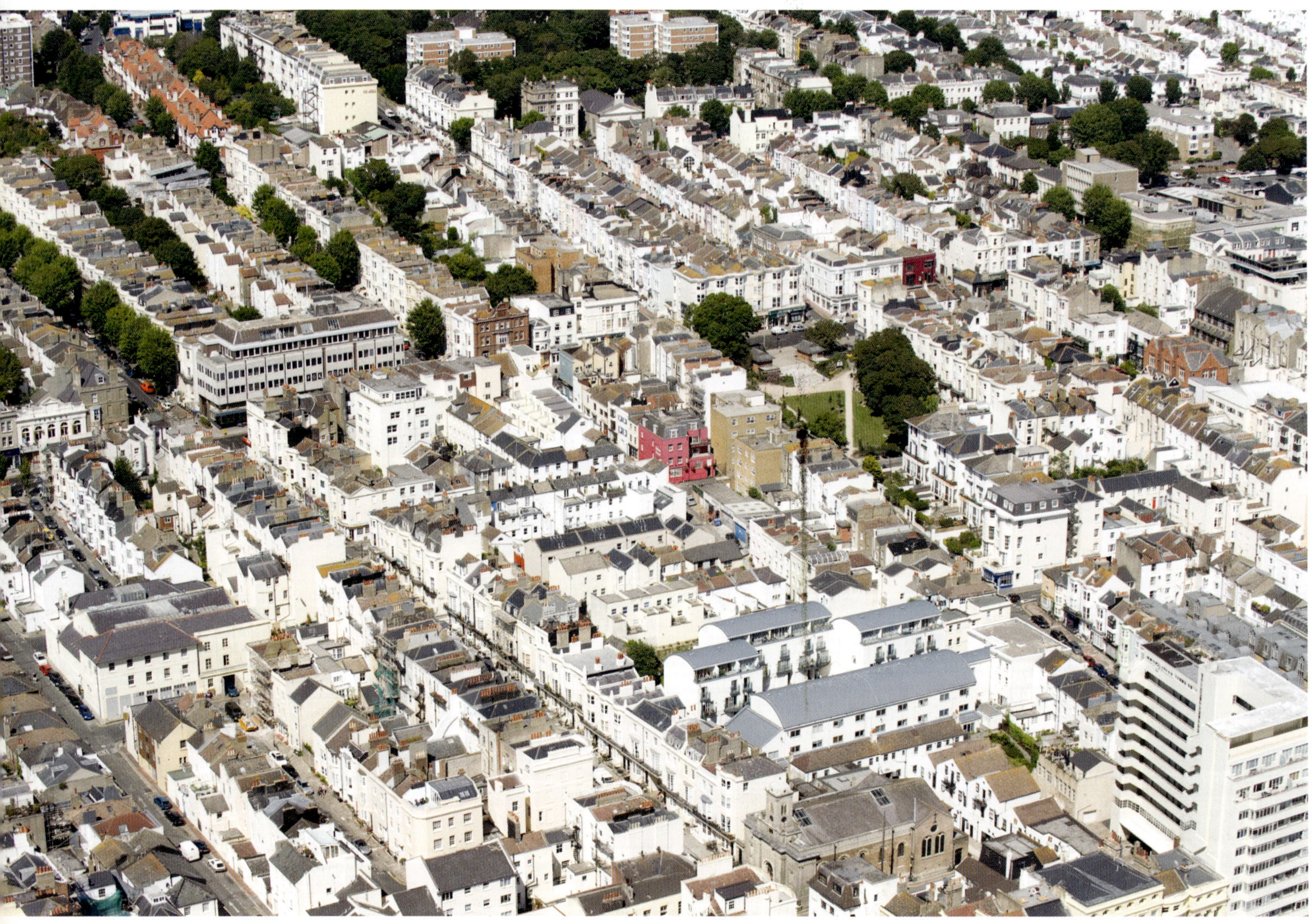

Above: Overlooking Waterloo Street and Norfolk Square, Brighton.

Right: Saltdean. Much of this area was open farmland until the early 1920s. The famous Lido can be seen centre foreground.

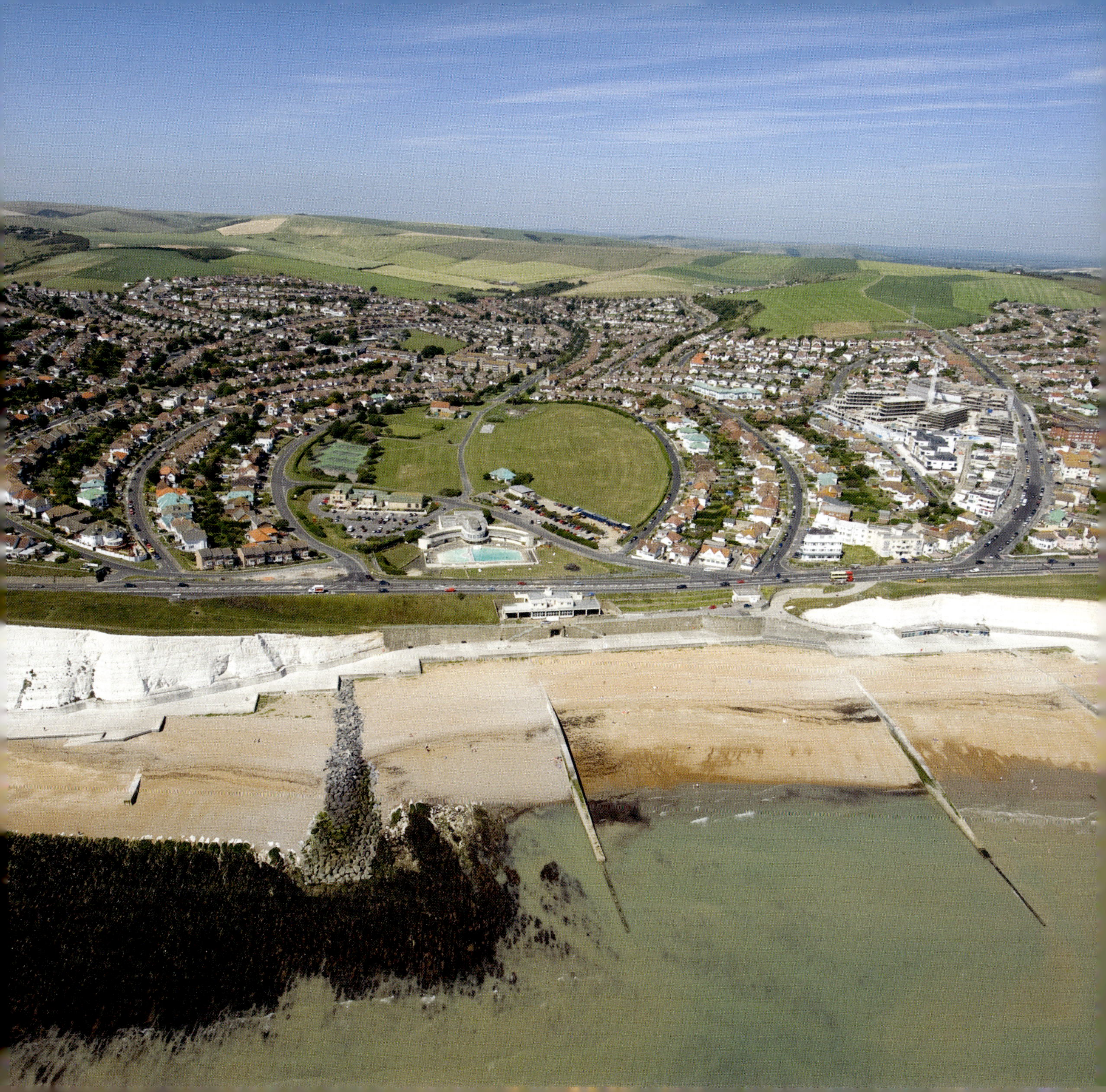

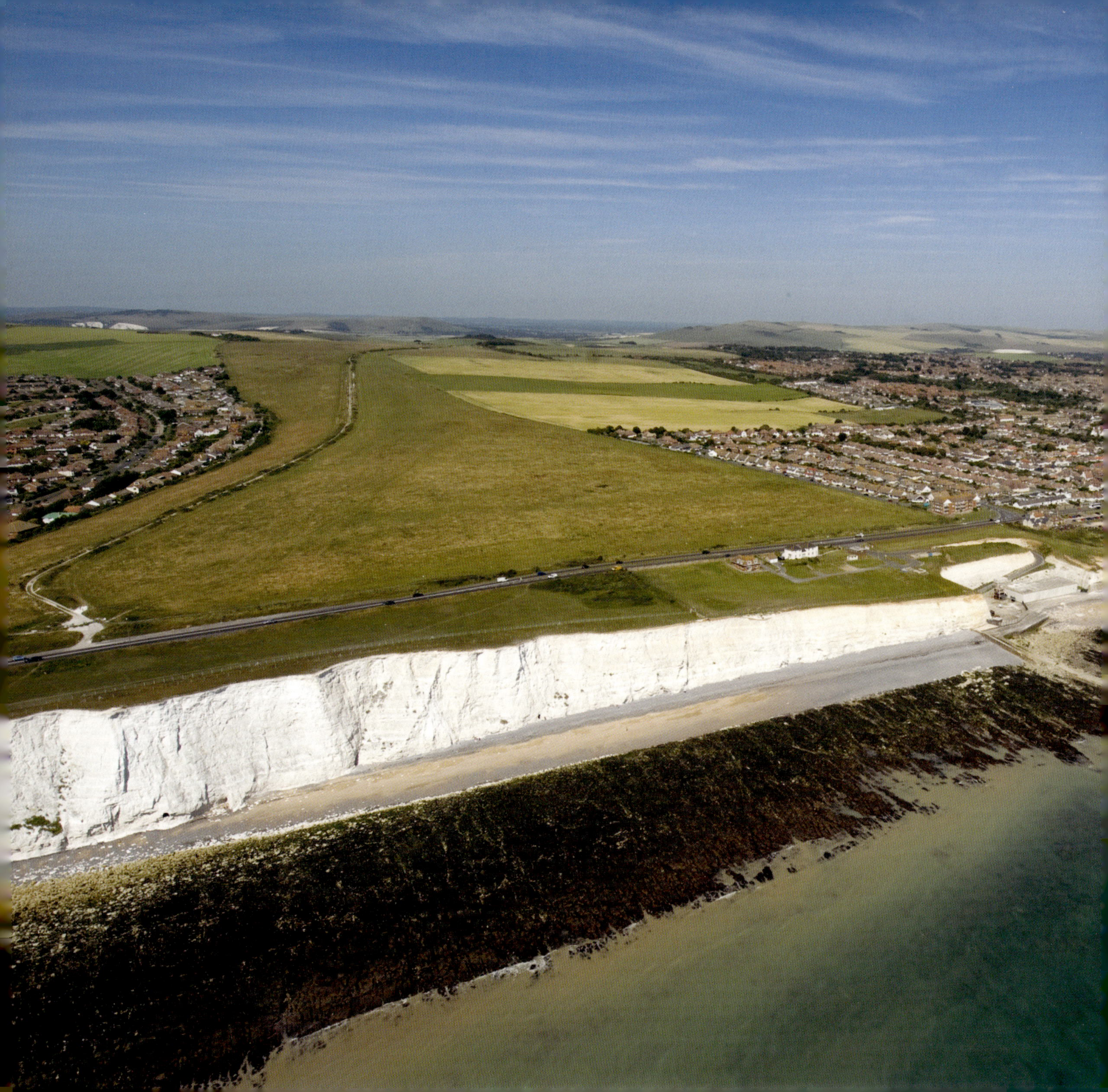

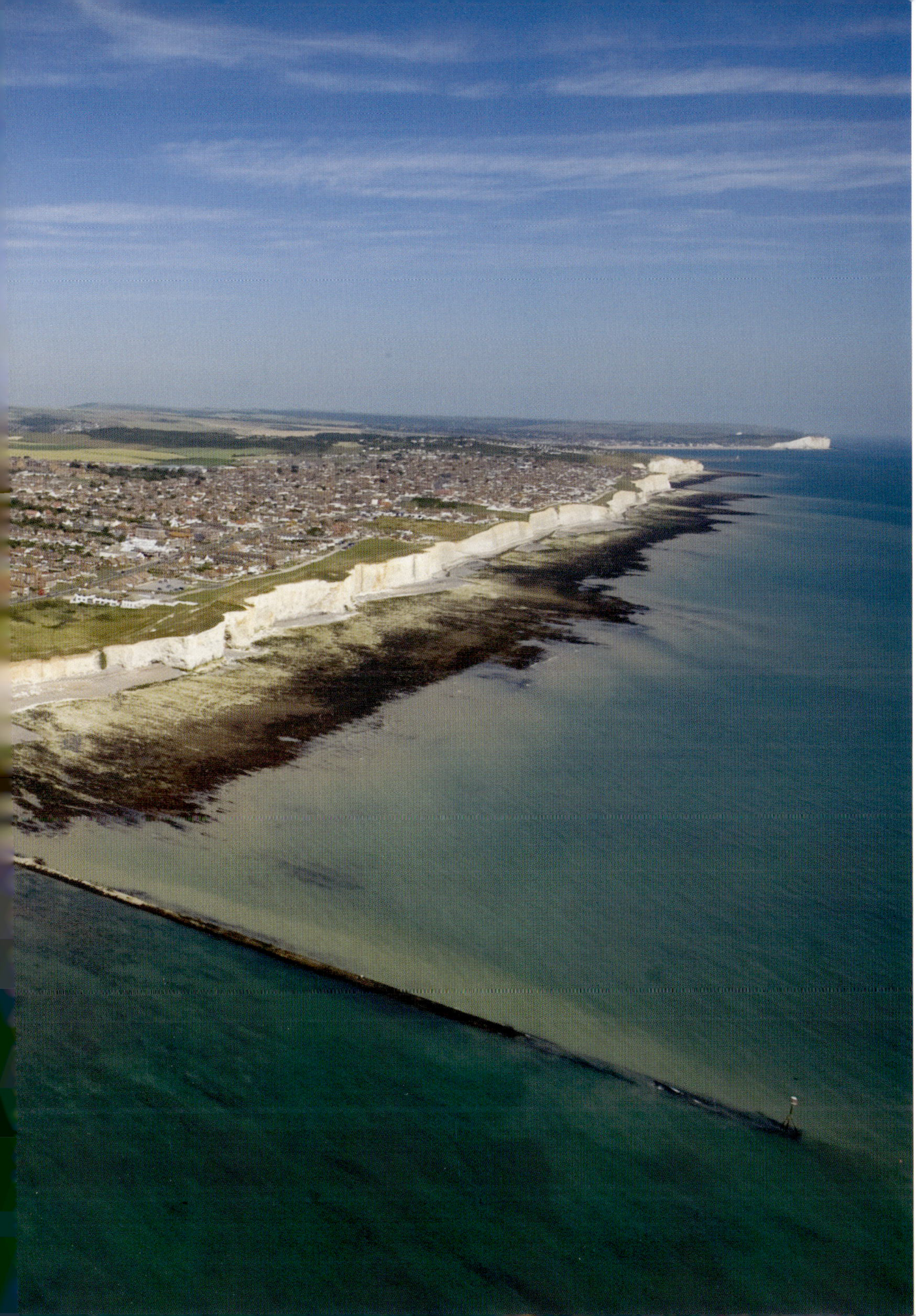

The view east along the shore from Saltdean, and onwards to Peacehaven and Beachy Head.

Peacehaven, Telscombe Cliffs and, far left, Saltdean.

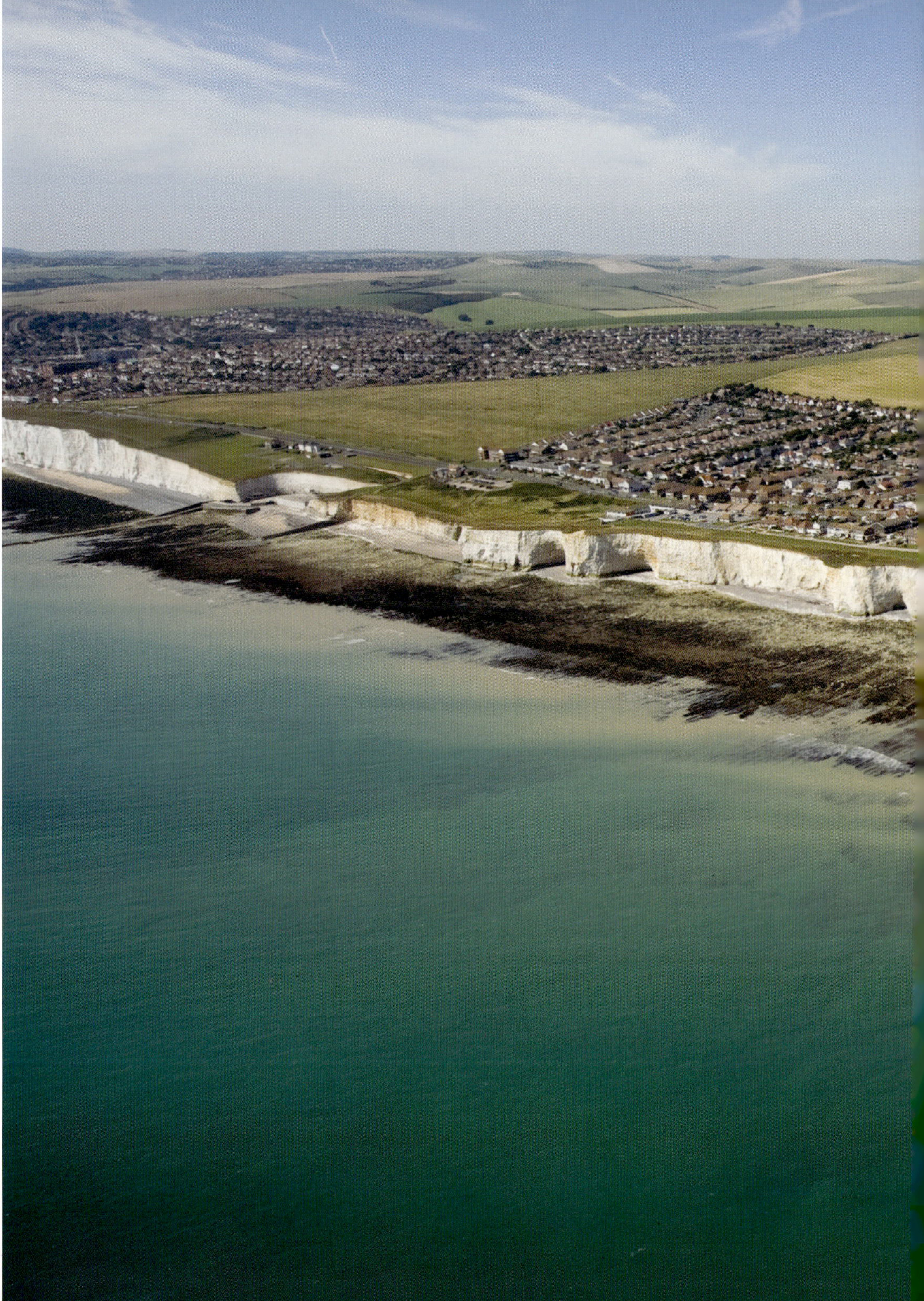

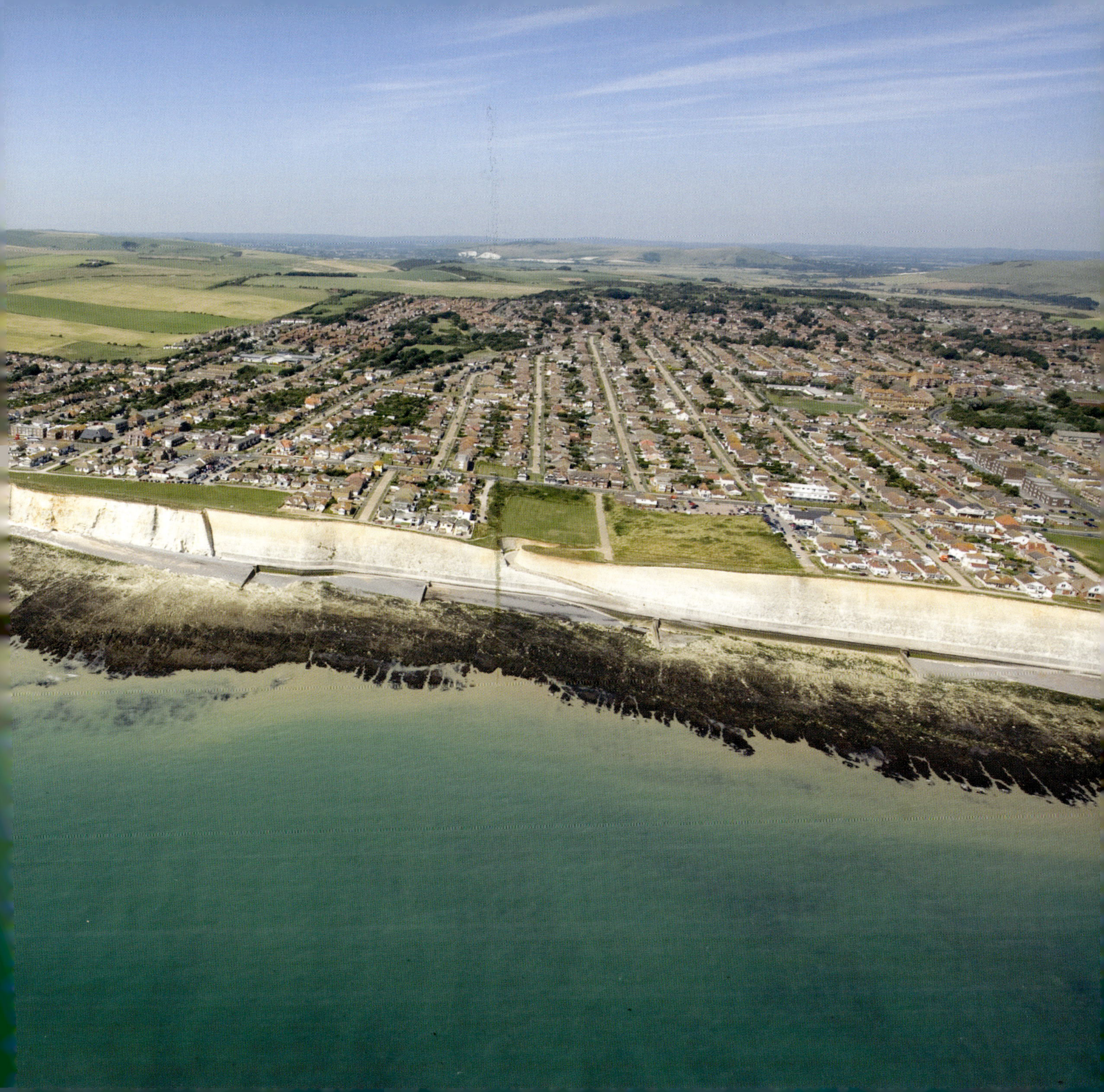

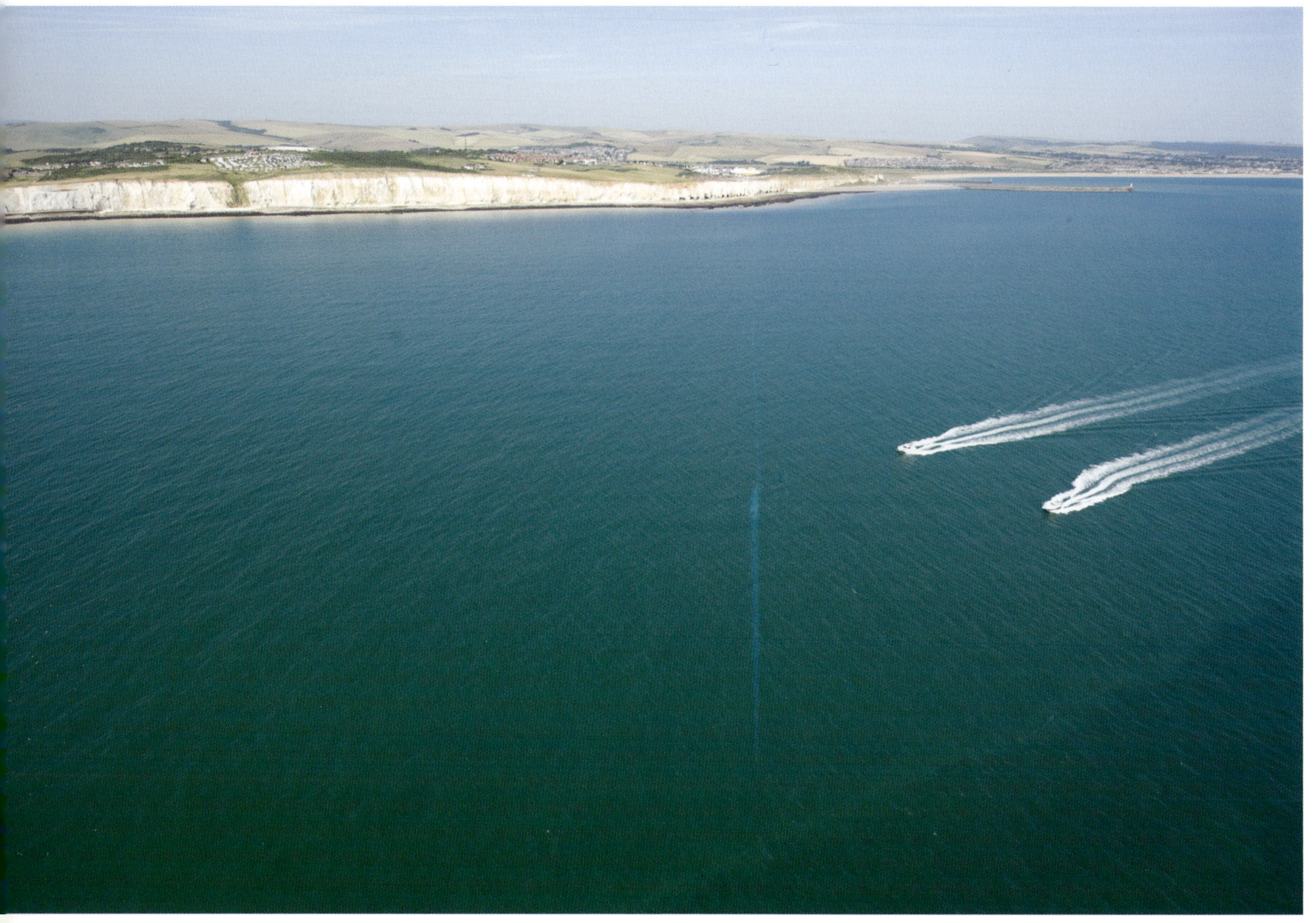

Above: Towards Seaford Bay and Newhaven.

Right: Newhaven is perhaps best known today as a ferry port. Standing on the River Ouse, the port has been subject to the threat of drifting sand and in 1791 a new entrance had to be cut below the old river mouth.

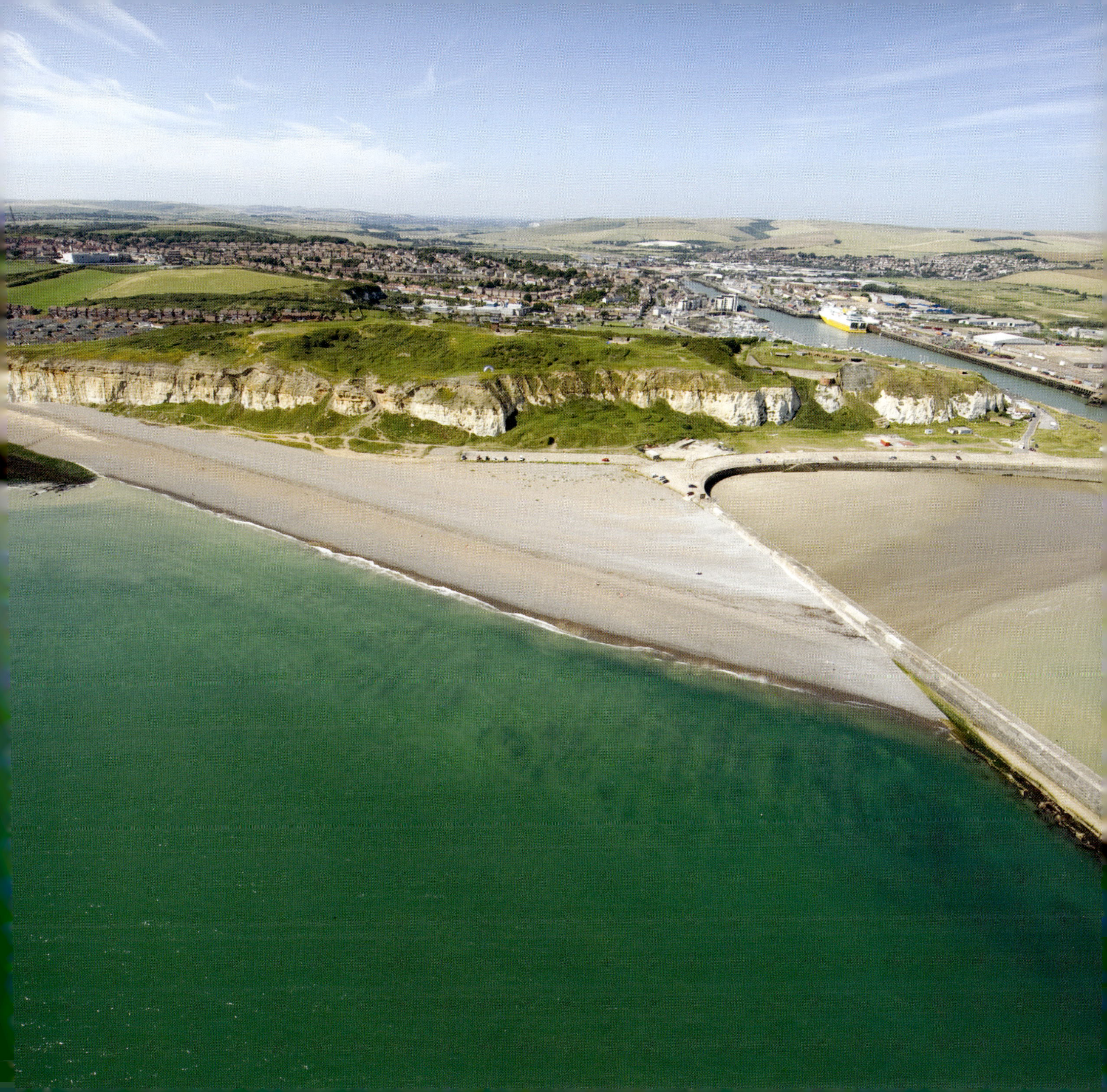

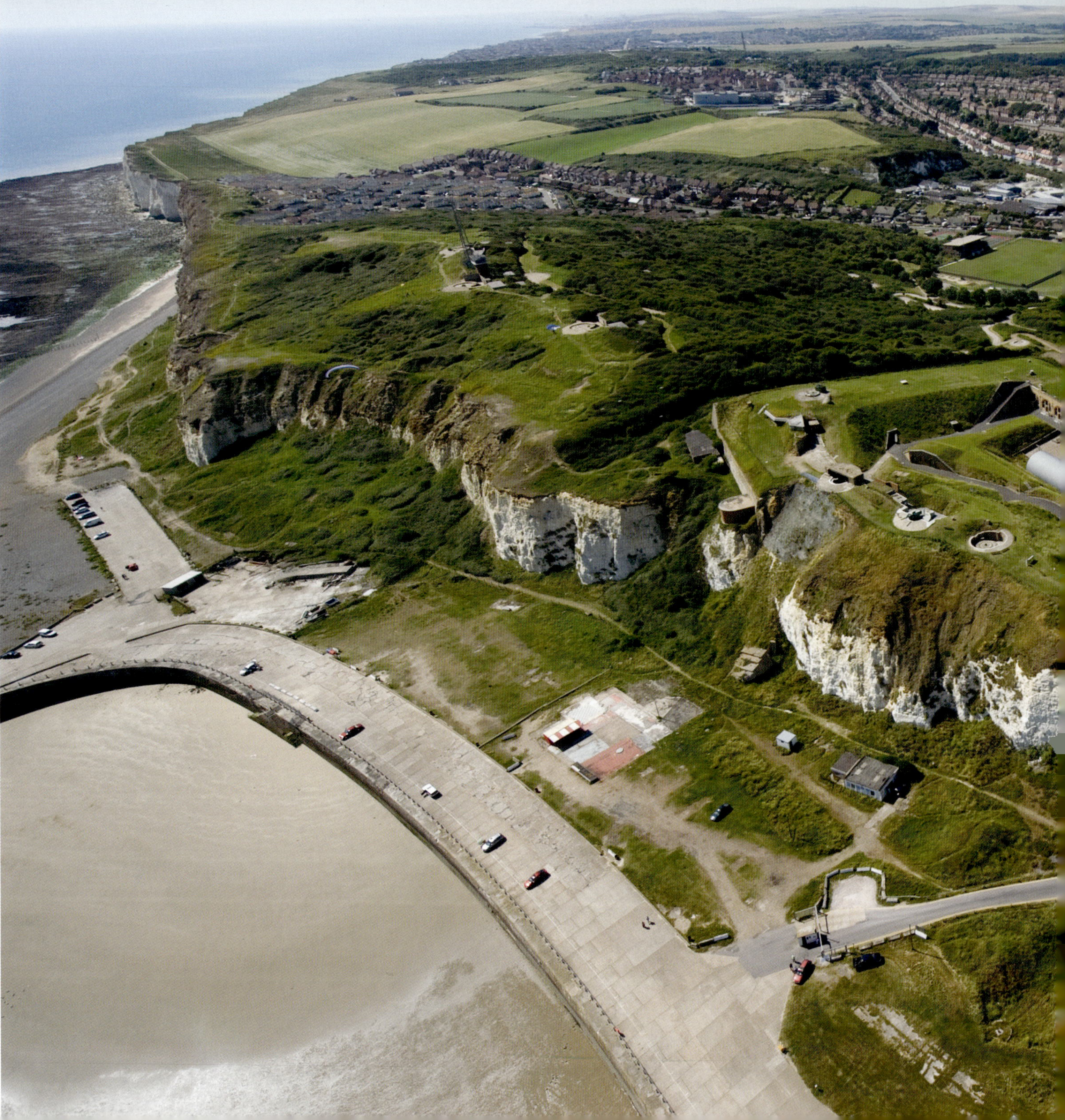

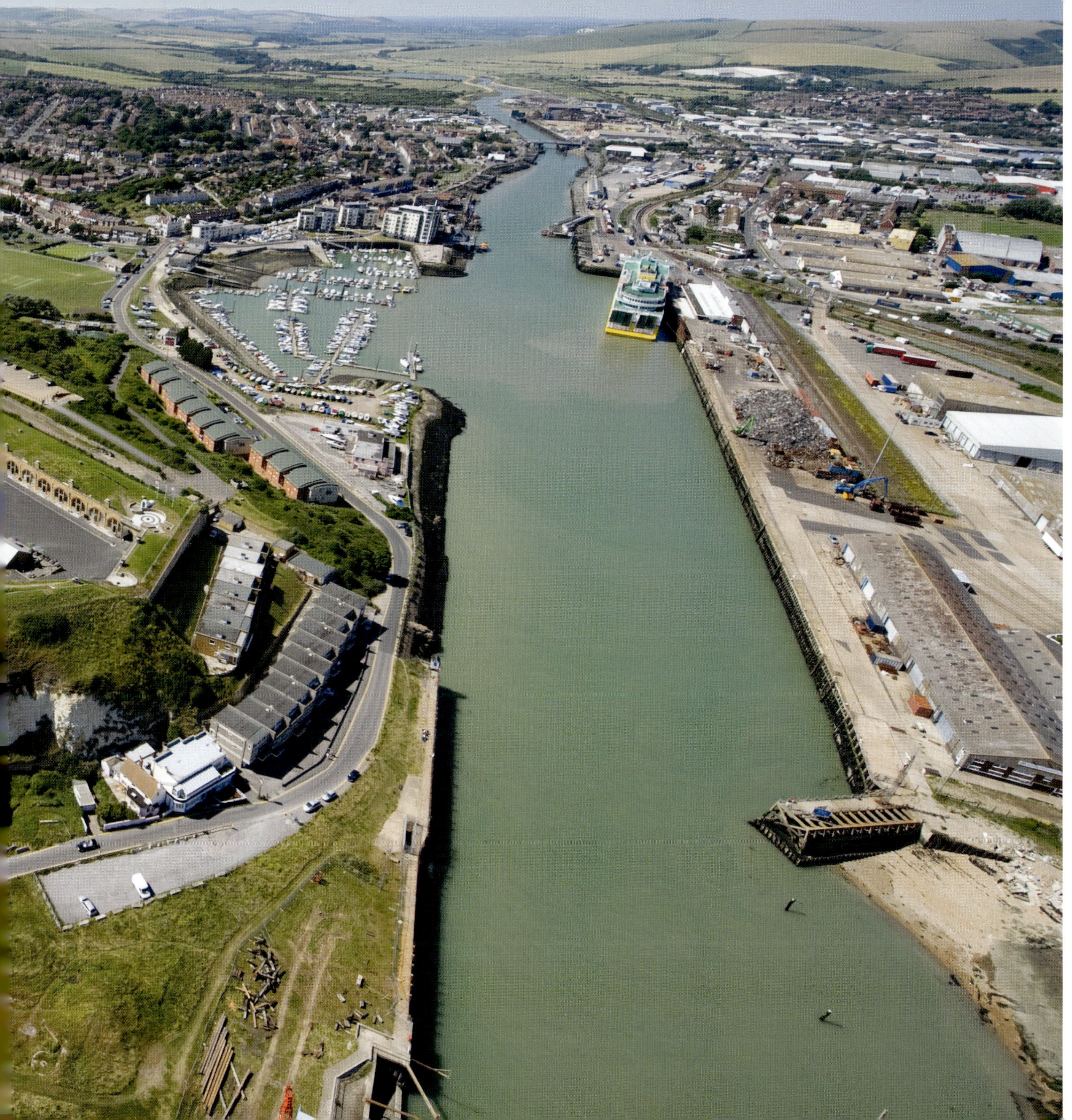

Previous page: A superb view of Newhaven looking along 'The Cut'. The fort, on the headland (left), was built around the 1860s and is the largest work of defence ever constructed in Sussex. It is now a tourist attraction.

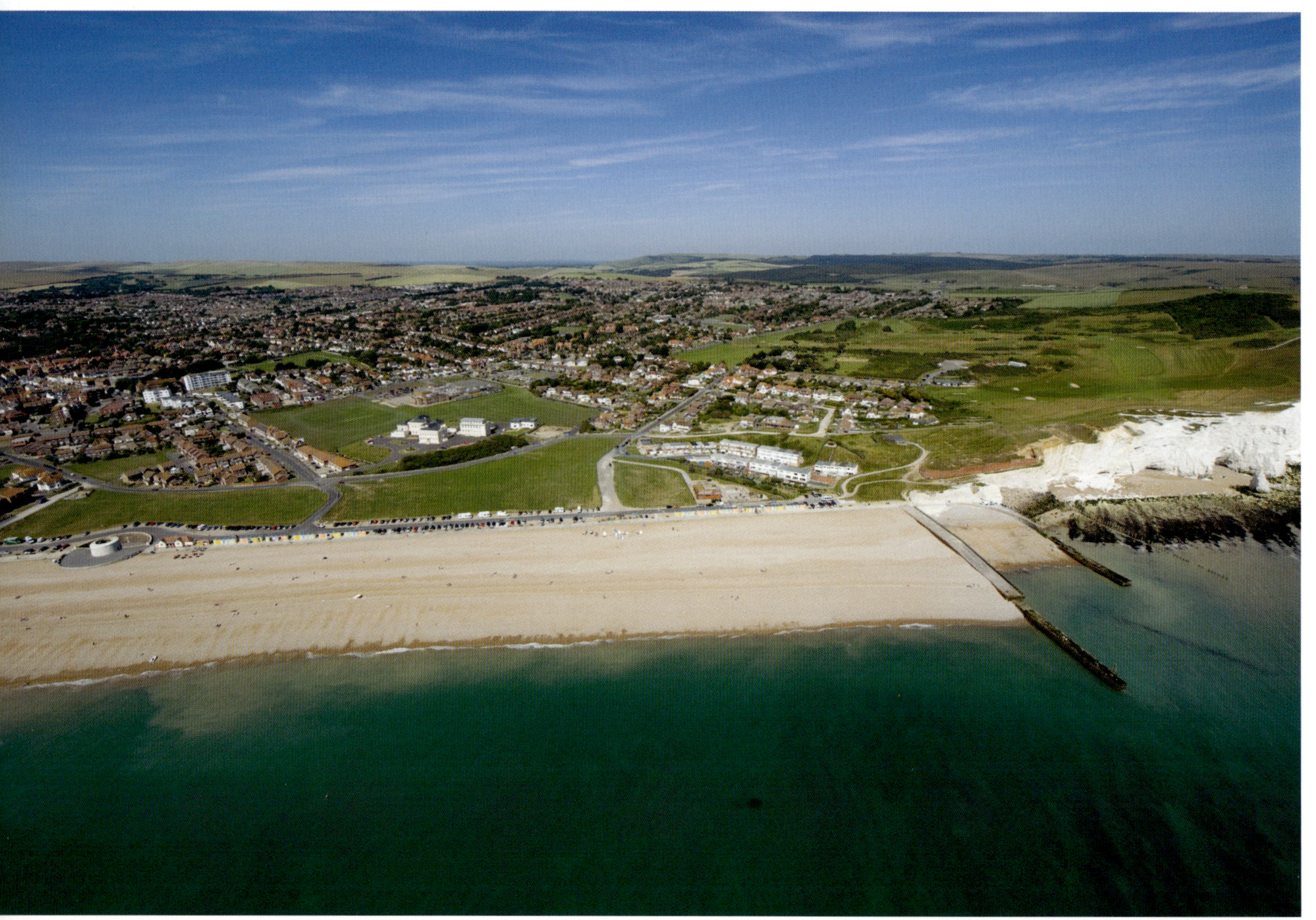

Above and right: Seaford, to the east of Newhaven, once had a reputation for wrecking and smuggling. A Martello Tower, visible on the beach, now does service as the town's museum.

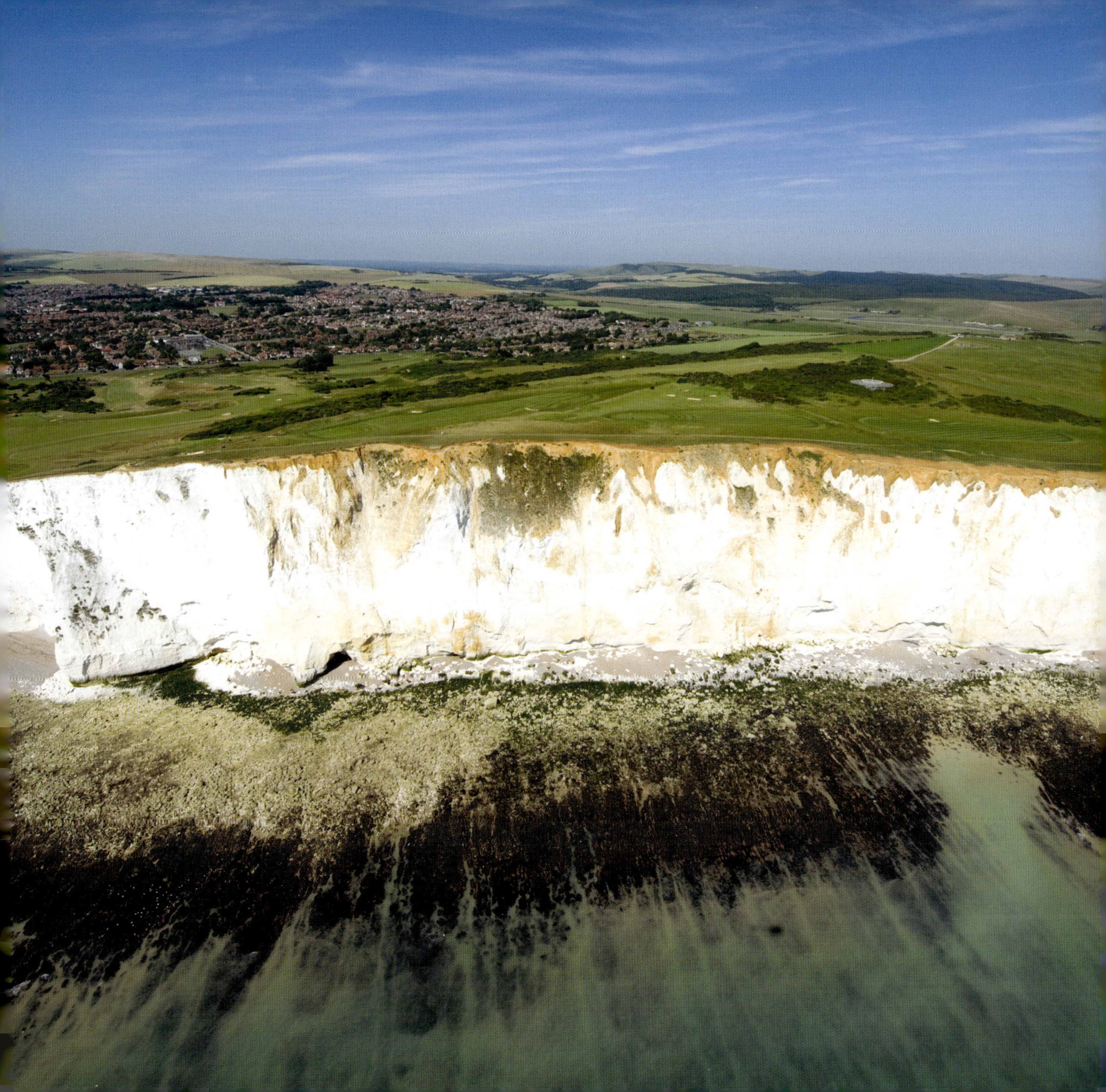

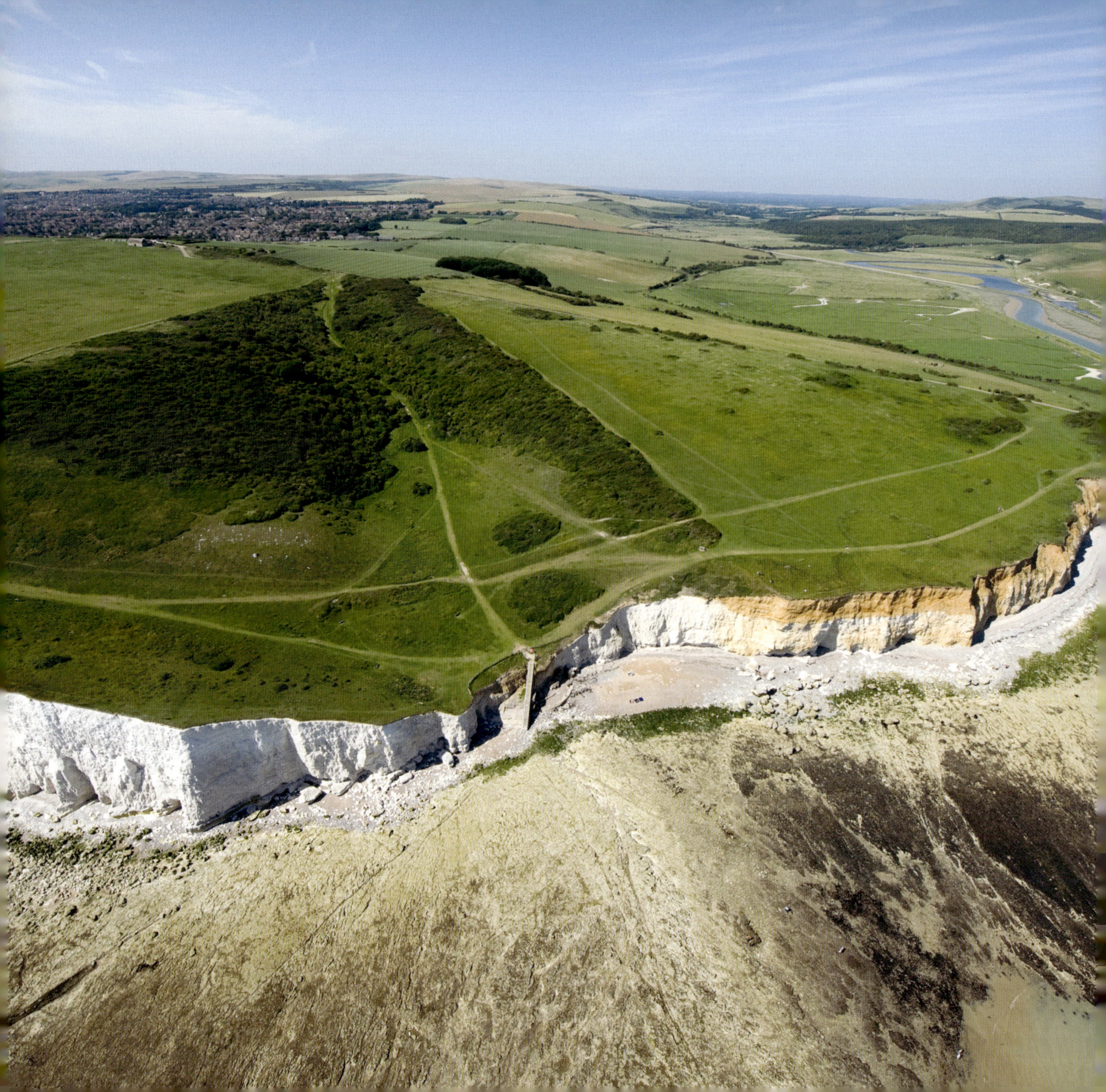

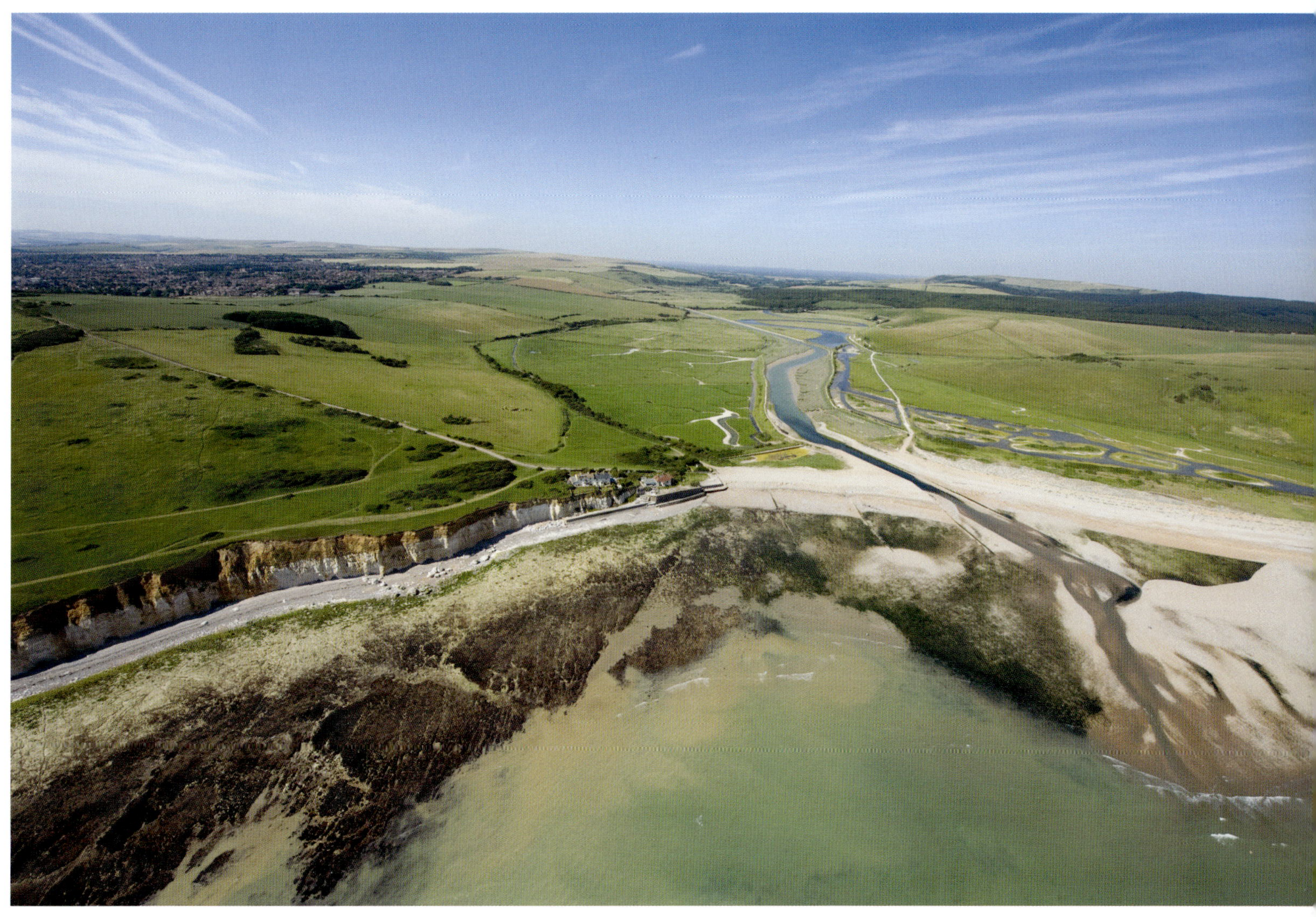

Left and above: Cuckmere Haven. Here the River Cuckmere enters the English Channel along a series of meanders. It is an area greatly favoured by walkers who can enjoy wonderful views along the coast, east and west.

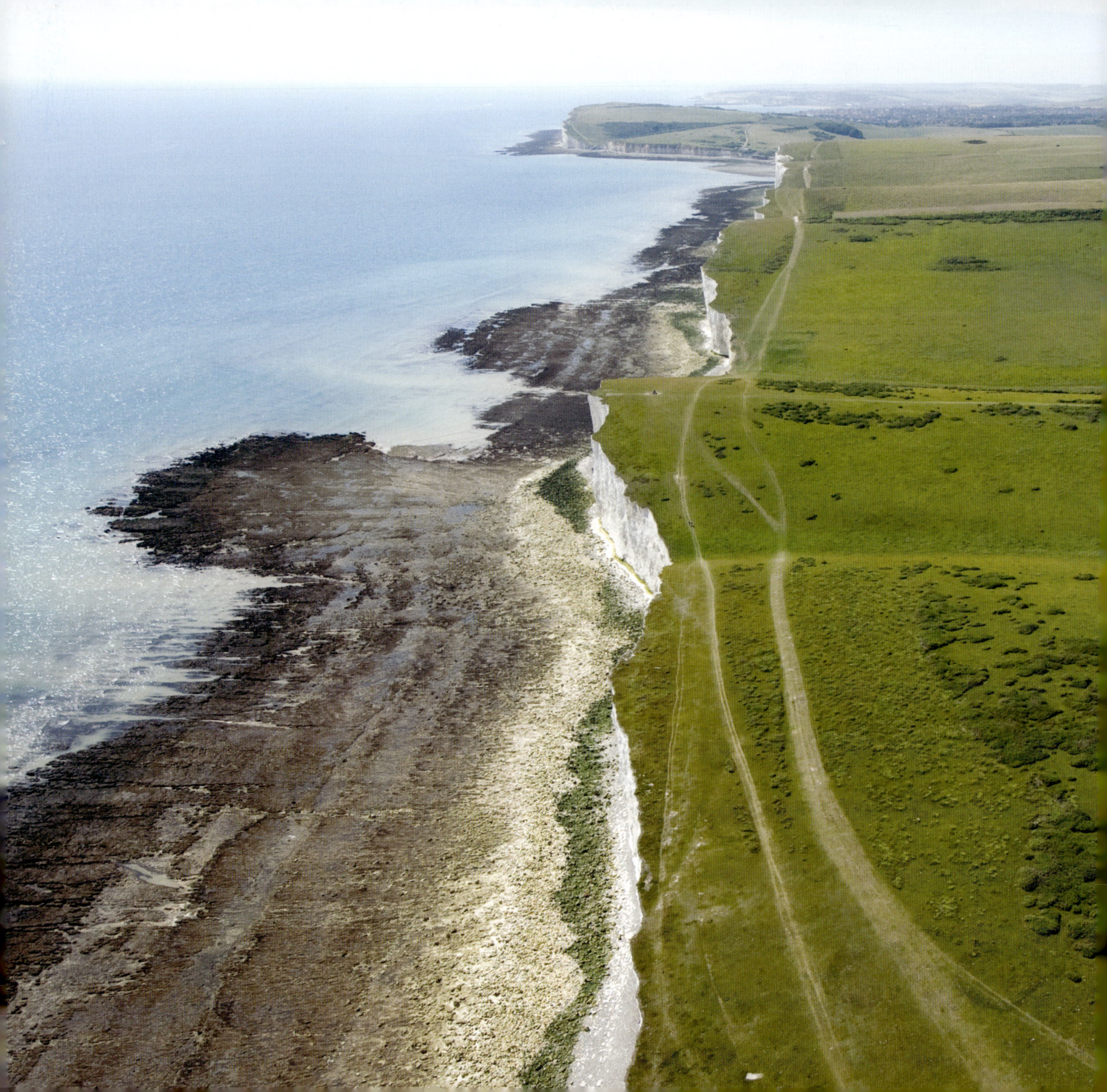

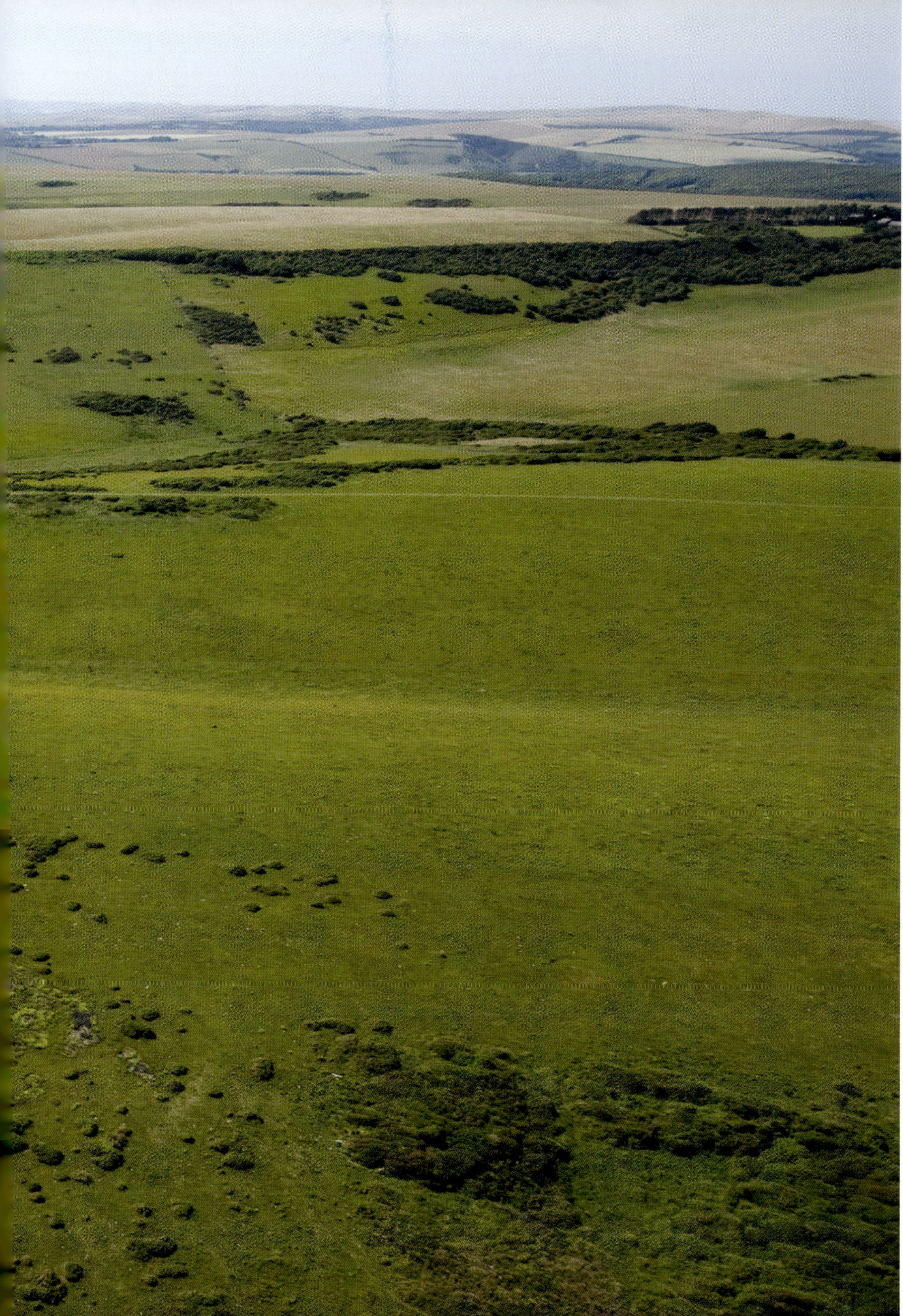

The famous Seven Sisters chalk cliffs, looking towards Cuckmere Haven. The cliffs have featured in numerous films, including the Harry Potter series.

Following page: Standing over 500 feet Beachy Head and the Seven Sisters are part of a designated Area of Outstanding Natural Beauty. The lighthouse, now fully automated, dates from 1902.

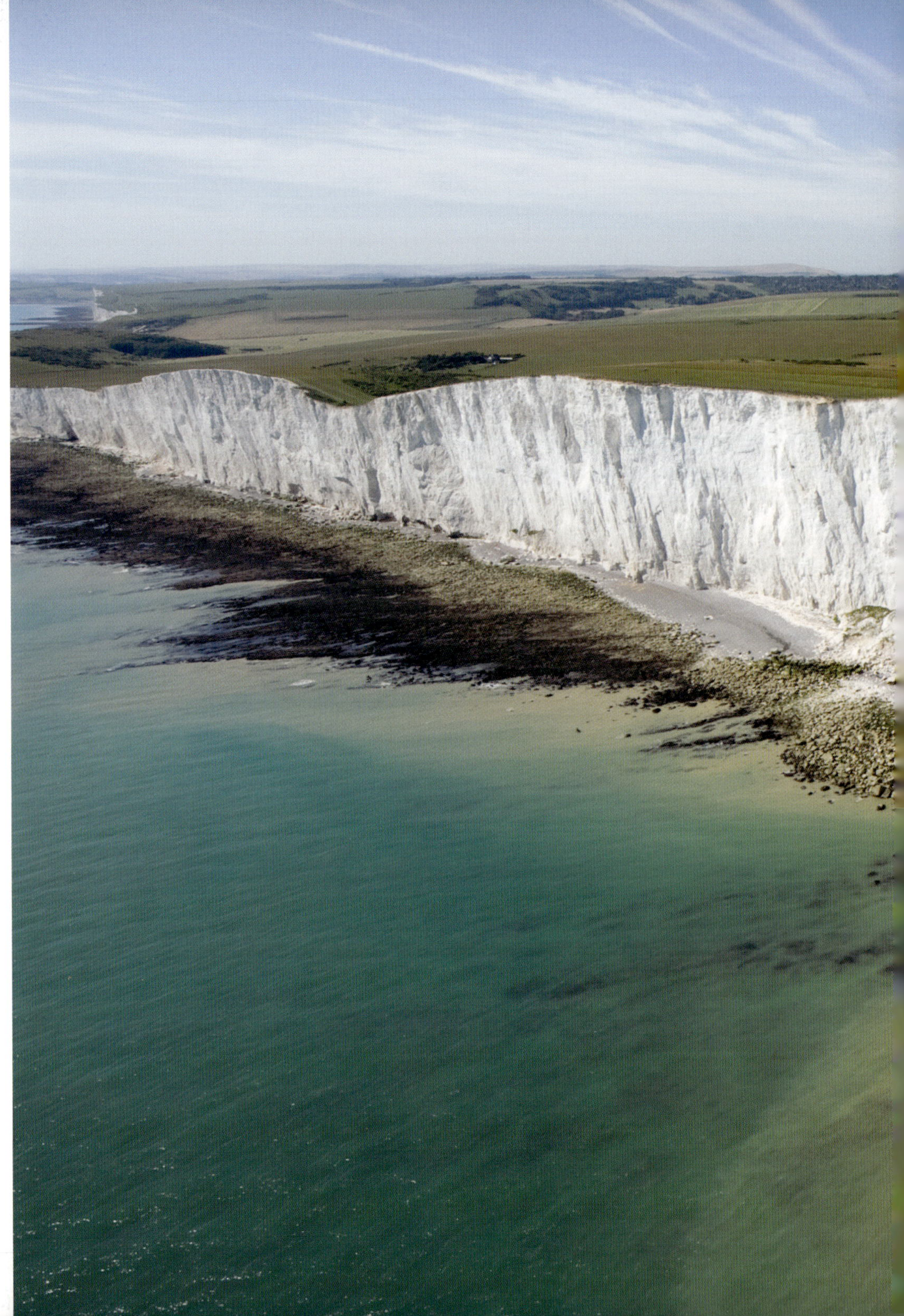

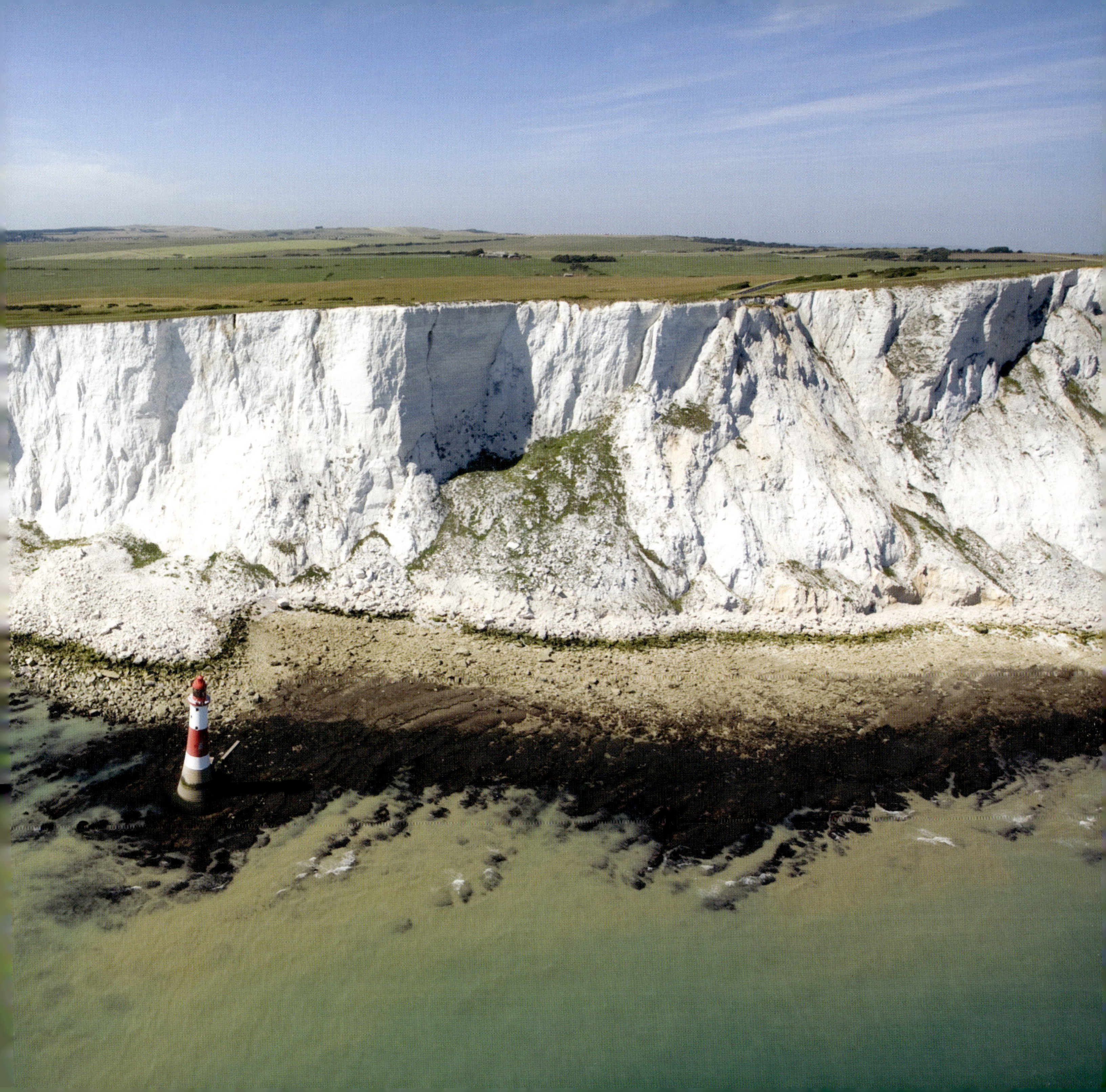

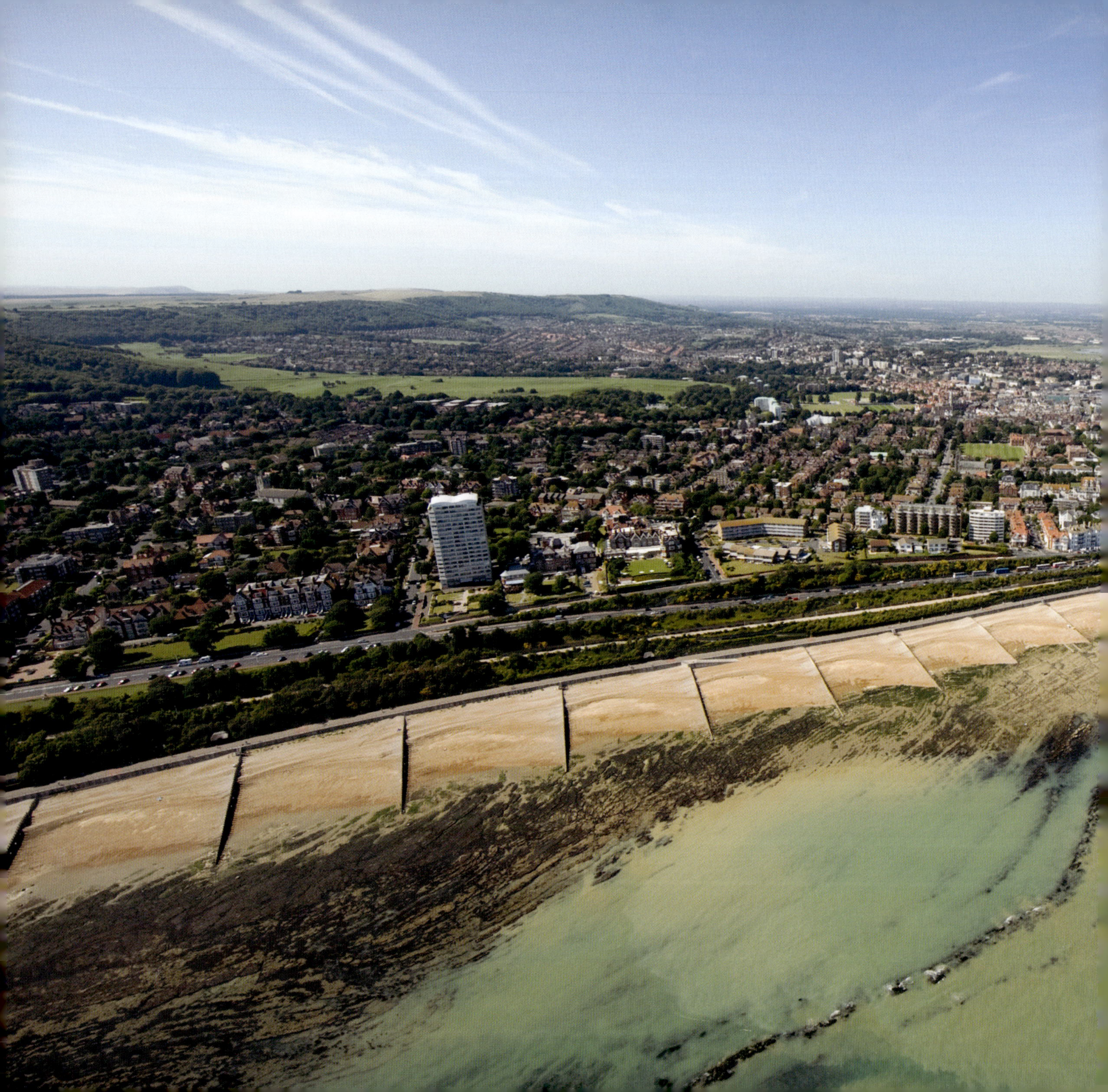

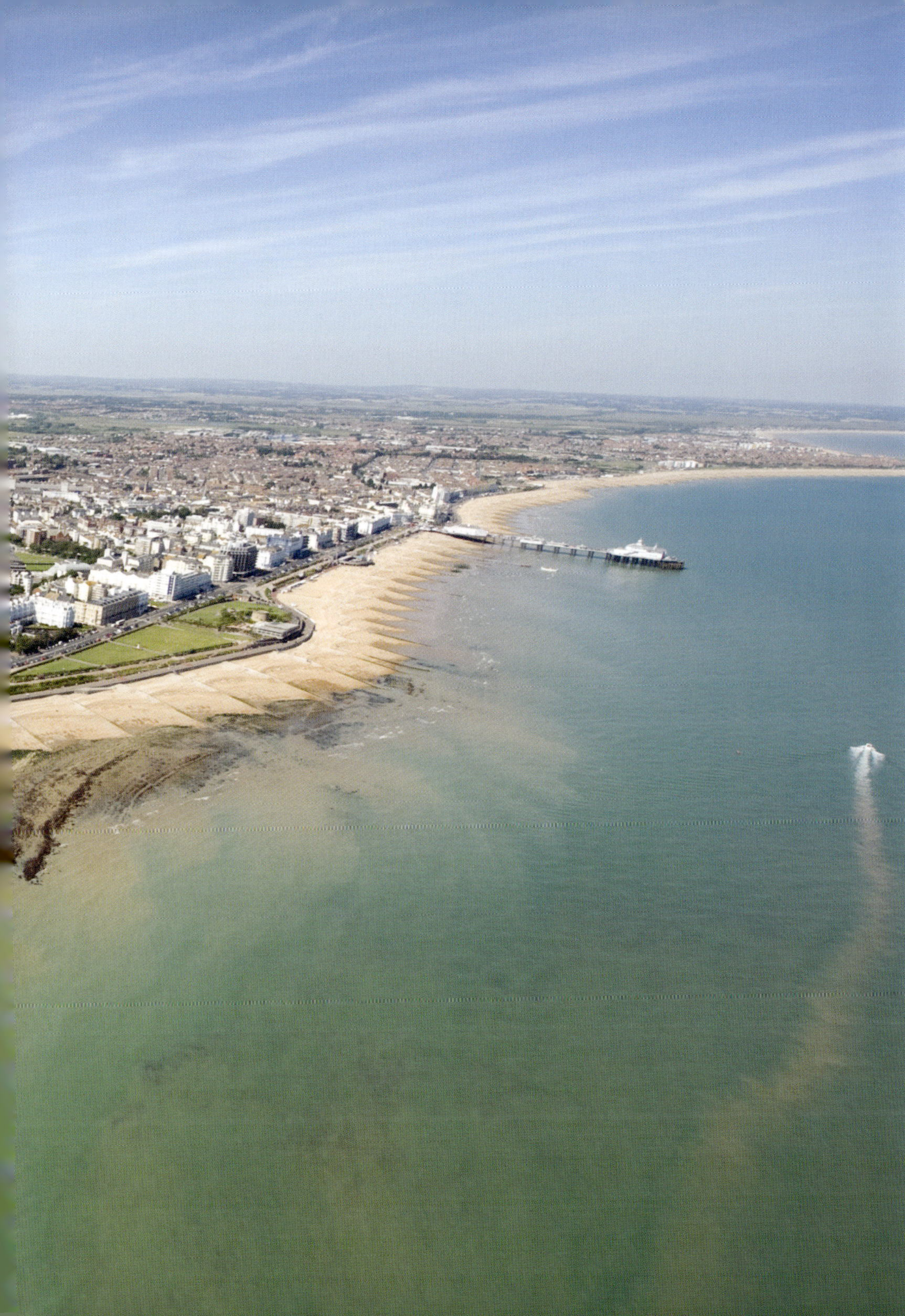

Eastbourne viewed from the west.

Eastbourne's pier was opened in 1870, although it was not actually completed until two years later. On New Years Day 1877 the landward half was swept away in a storm and it was later rebuilt 1000 feet in length.

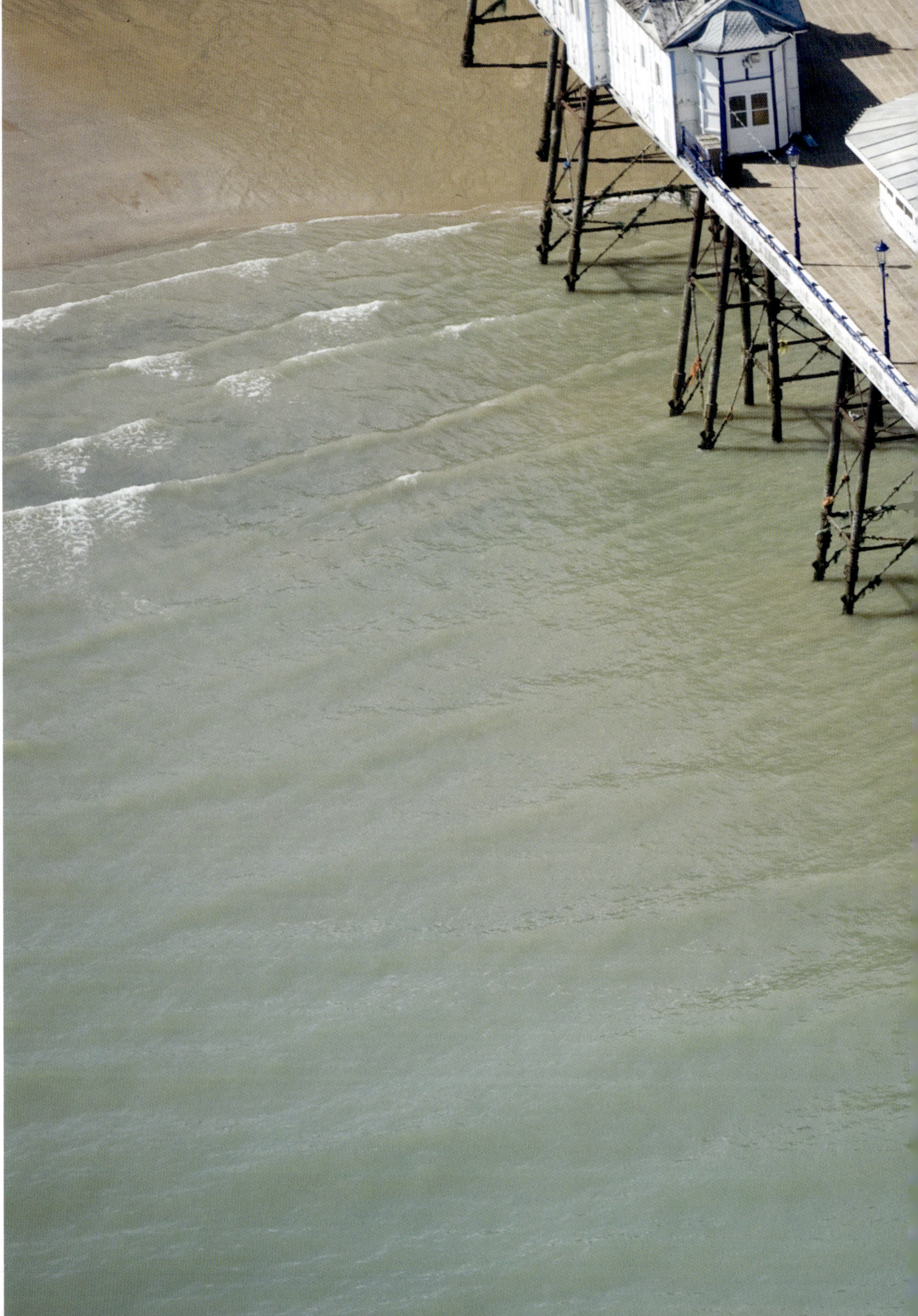

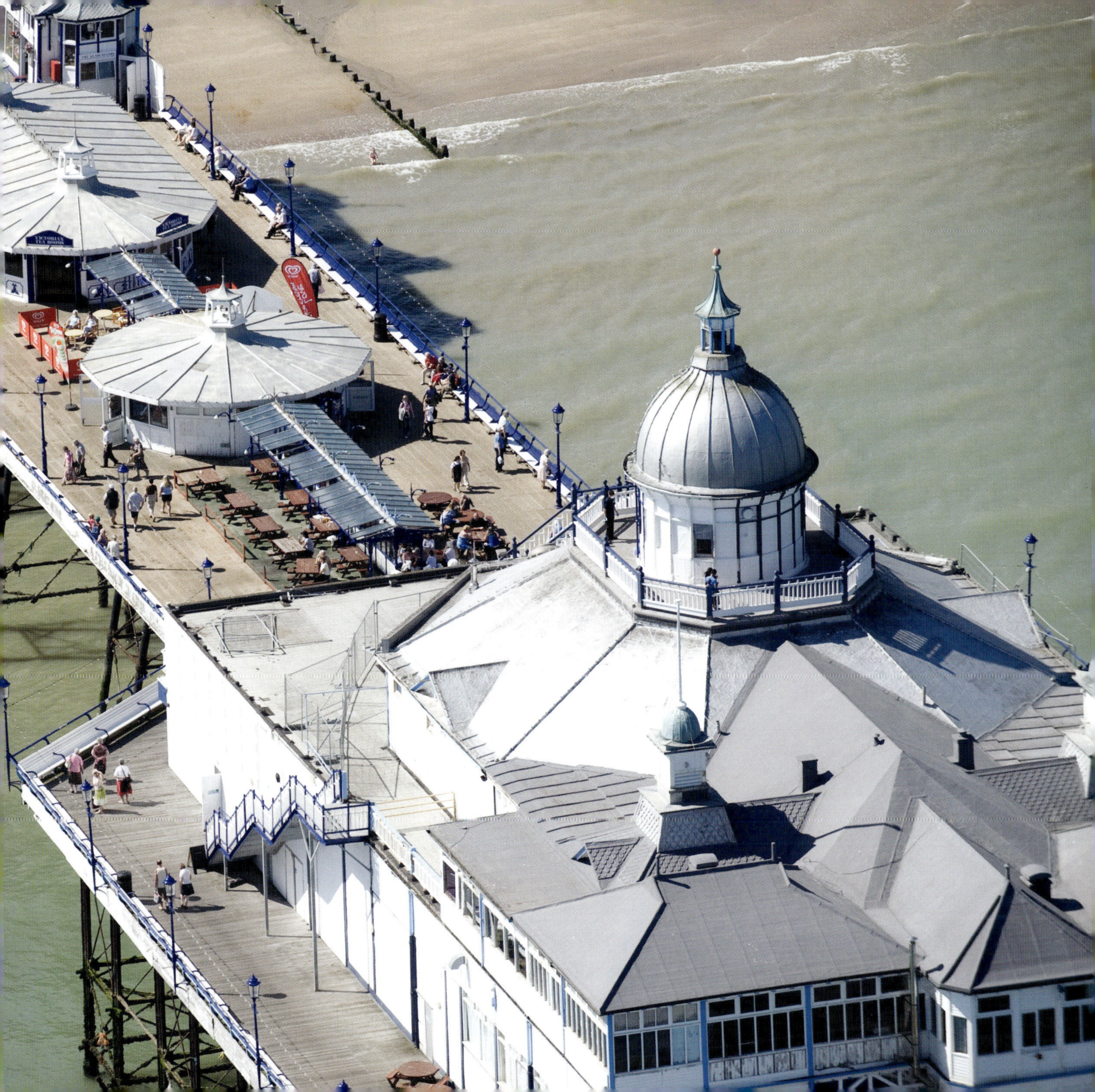
VICTORIAN TEA ROOMS

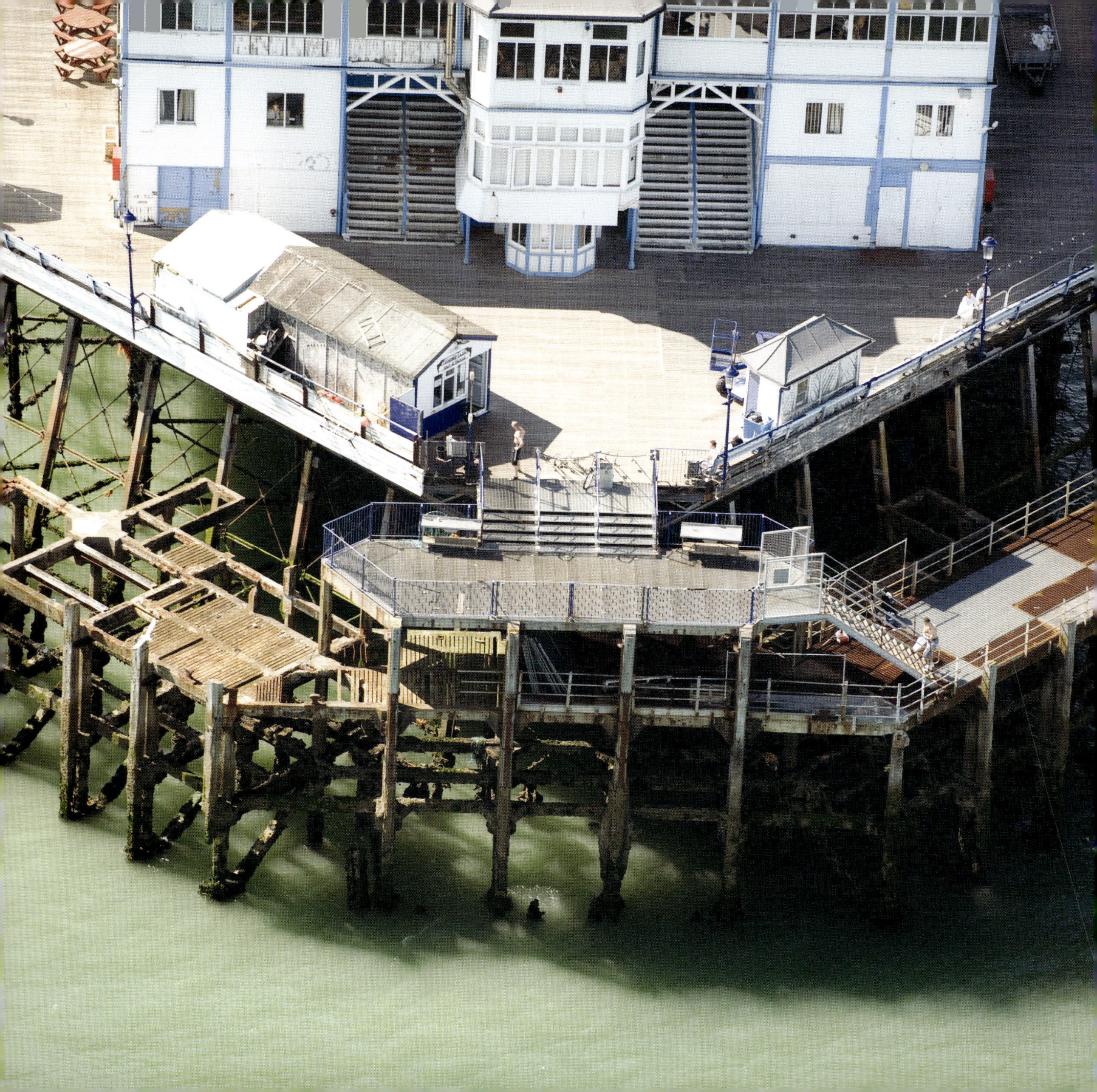

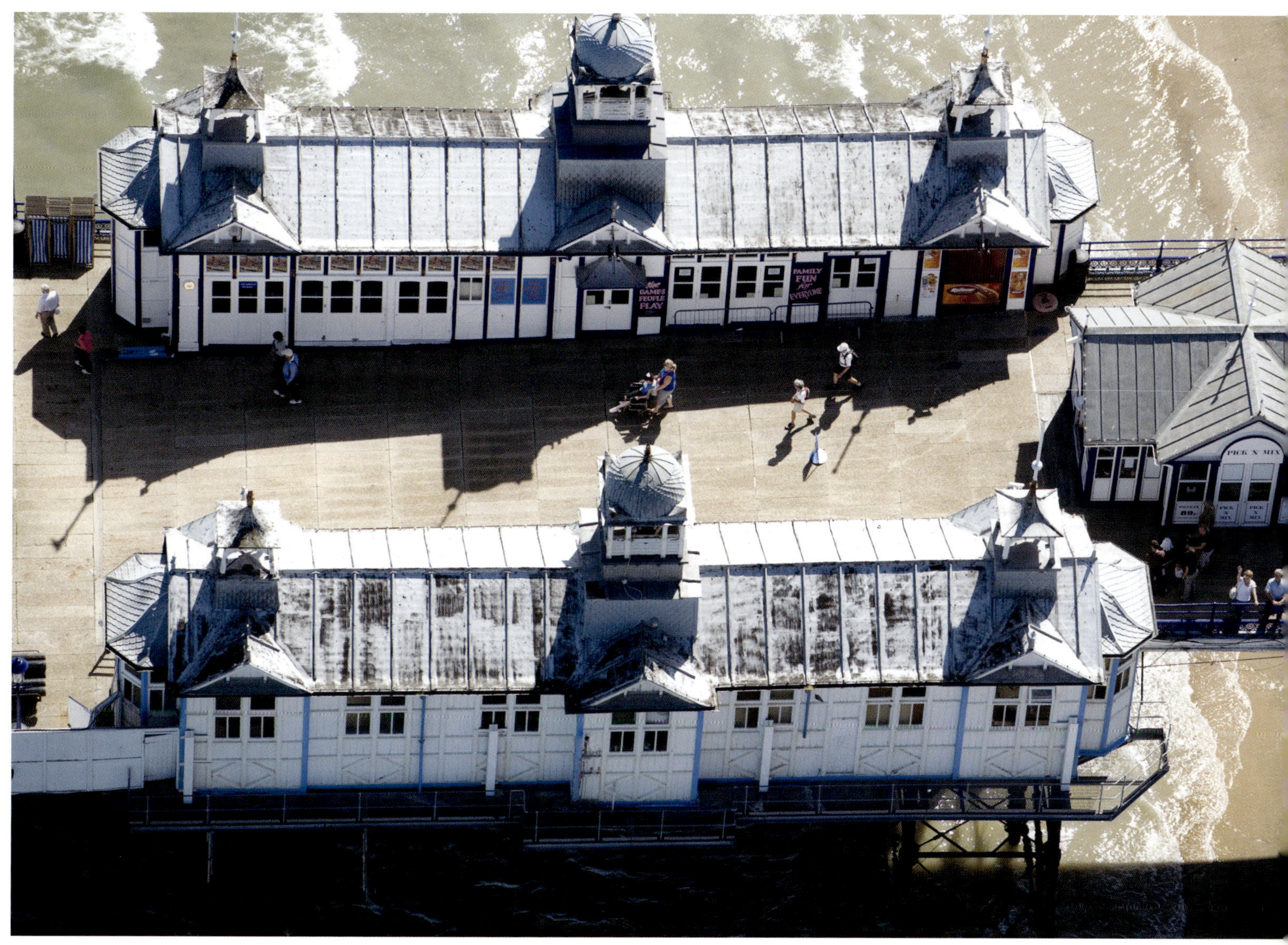

Left and above: Eastbourne pier.

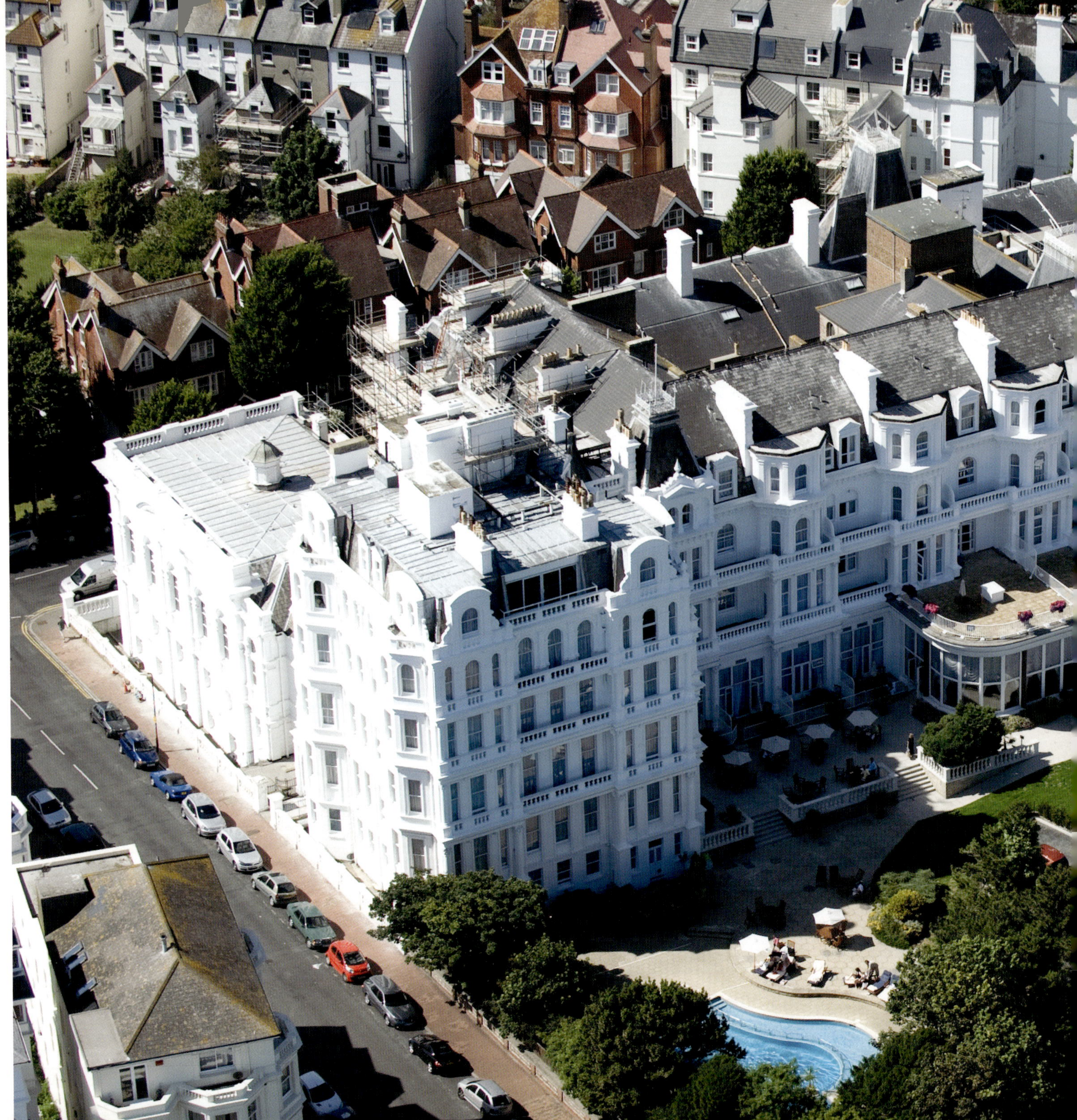

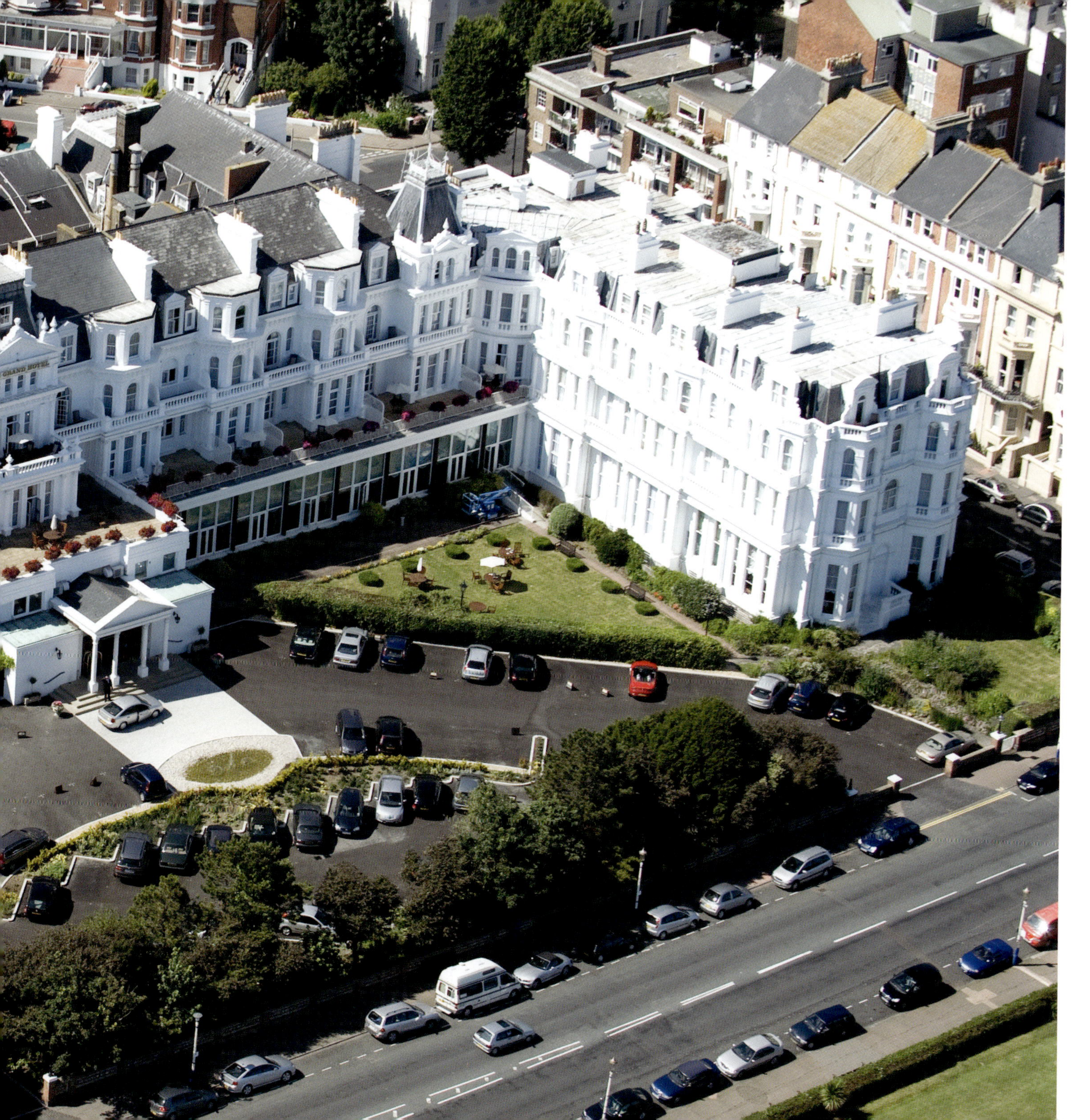
GRAND HOTEL

Previous page: The aptly named Grand Hotel, Eastbourne.

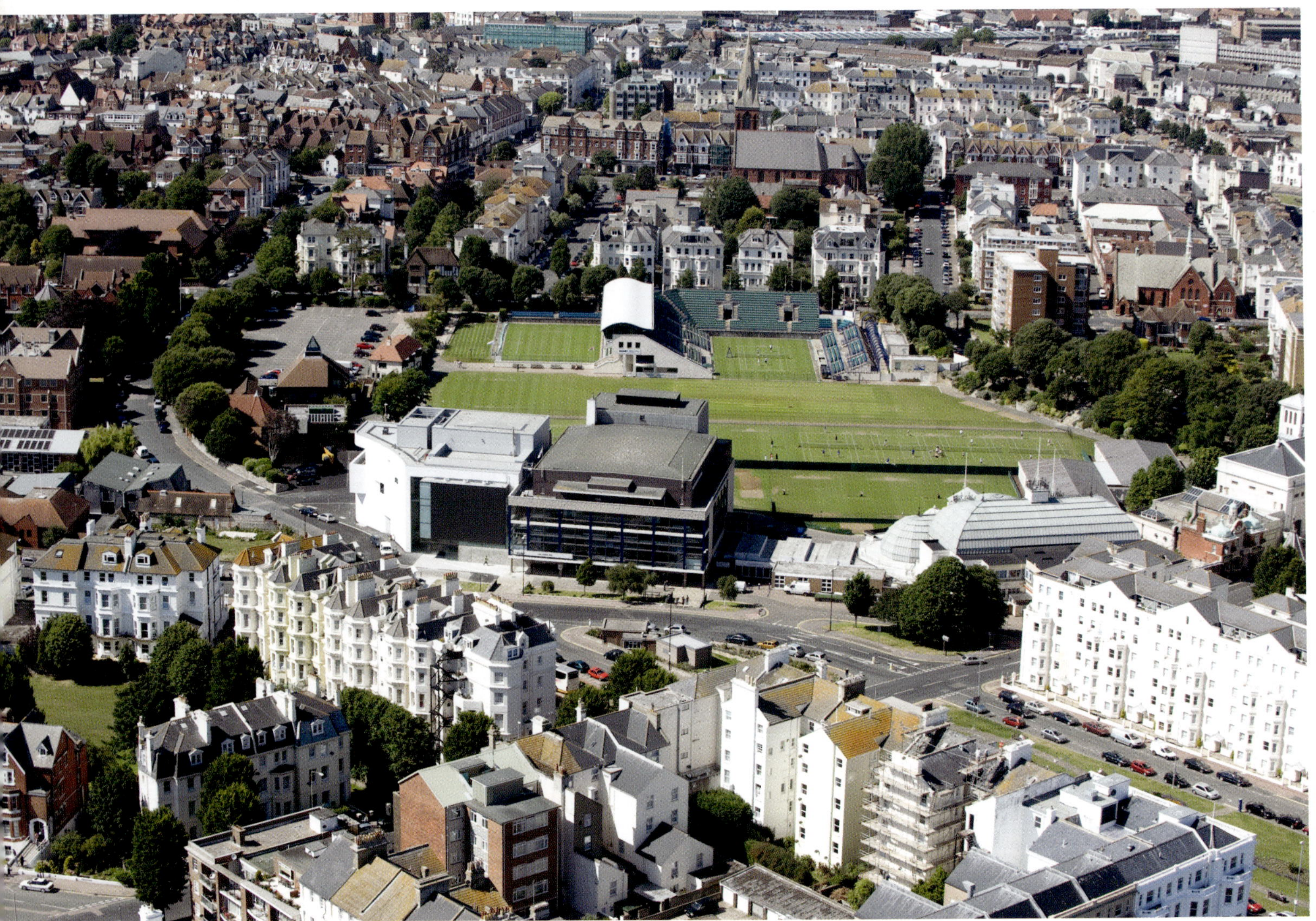

Above: Eastbourne, looking over College Road.

Right: The Wish Tower, King Edward's Parade.

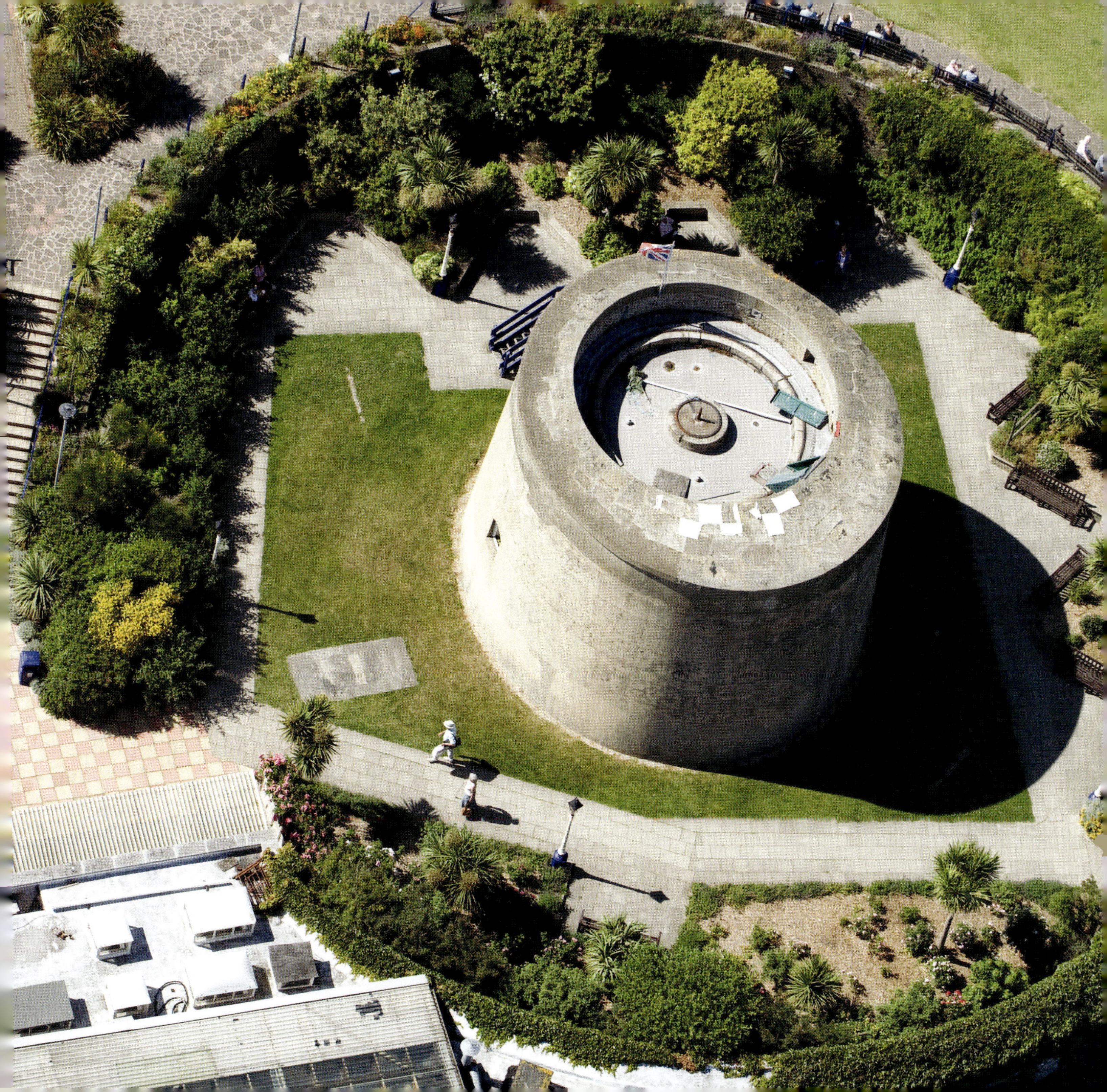

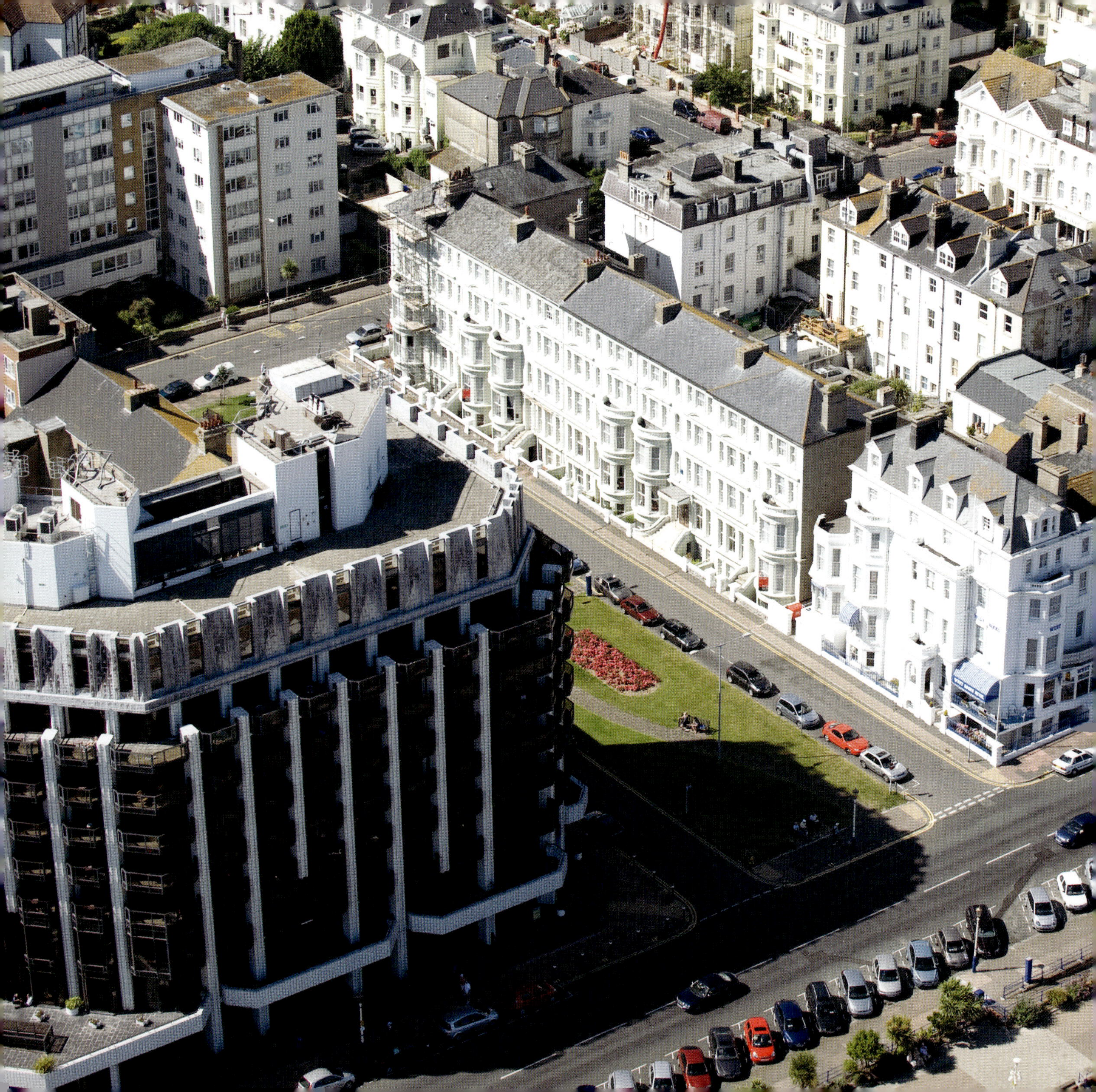

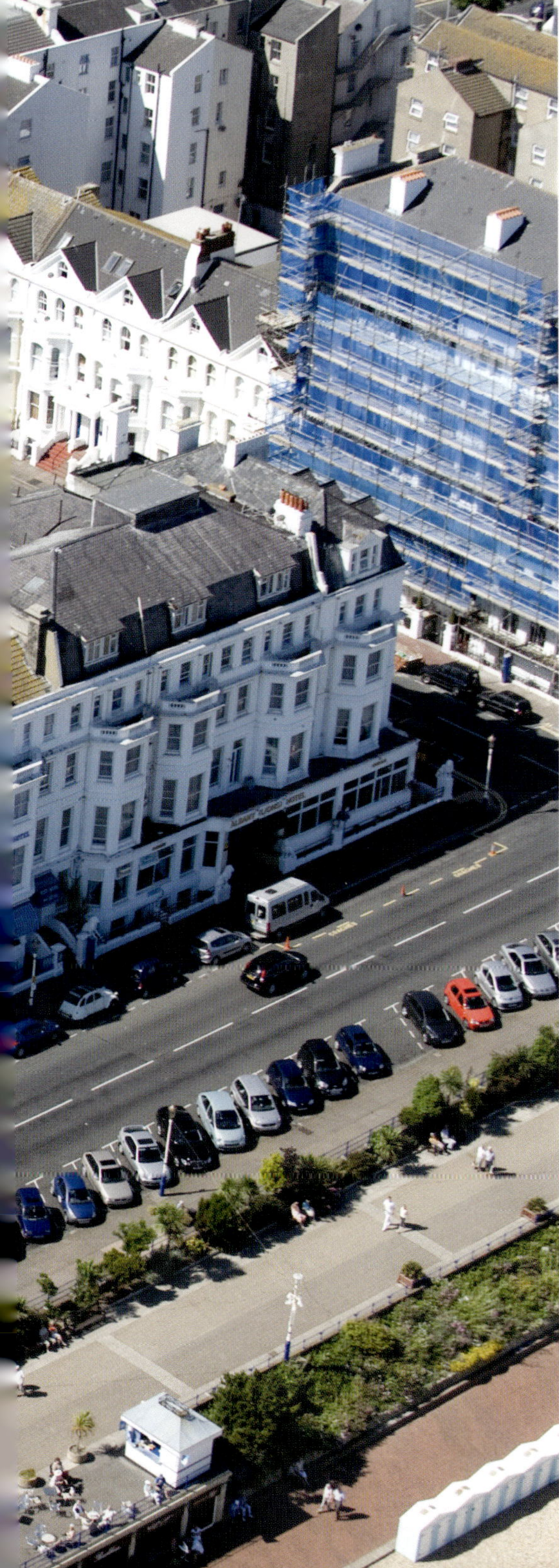

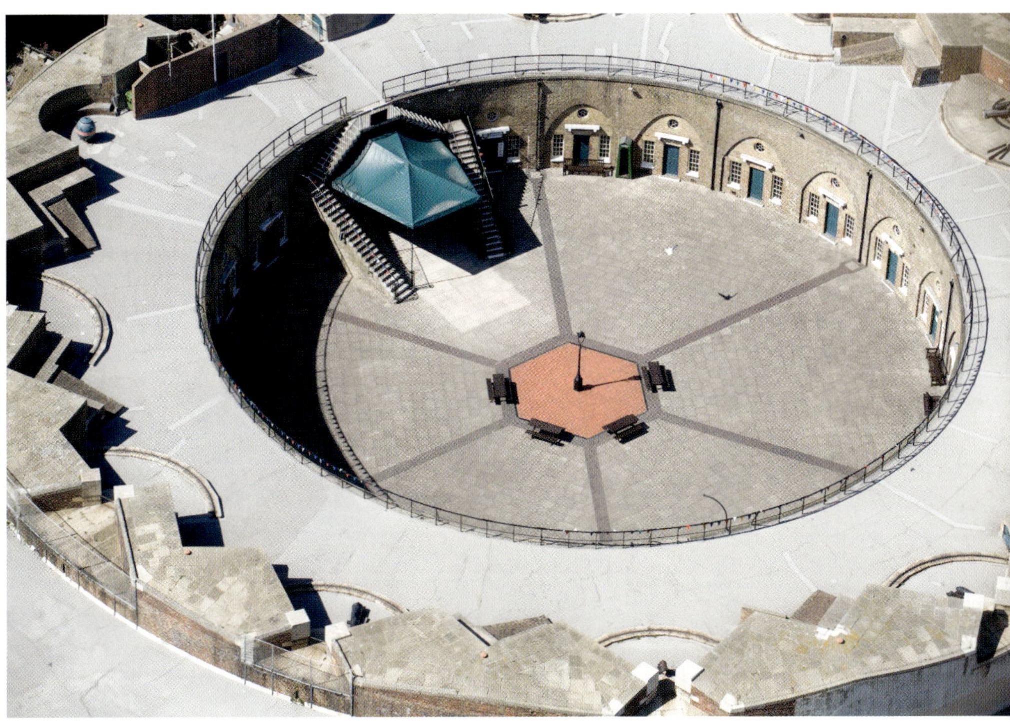

Above: The Redoubt was built between 1804 and 1810 to support the associated Martello Towers in defending against the threat of an invasion by Napoleon. It now houses a military museum.

Left: The view above Howard Square, Eastbourne.

Eastbourne Harbour.

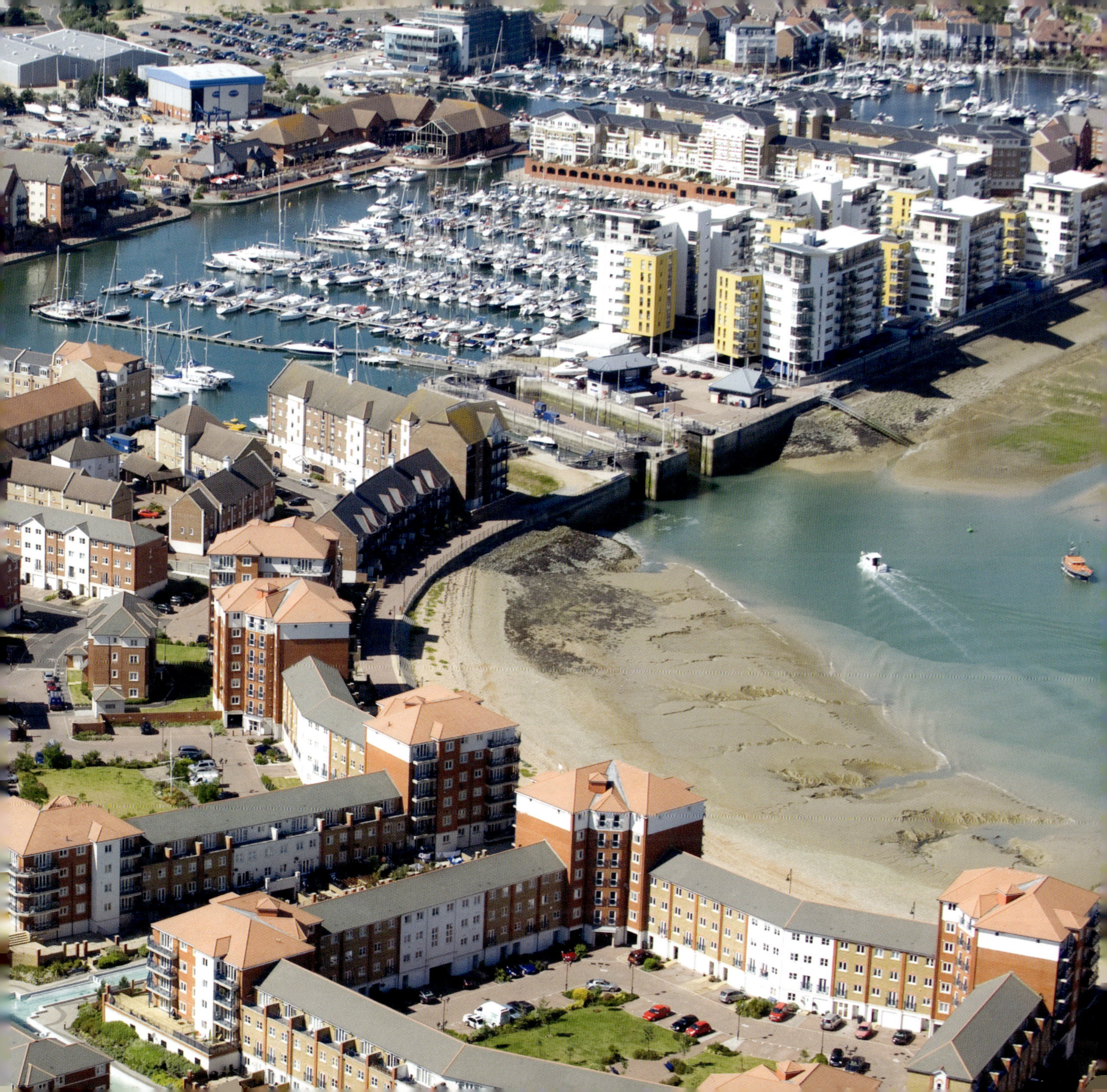

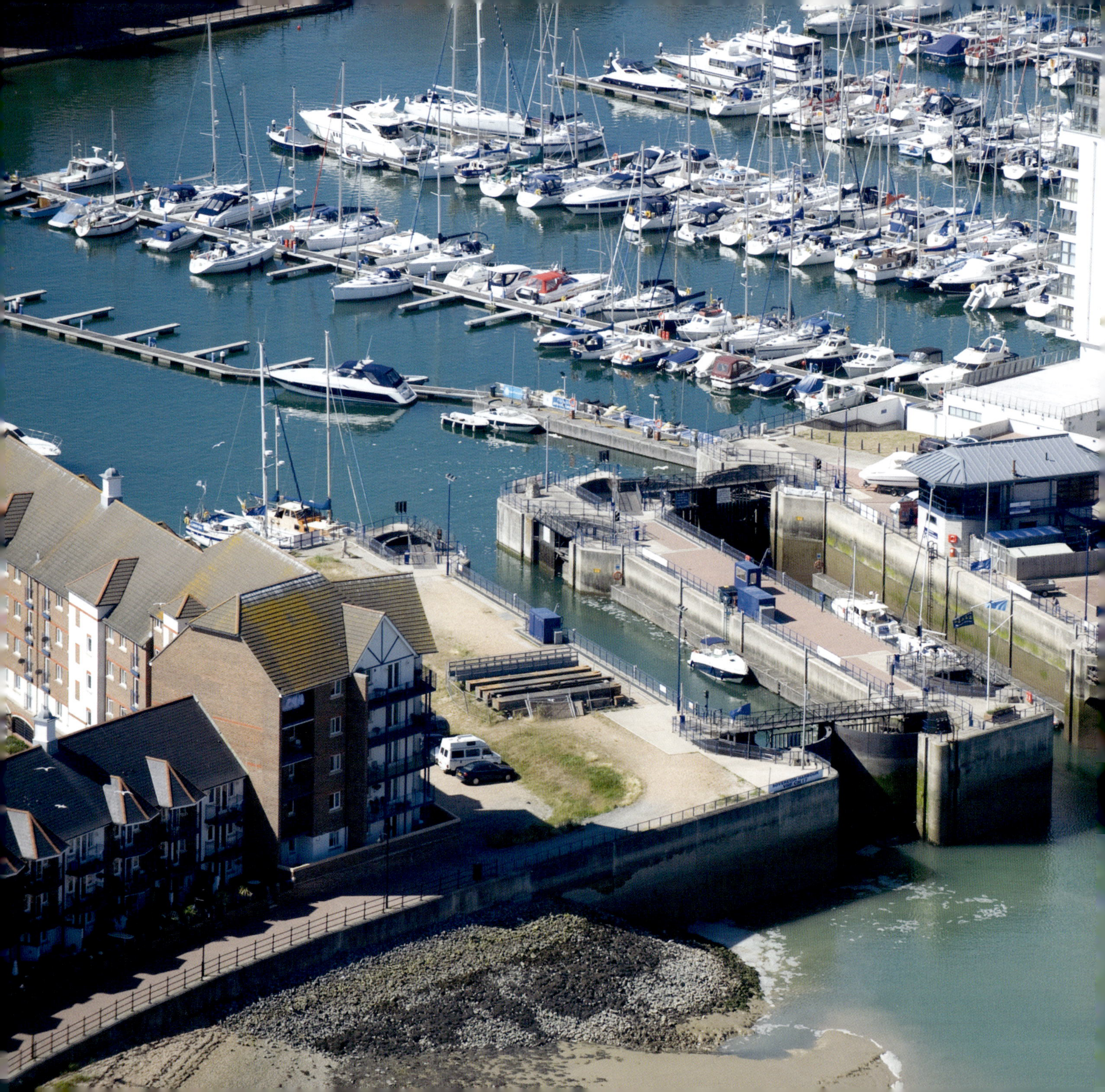

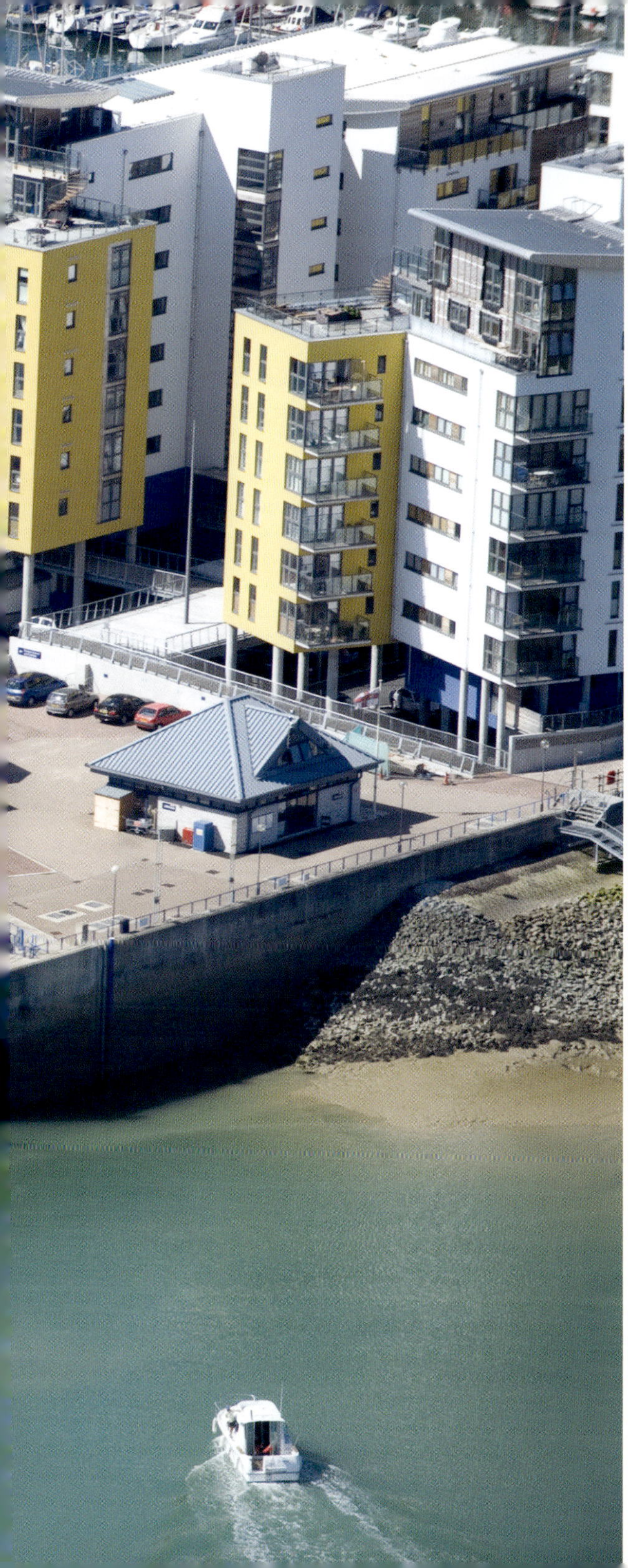

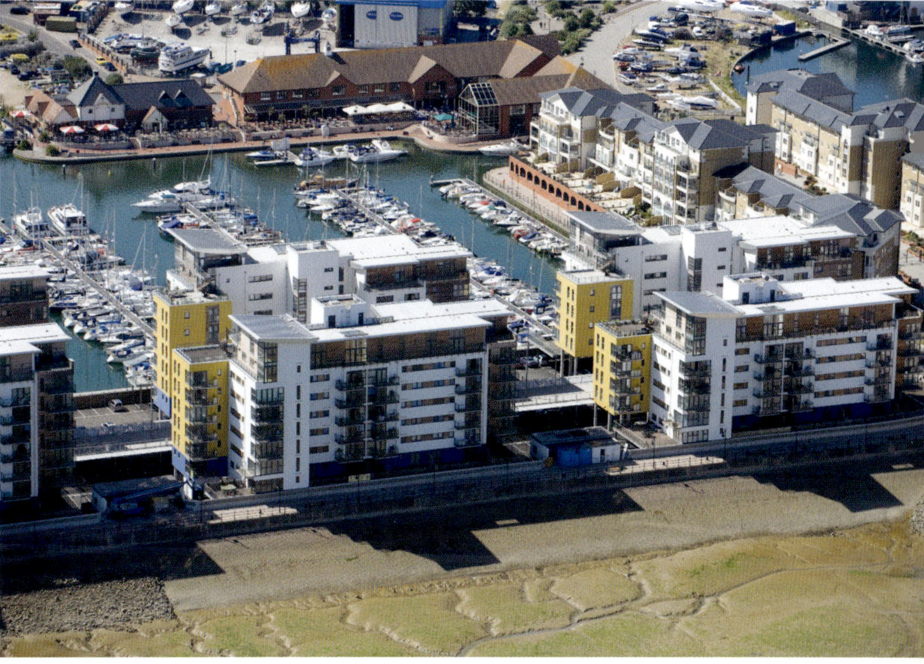

One of the south coast's premier marinas, Eastbourne Harbour.

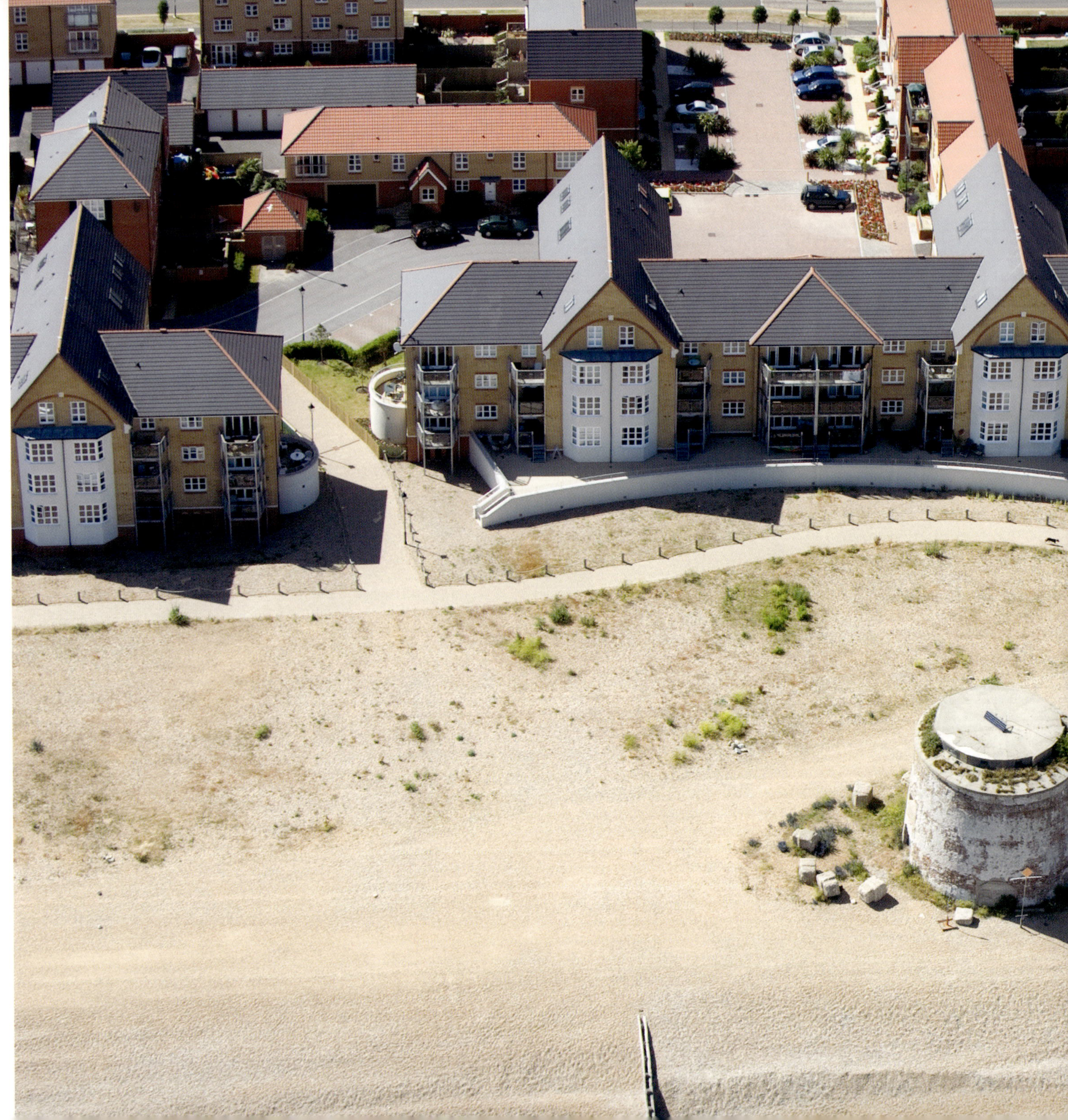

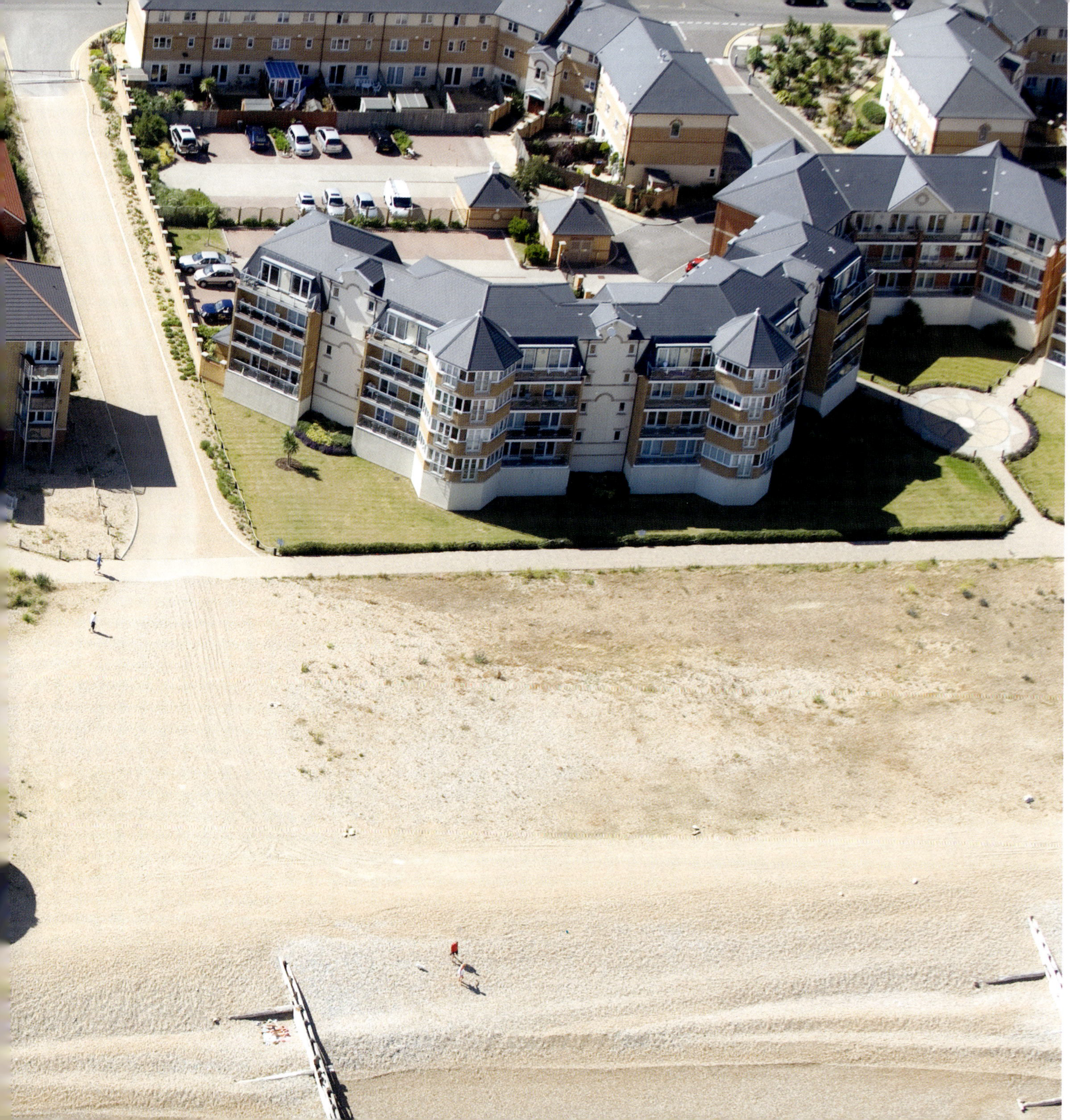

Previous page: New beach-side homes stand alongside the remains of a Martello Tower, Eastbourne Harbour.

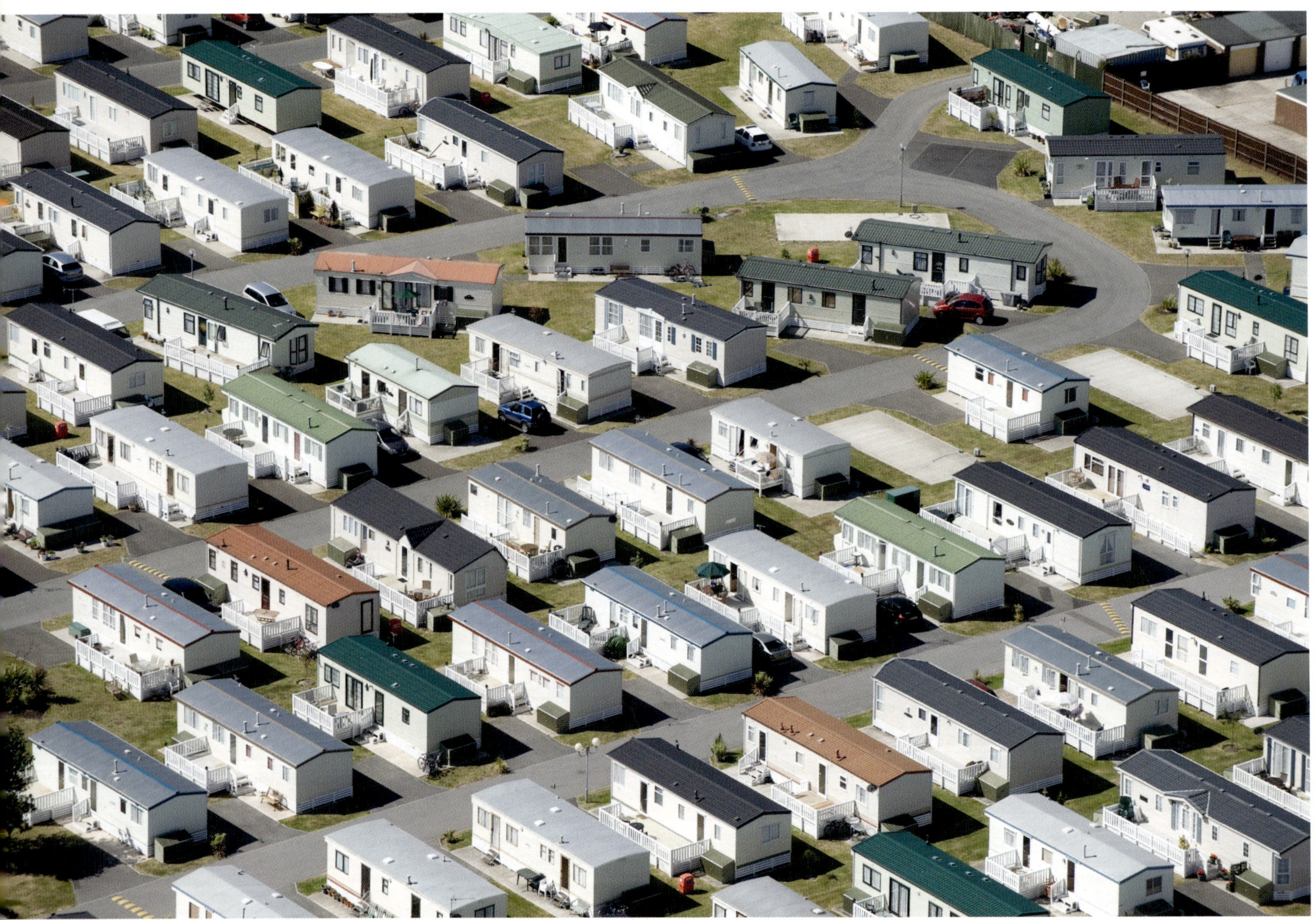

Above: Caravans at Pevensey Bay.

Right: A Martello Tower at Pevensey Bay, now a residence.

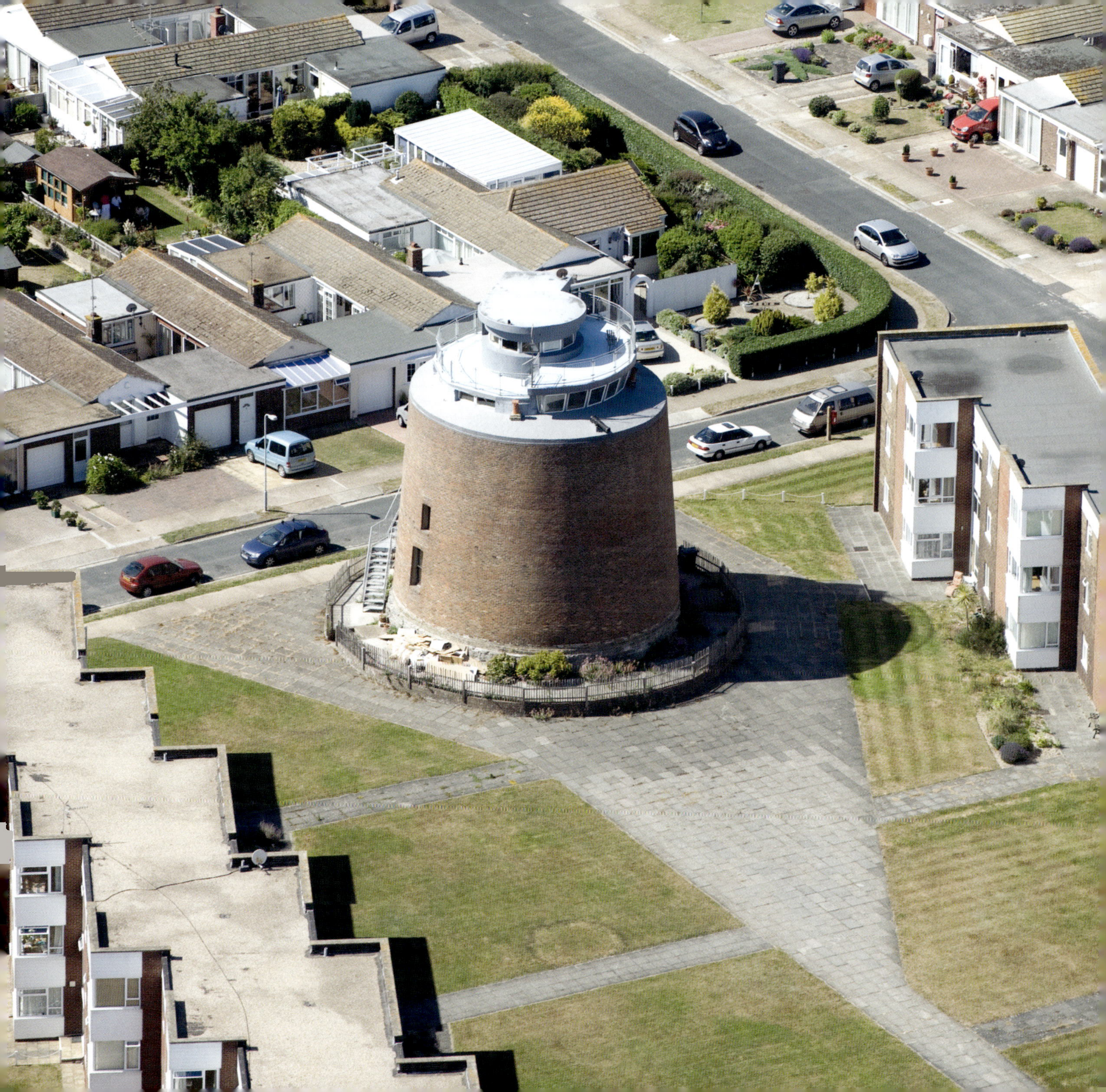

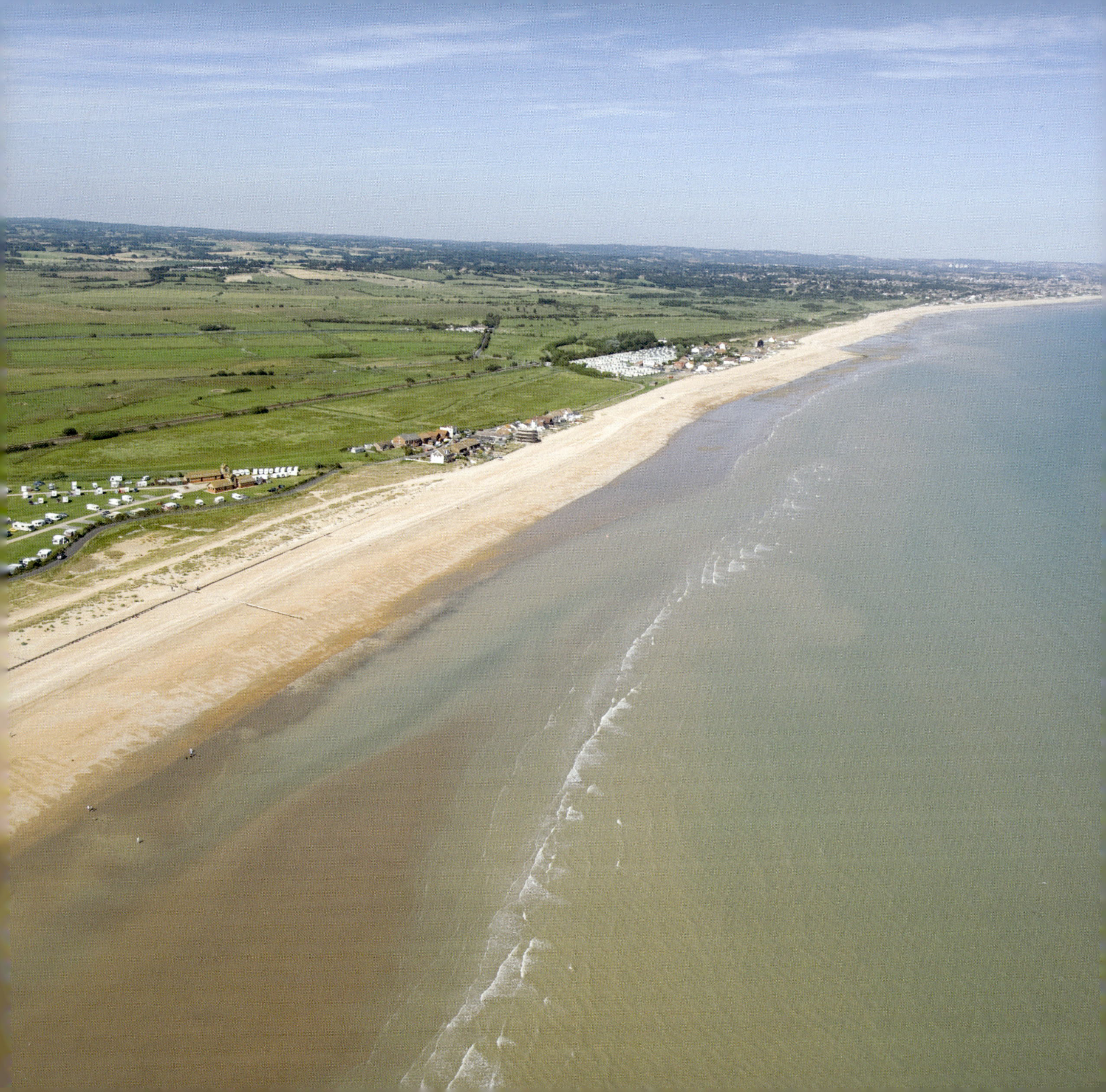

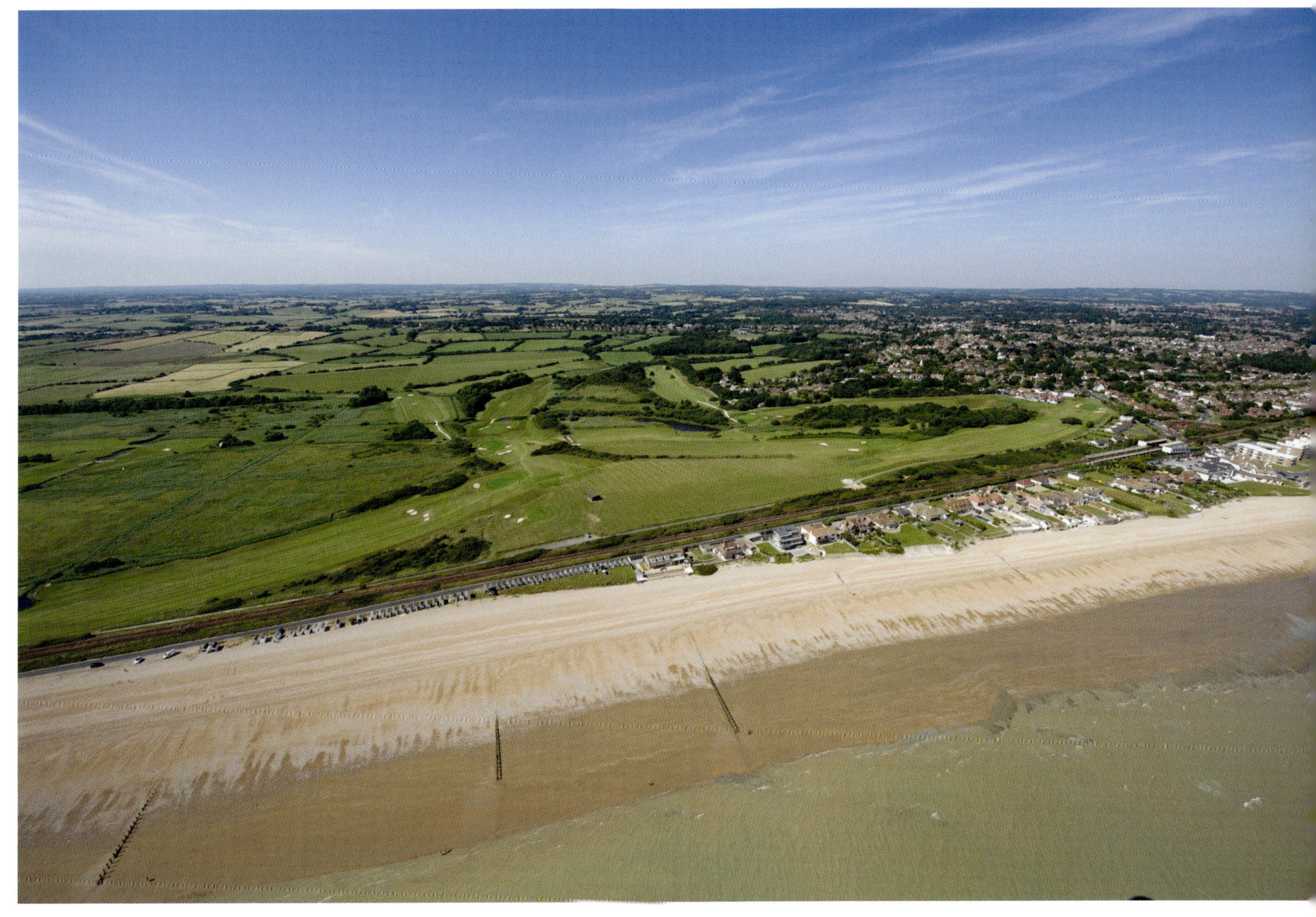

Left: Twixt Pevensey and Bexhill in Norman's Bay.

Above: Little Common on the outskirts of Bexhill.

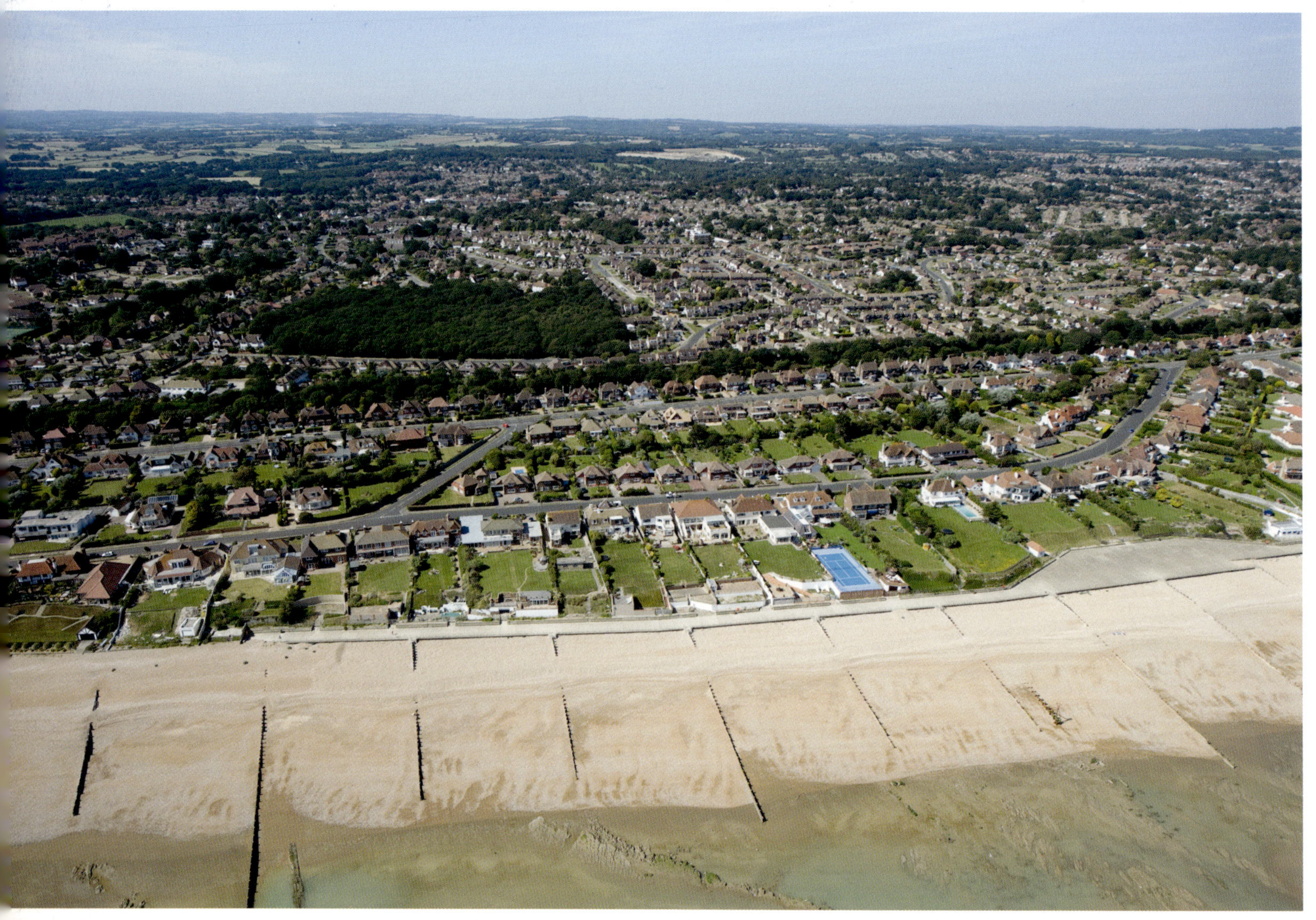

Above: Beach front properties line Cooden Drive west of Bexhill.

Right: Properly, Bexhill-on-Sea, Bexhill was once the epitome of genteel seaside living. In many respects this atmosphere still pervades the town.

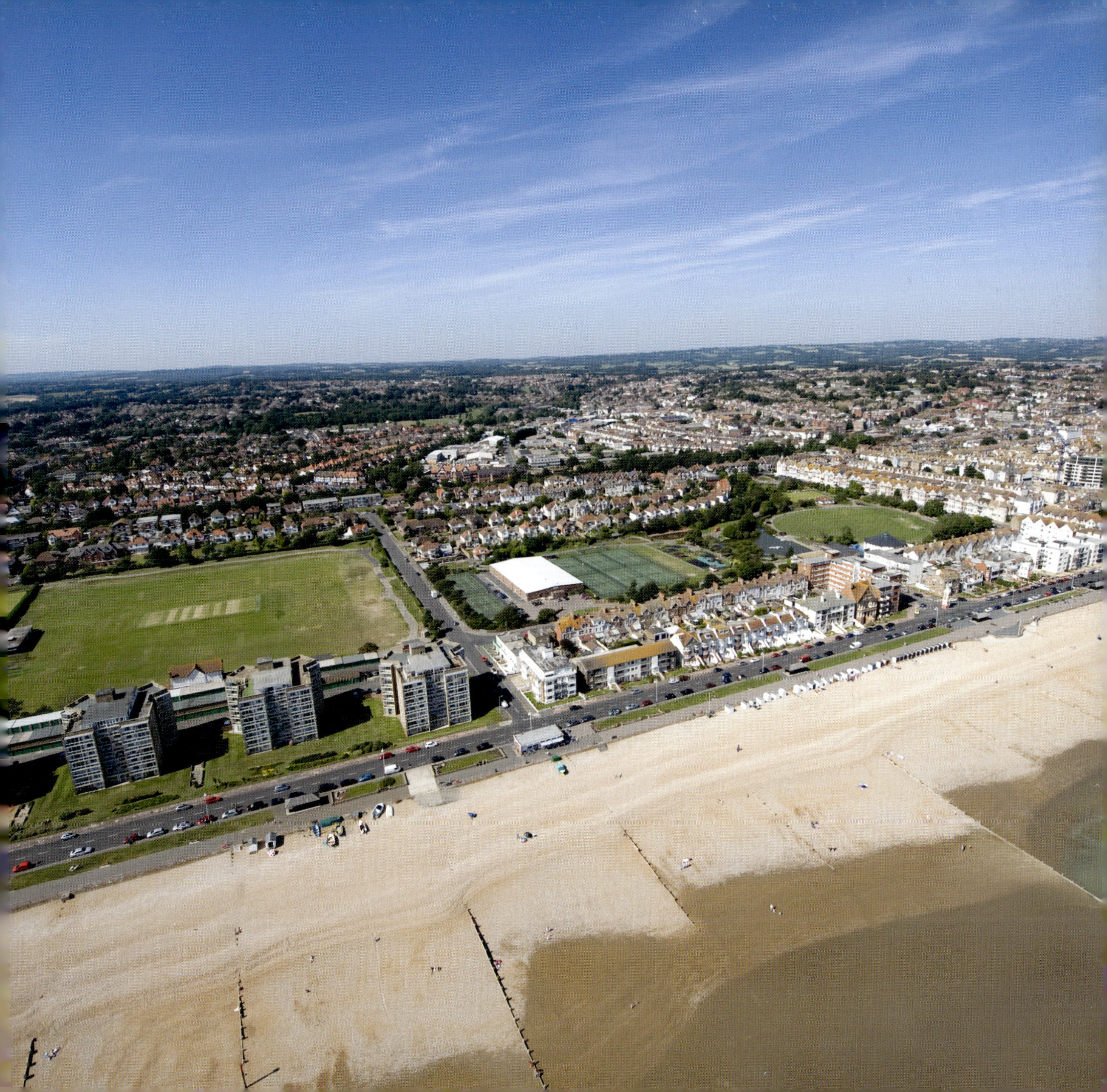

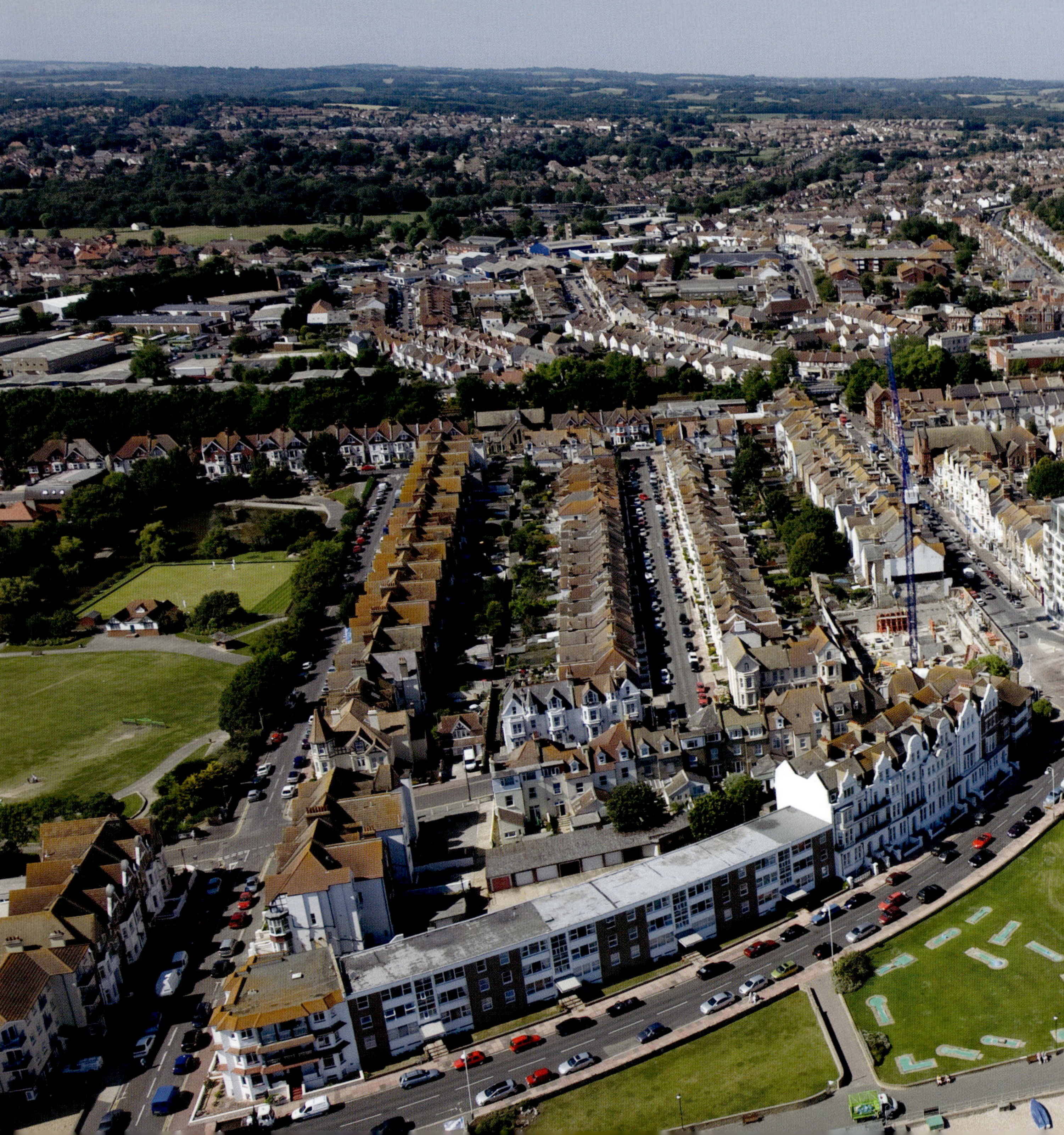

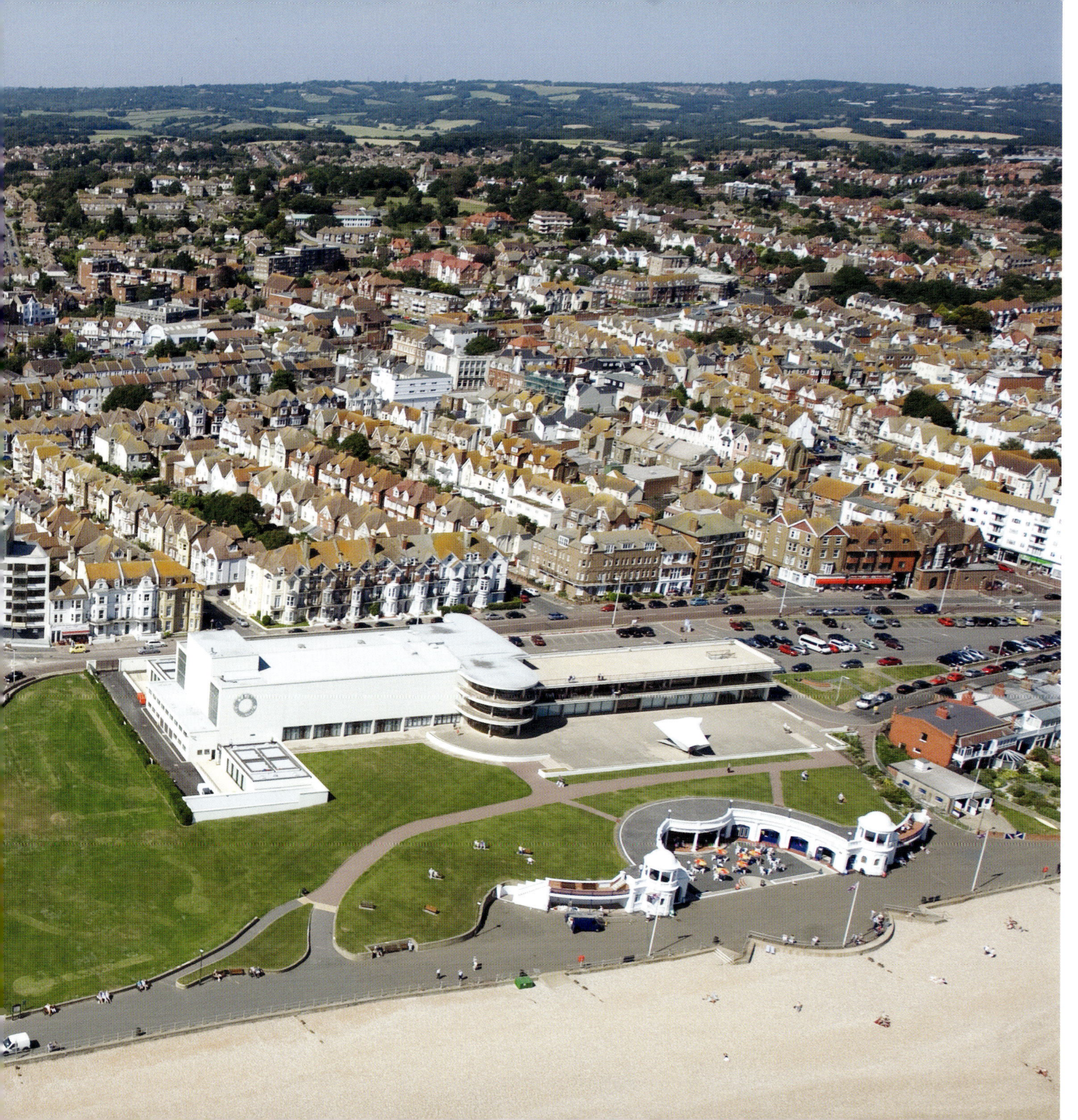

Previous page: West Parade, Bexhill.

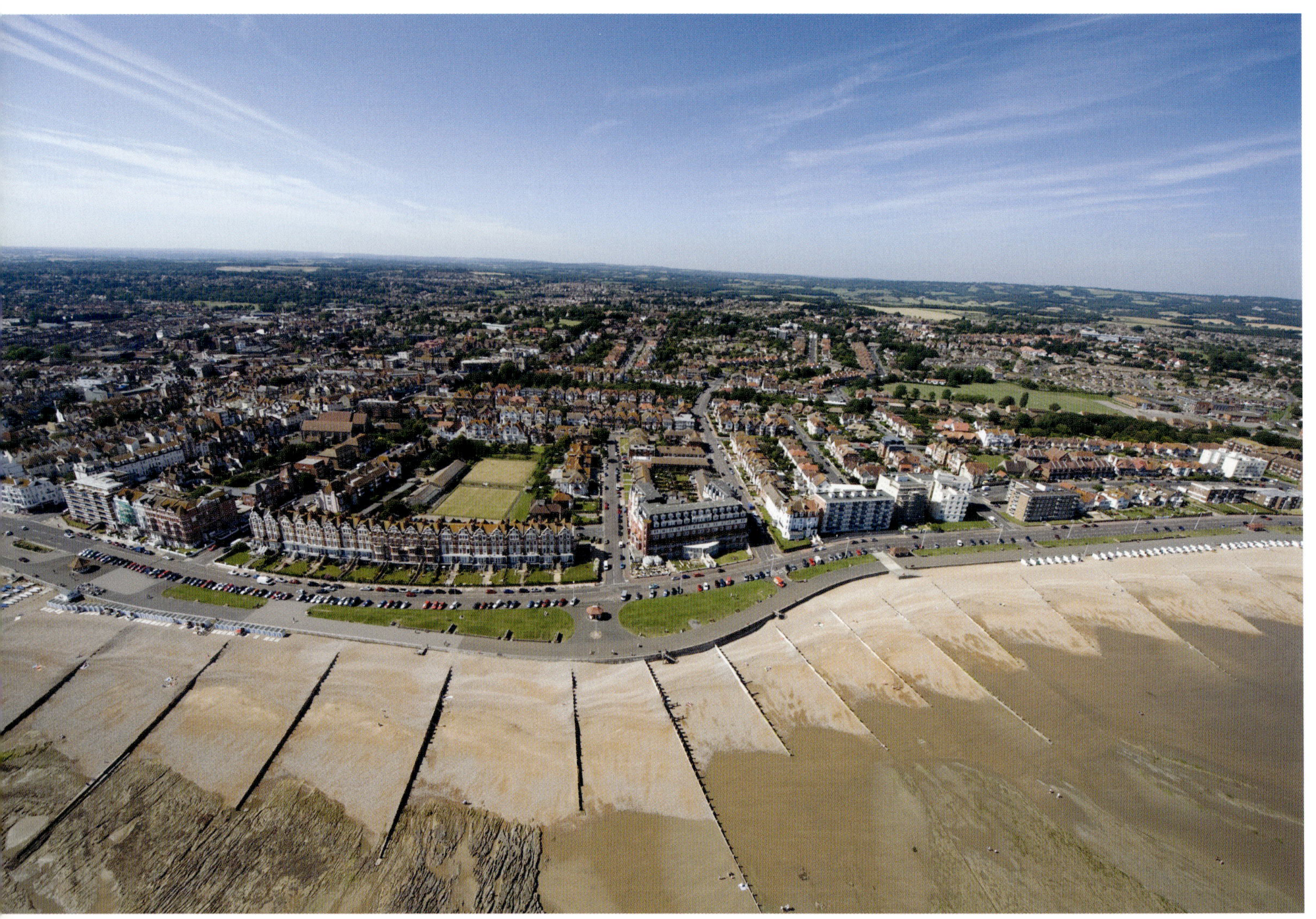

Above: A panoramic view of Bexhill overlooking De La Warr Parade

Right: Beach huts.

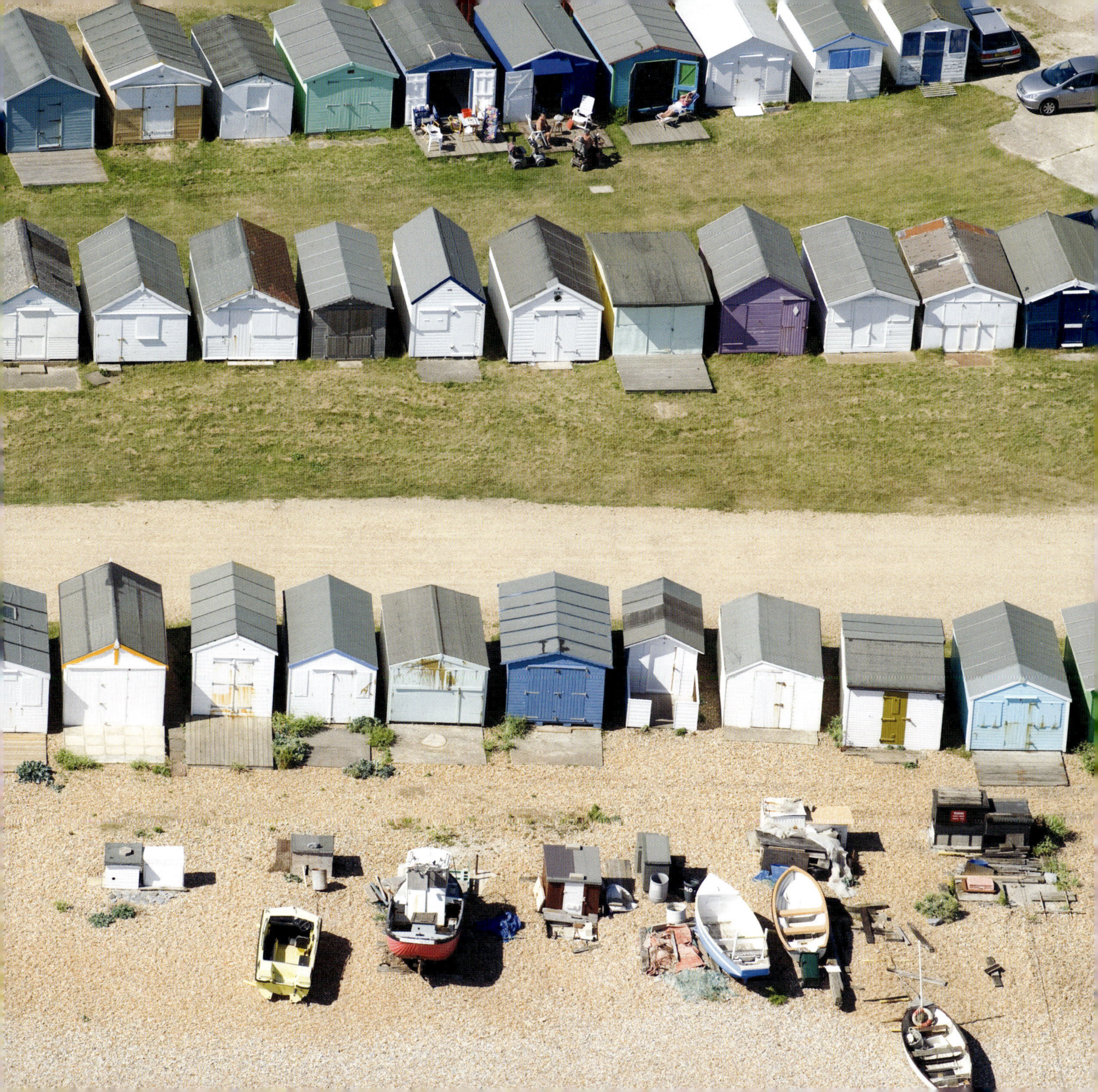

The railway follows the sandy shoreline between Bexhill and St Leonard's-on-Sea, passing Bulverhythe, seen in this photograph, with the eastern end of Bexhill on the left.

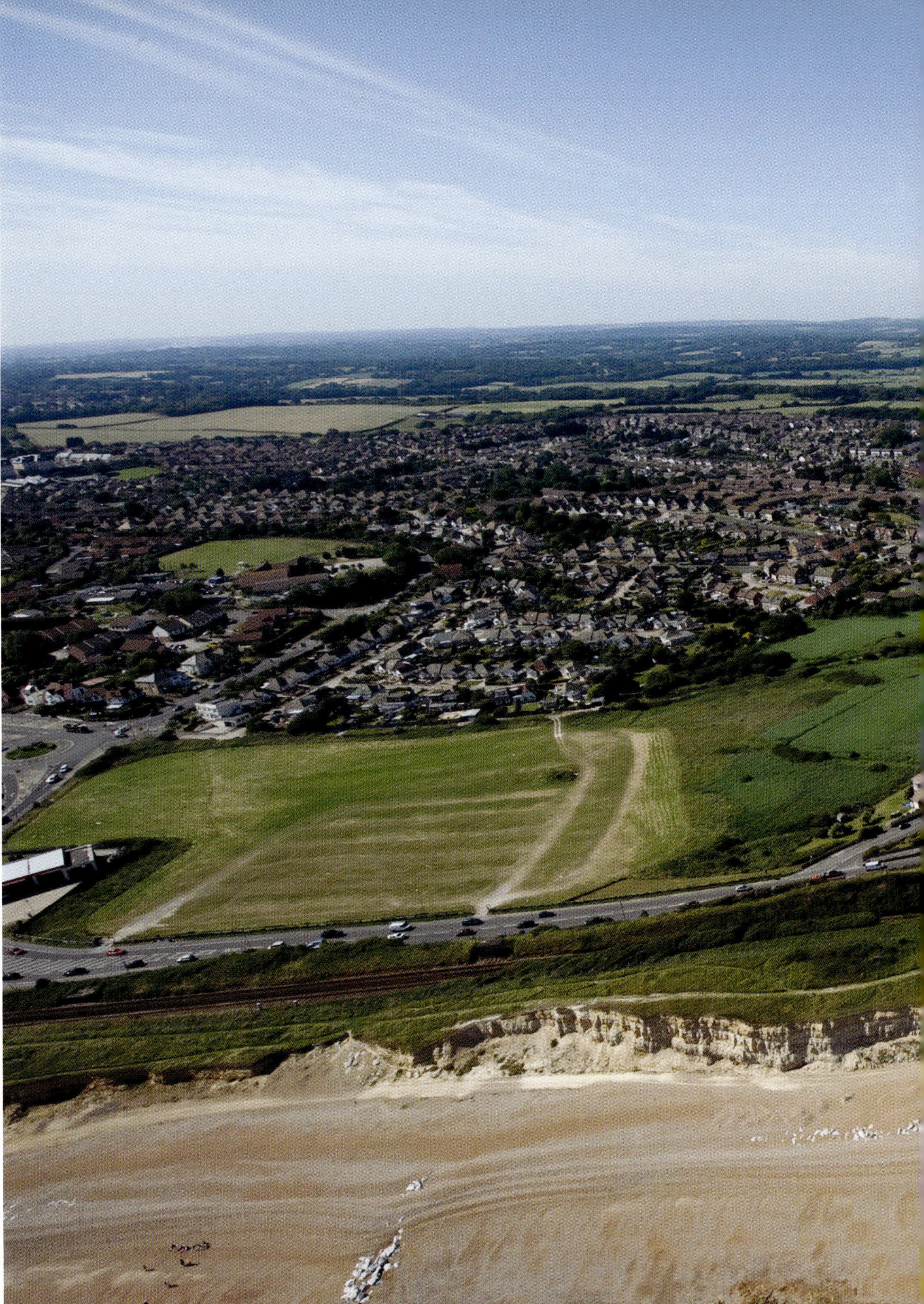

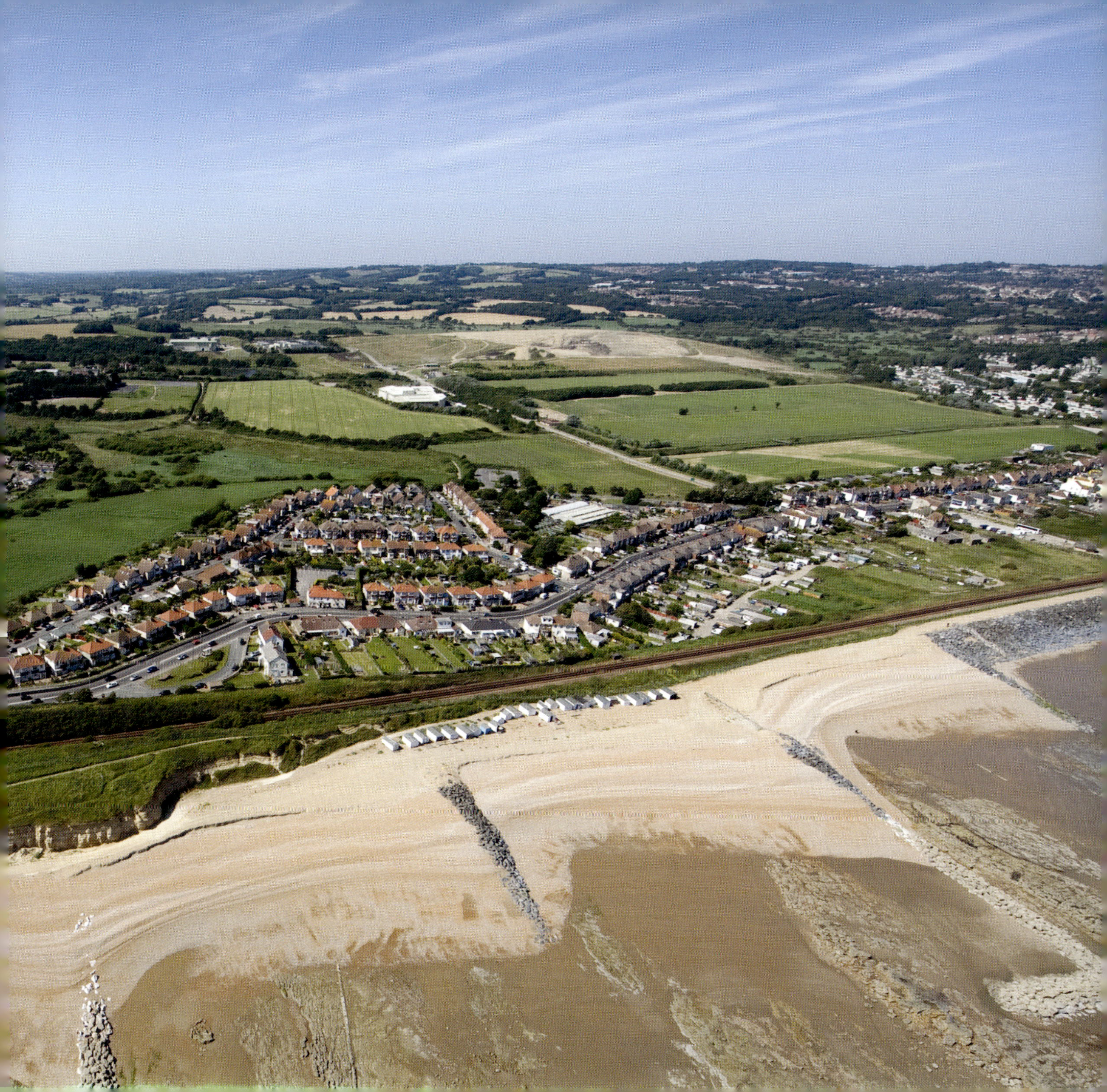

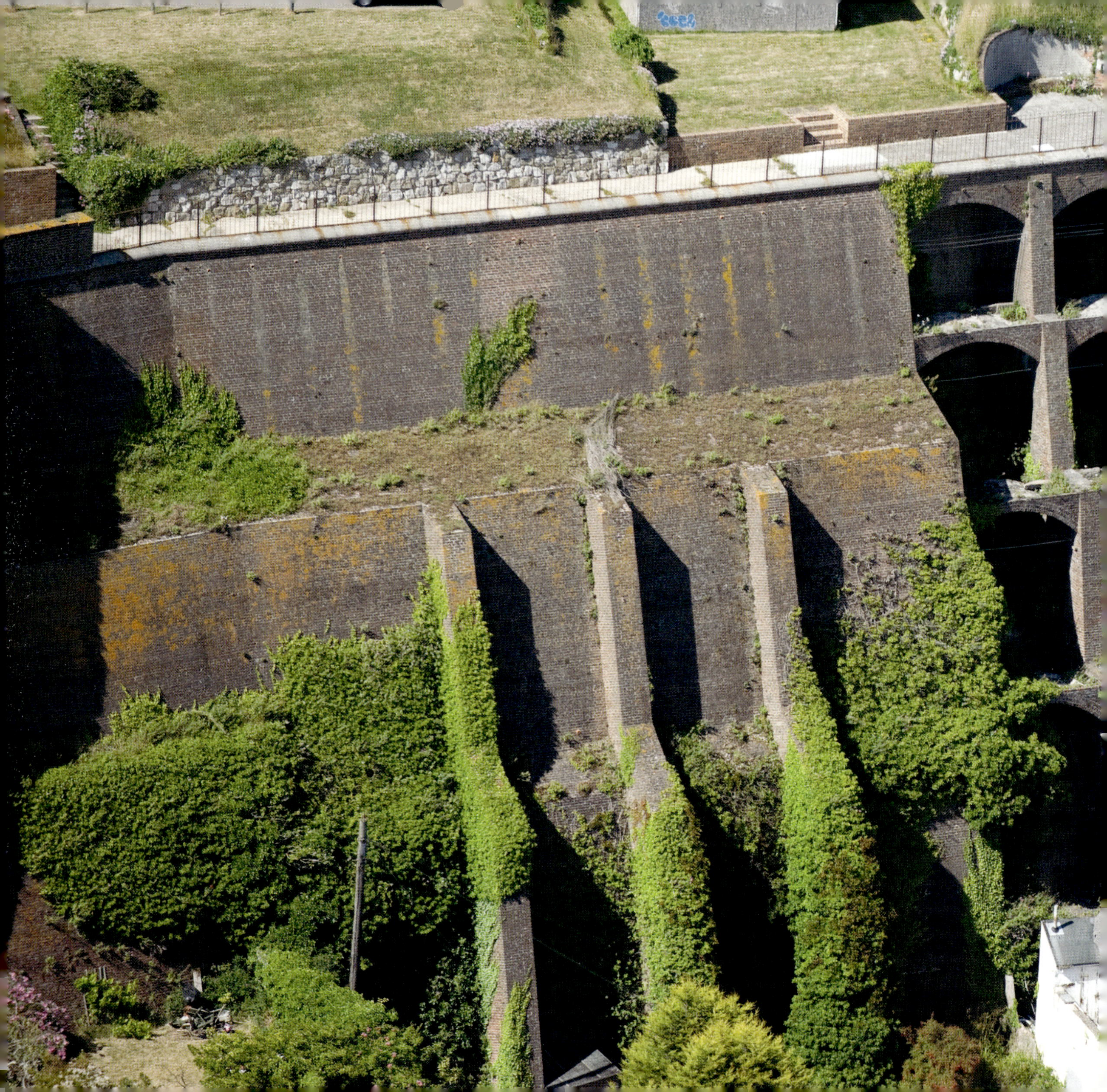

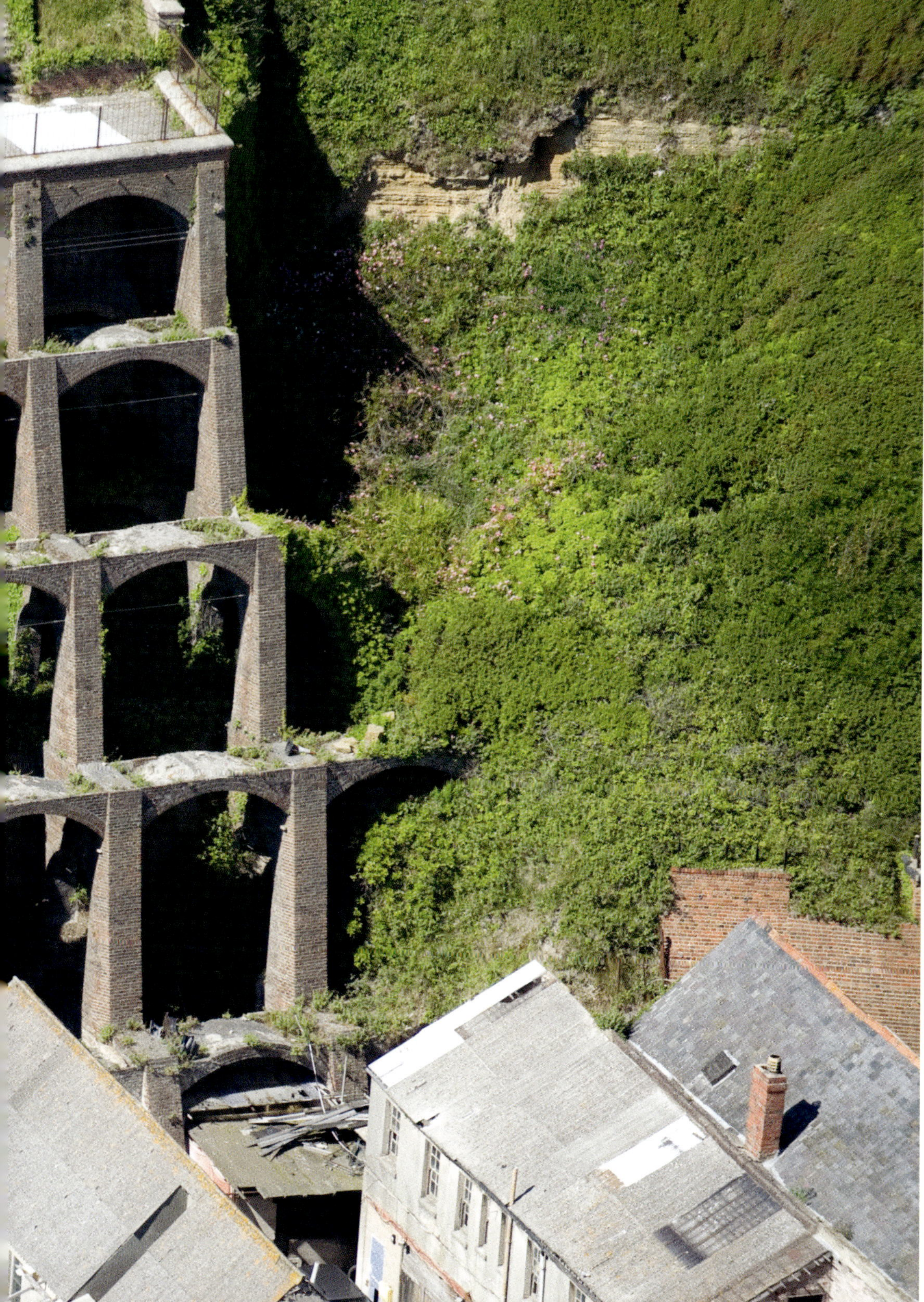

The hanging gardens of
St Leonard's-on-Sea.

View over the Marina
St Leonard's-on-Sea.

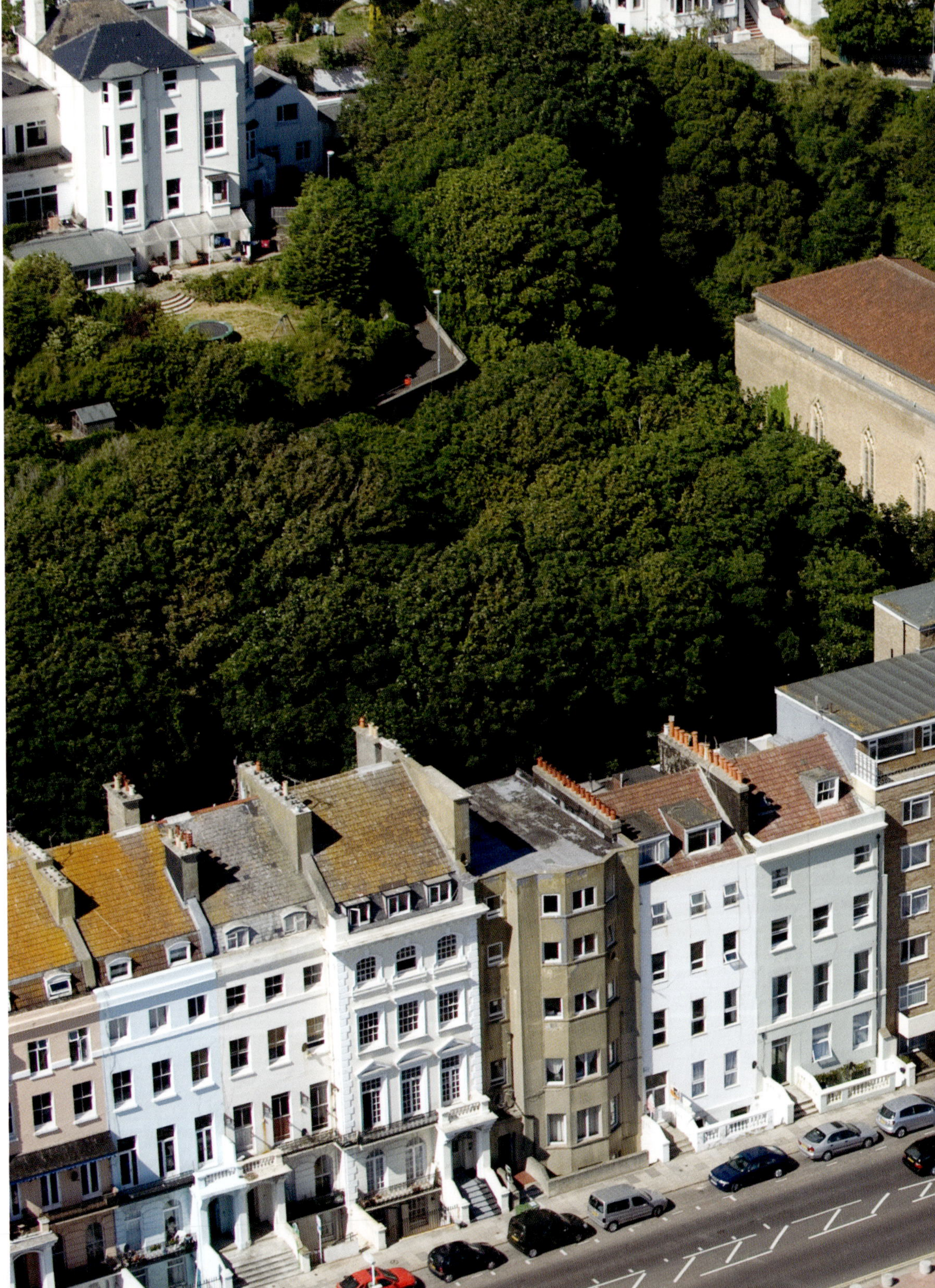

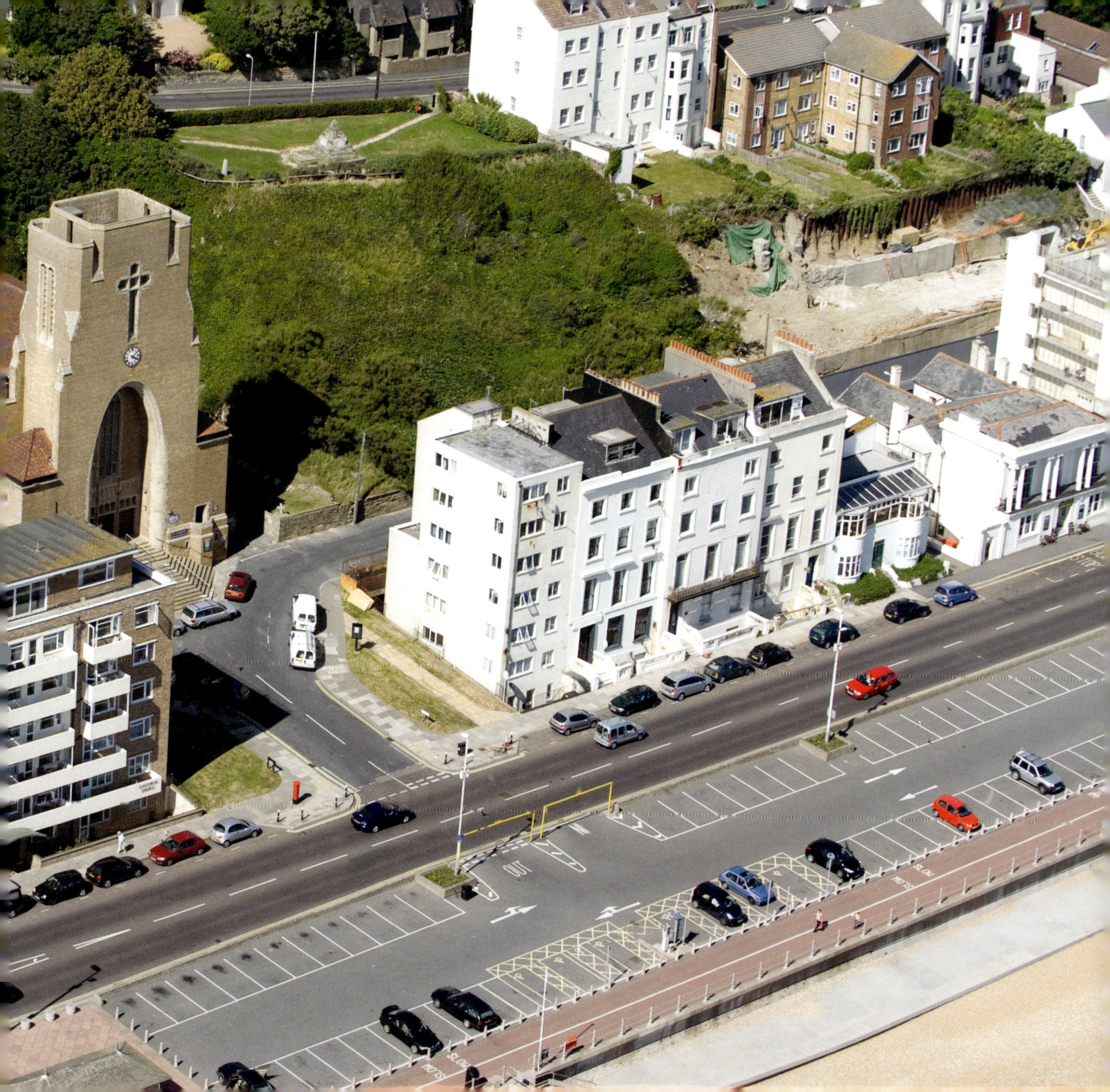

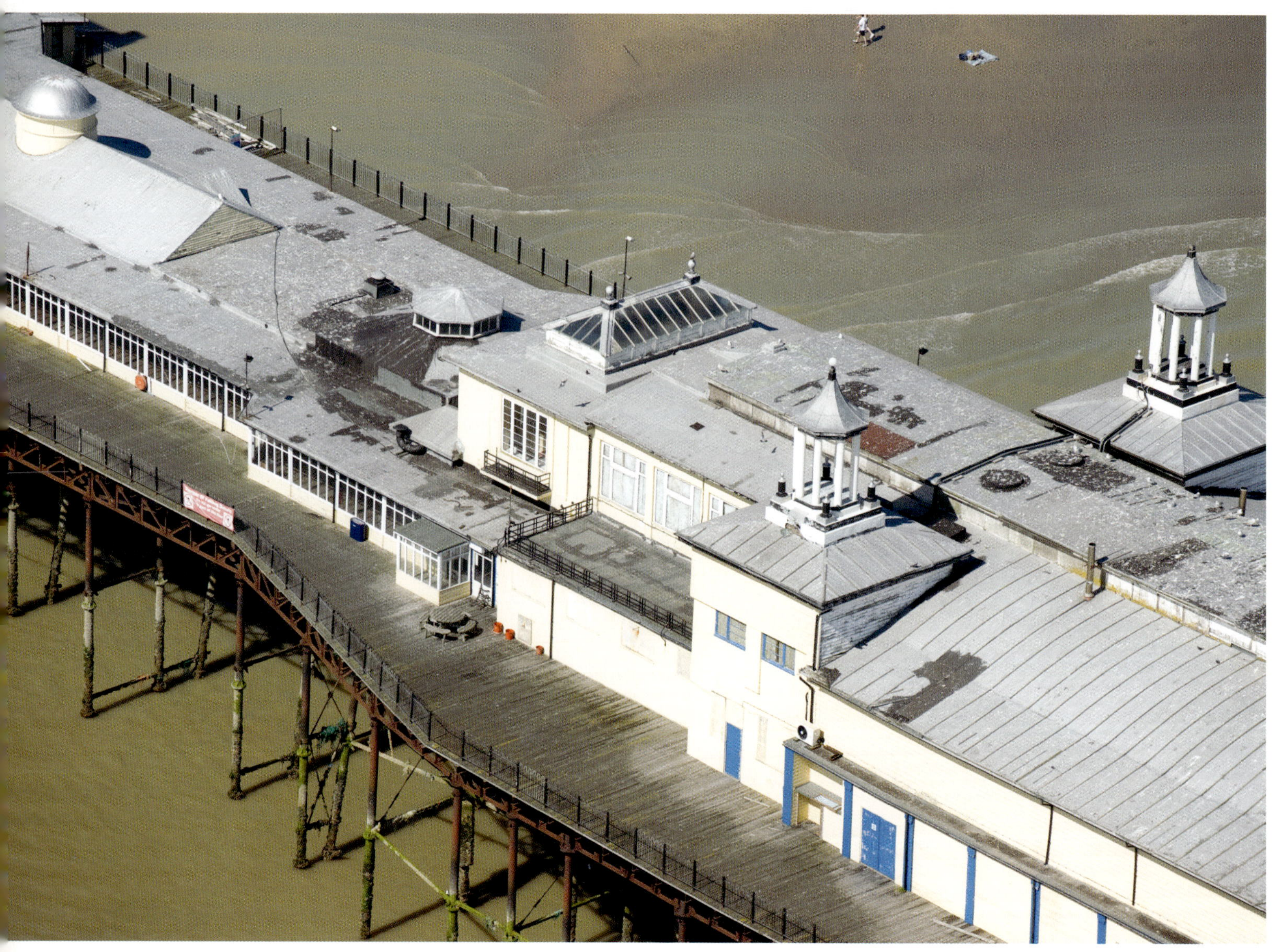

Above: Now closed to the public, Hastings pier was originally opened in 1872.

Right: The view from the sea over White Rock Road

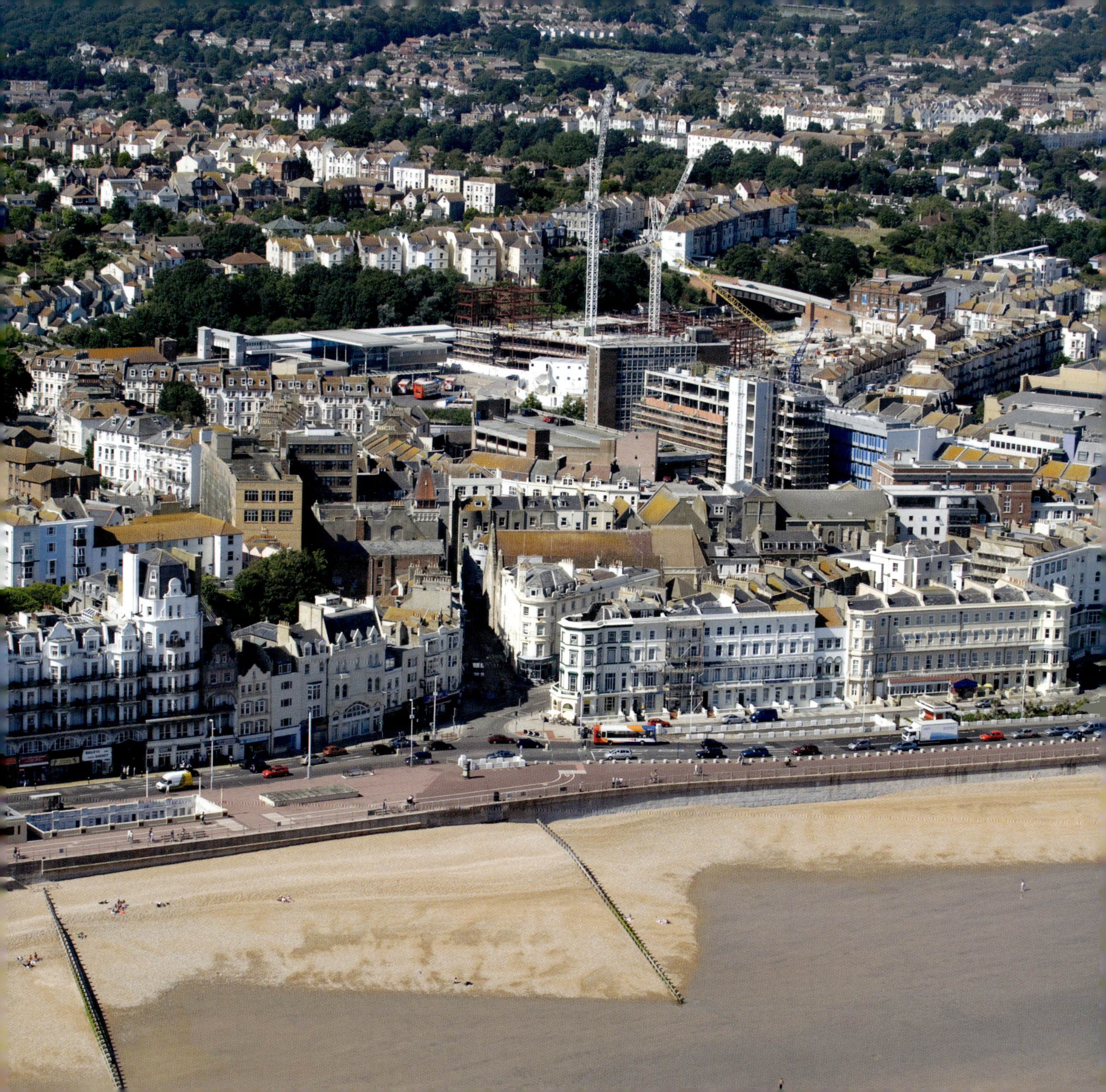

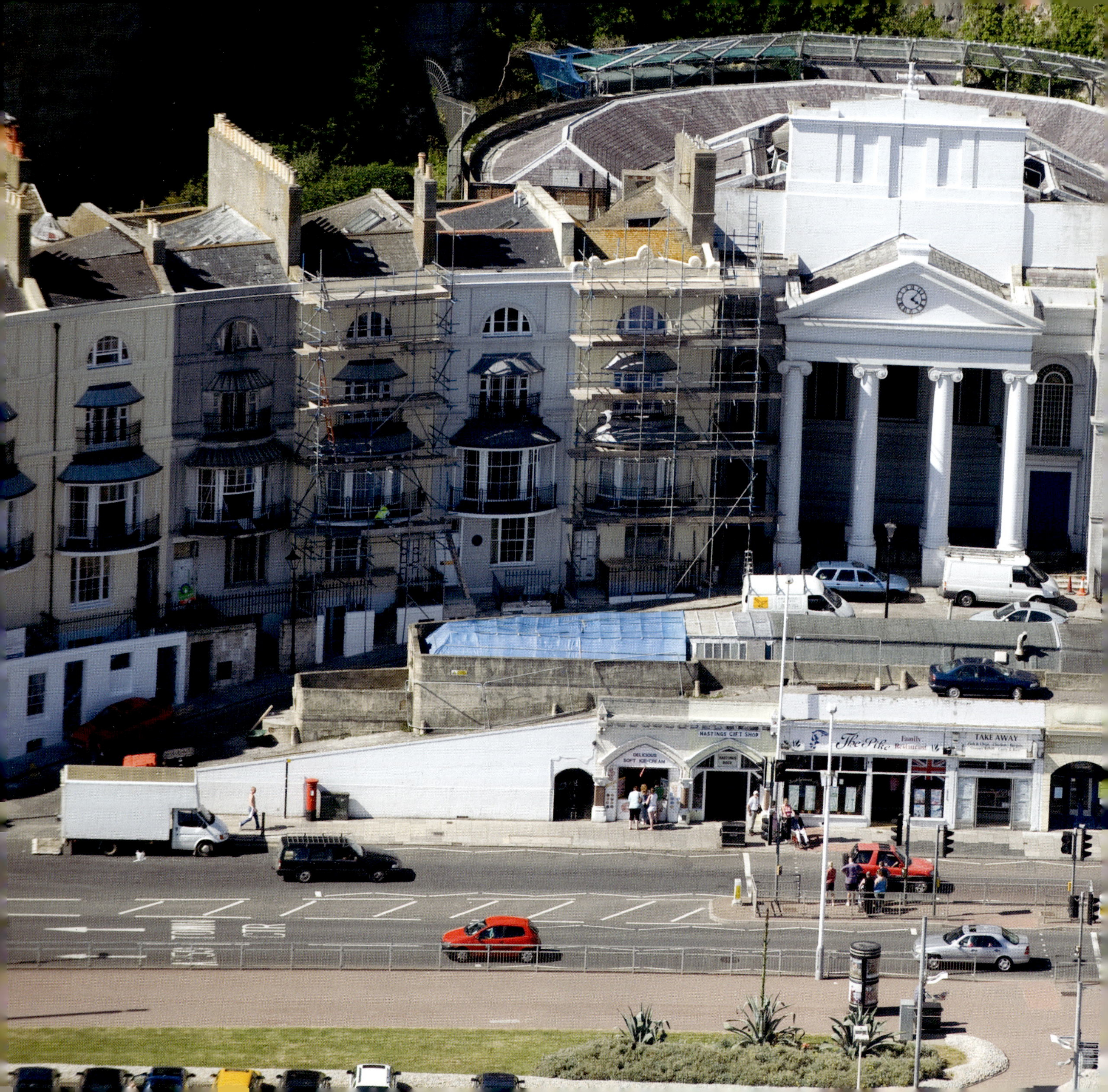
HASTINGS GIFT SHOP
DELICIOUS
SOFT ICE-CREAM
The Pike
Family
Restaurant
TAKE AWAY

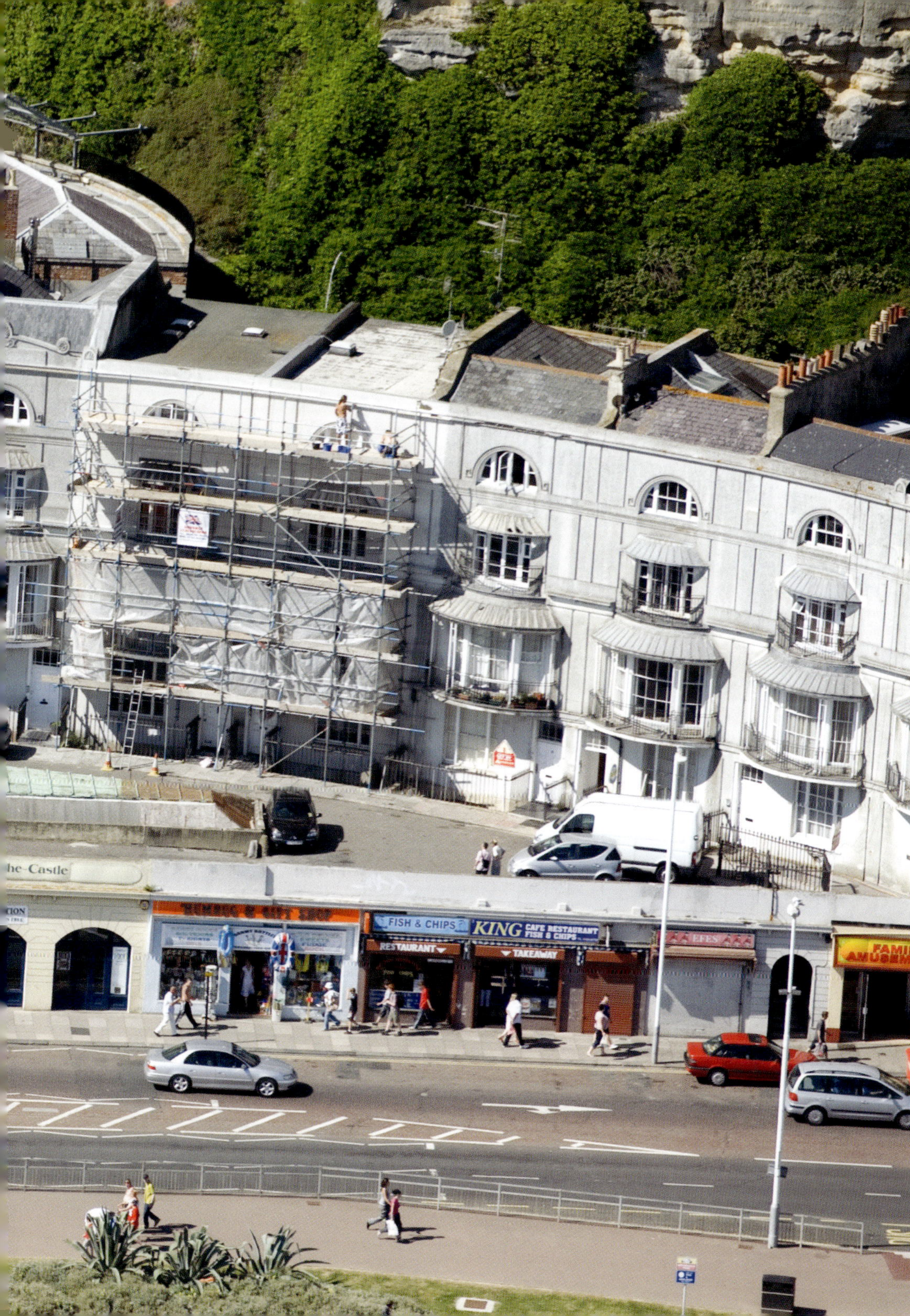

Pelham Crescent, Hastings, undergoing much-needed refurbishment.

Wonderful jumble. On the beach at Hastings near Rock-a-Nore Road.

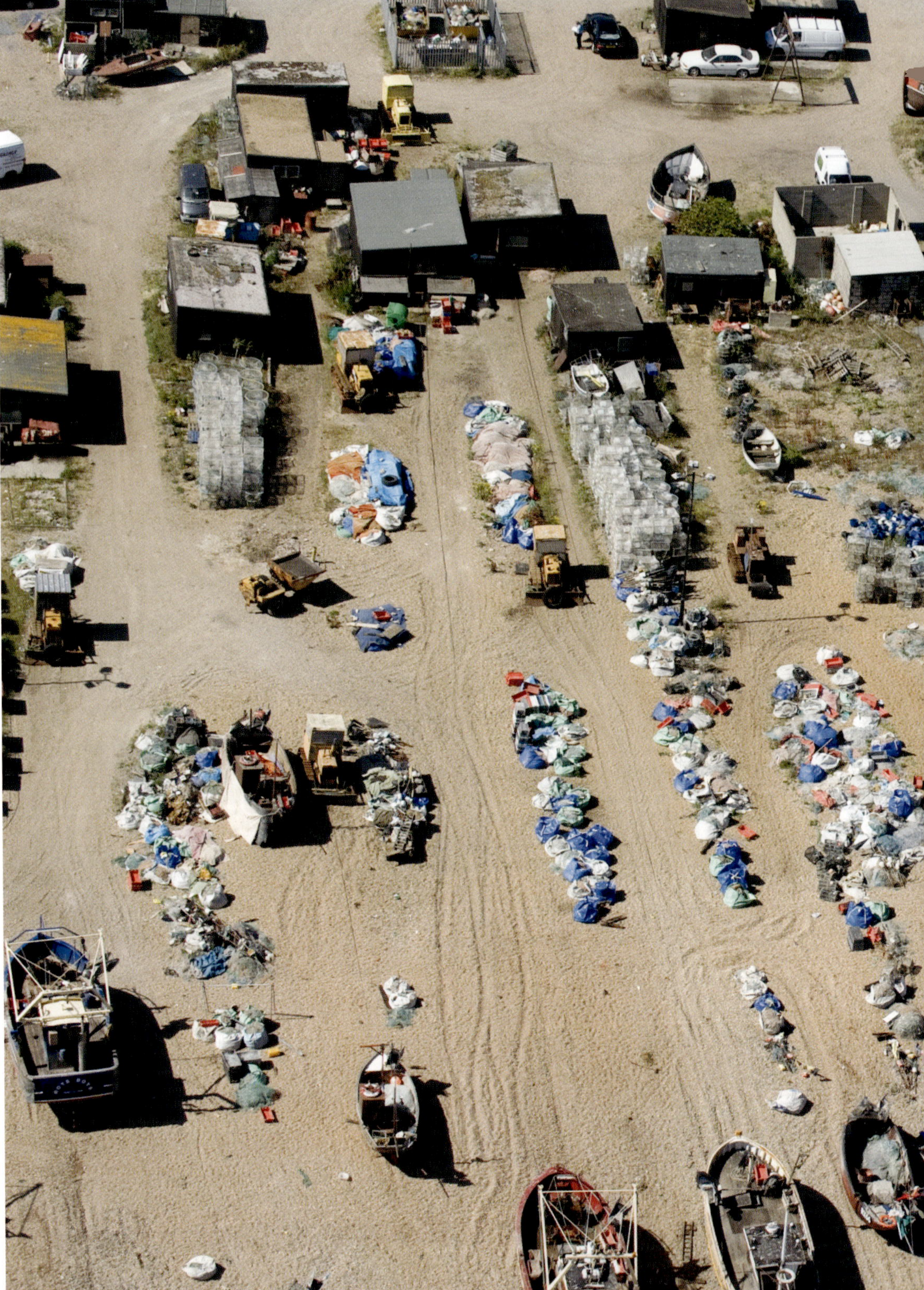

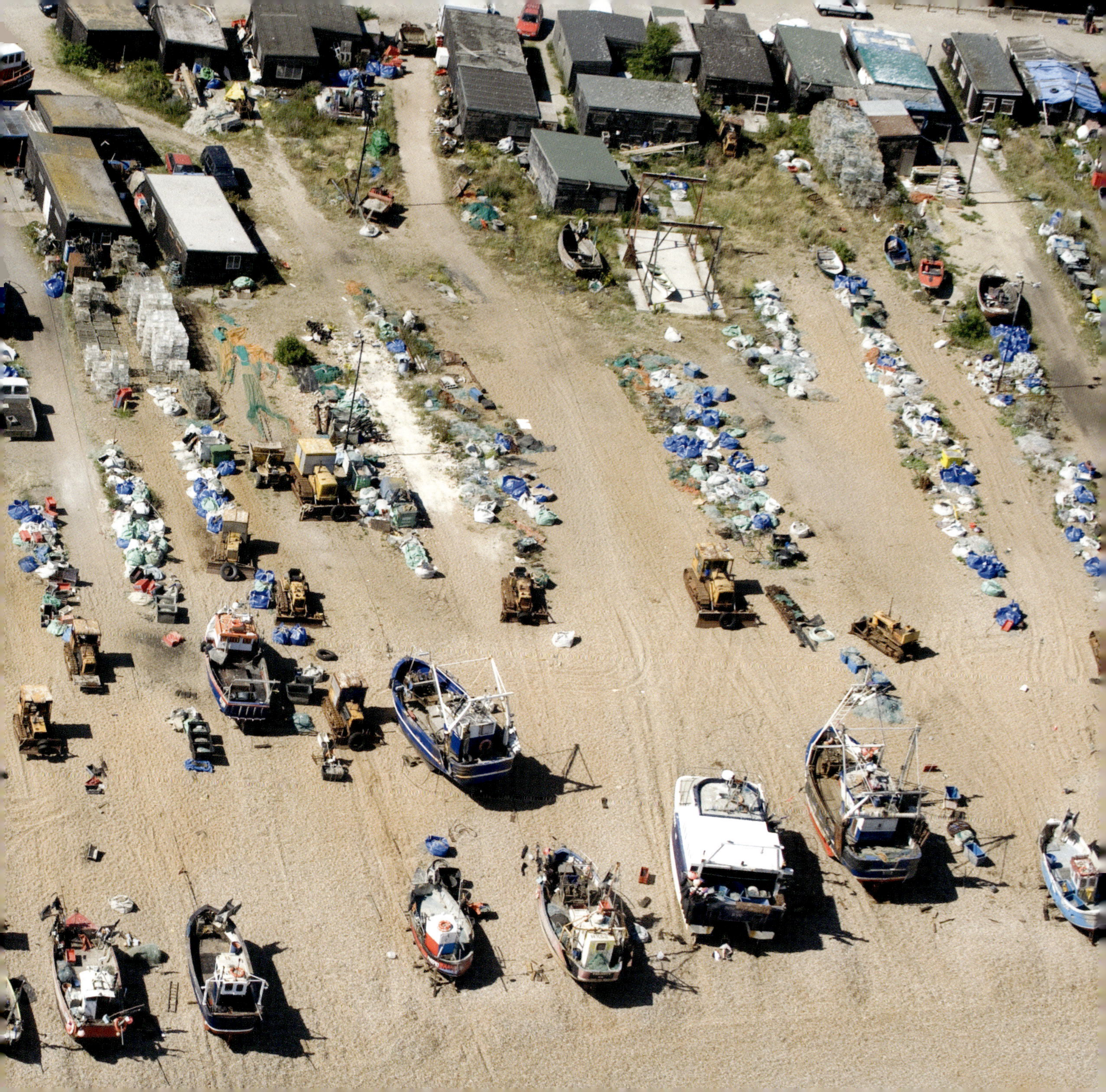

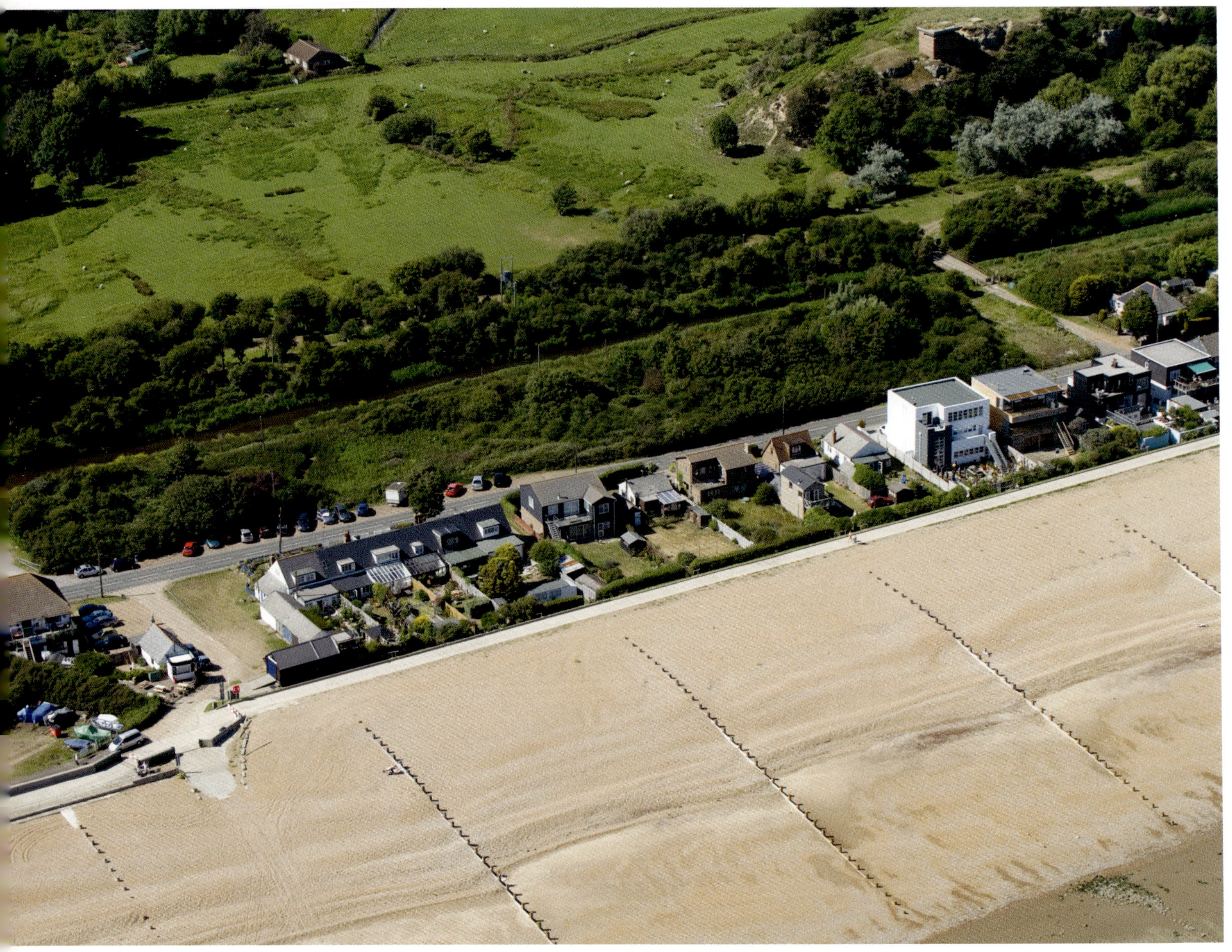

Above: Cliff End, east of Hastings.

Right: Winchelsea, an ancient port and once one of the richest towns in England.

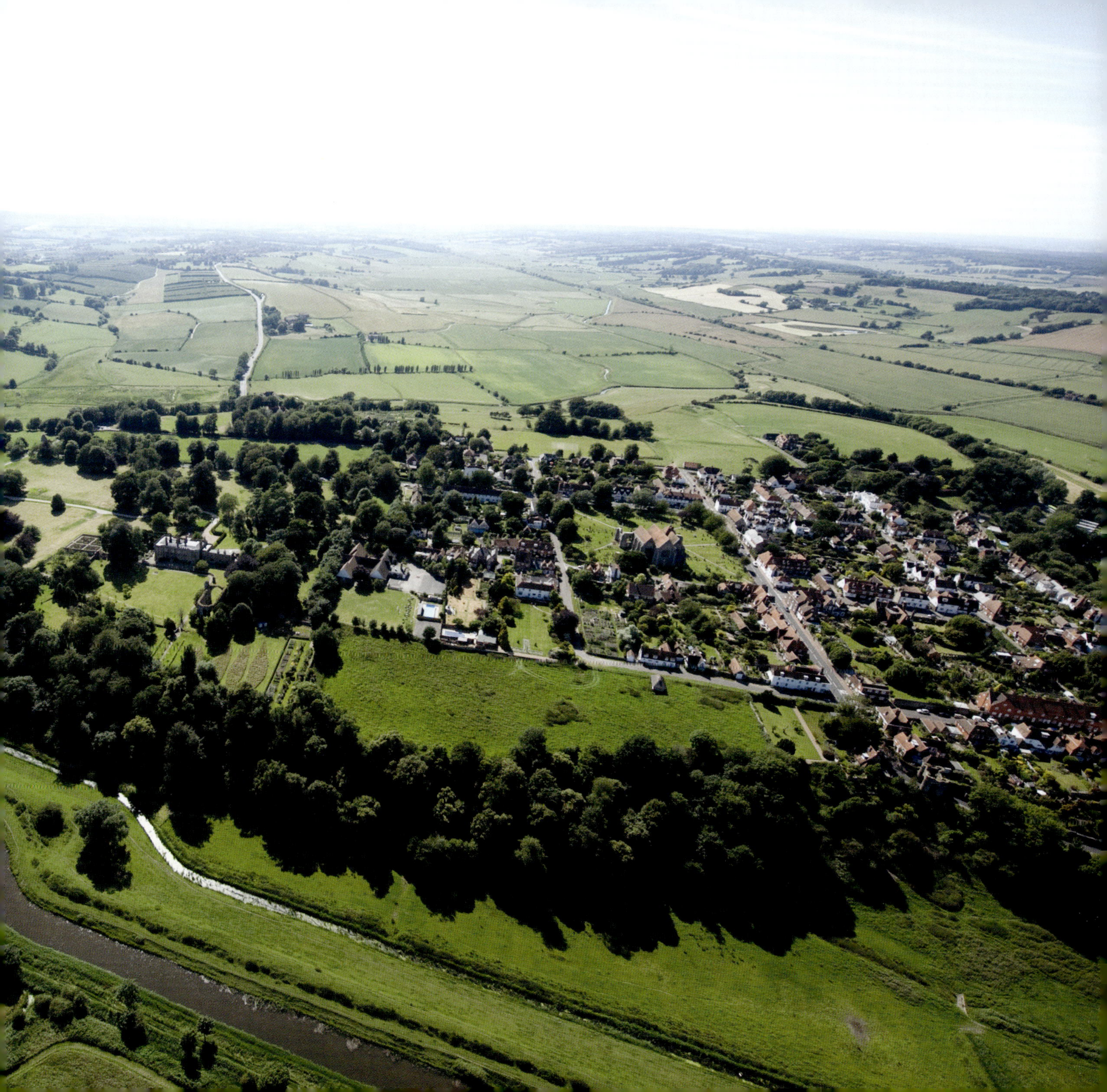

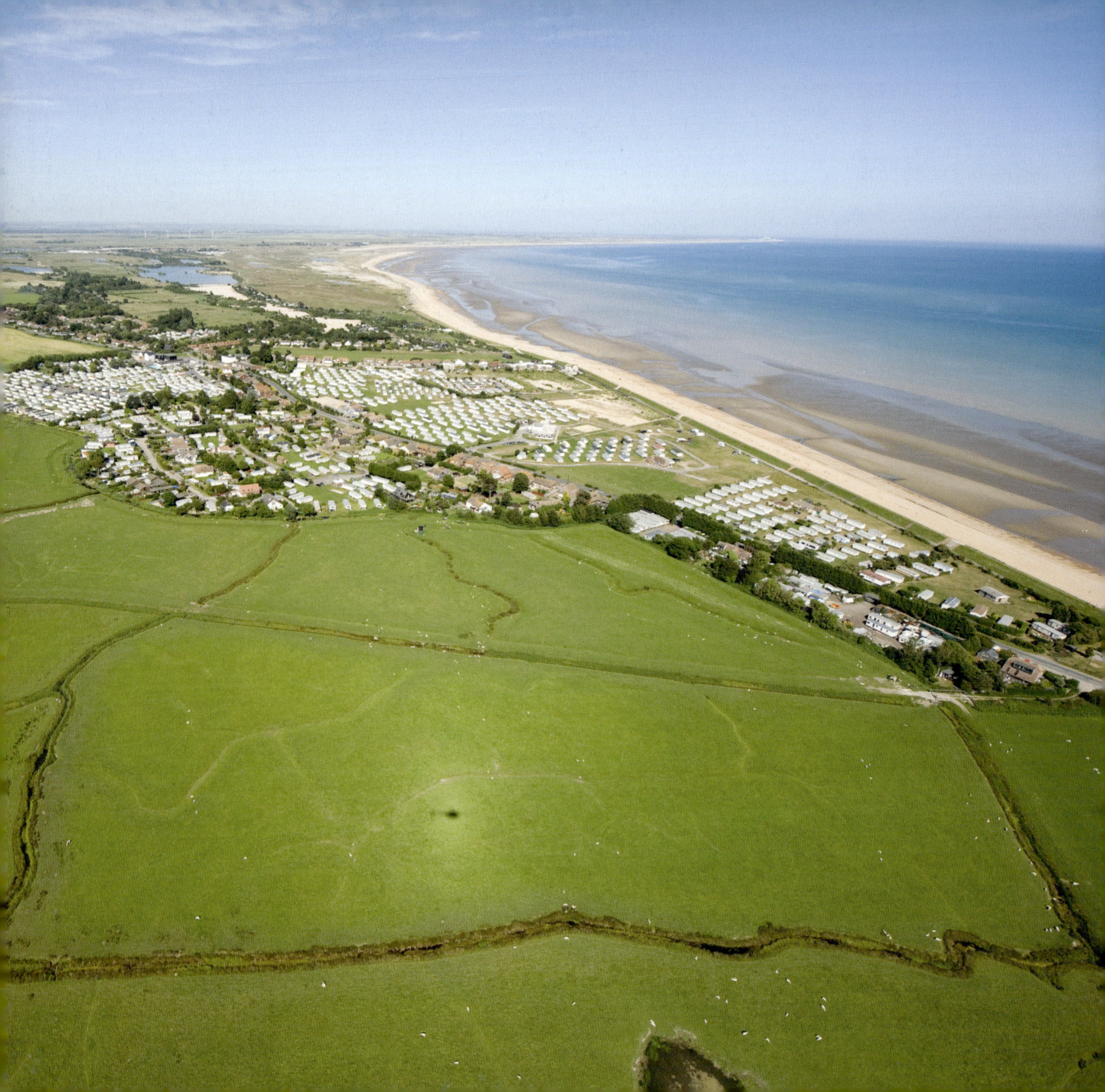

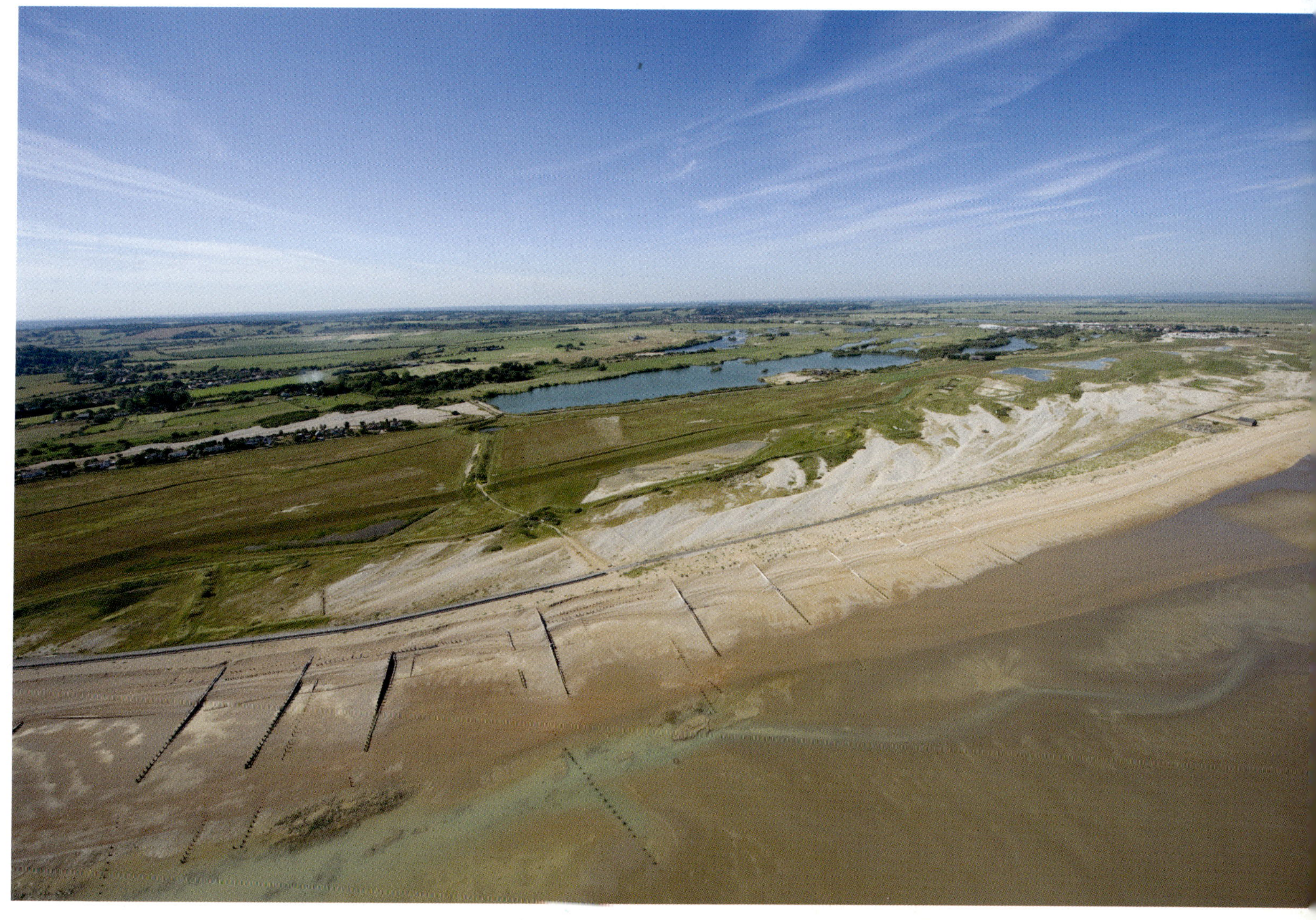

Left: Winchelsea Beach viewed from the west, with Camber and Dungeness far distant.

Above: Looking inland towards Rye.

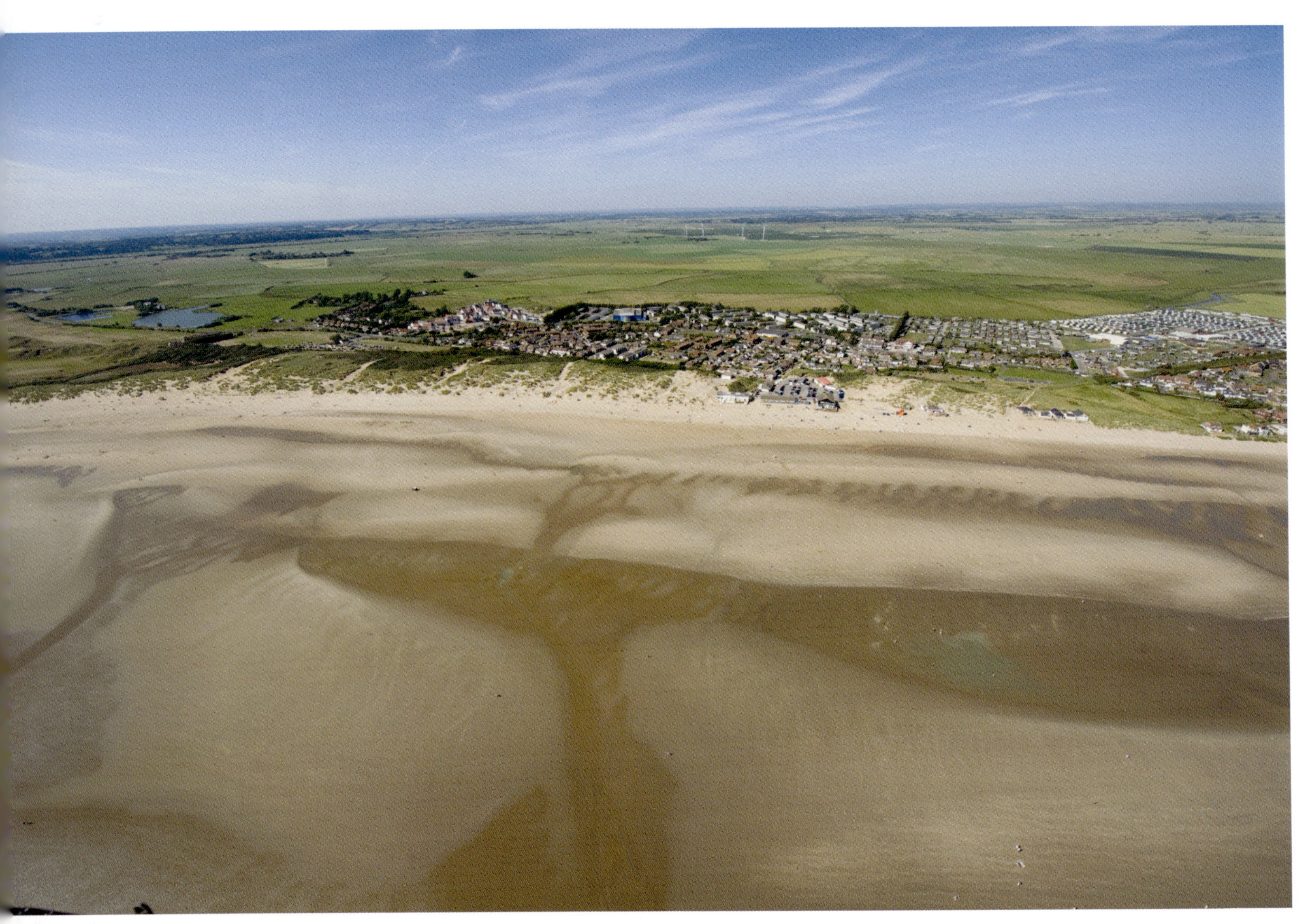

Camber, Rye Bay, at low tide.